Finding Josie

Finding Josie

WENDY BILEN

Wisconsin Historical Society Press

Published by the Wisconsin Historical Society Press
Publishers since 1855

© 2008 by the State Historical Society of Wisconsin

Publication of this book was made possible in part by a grant from the Amy Louise Hunter fellowship fund.
. . . .

Portions of this work have appeared in the *North Dakota Quarterly*, in *The Country Today*, and on North Dakota Public Radio.

All photographs in this work are from the author's family photo collection.

www.wisconsinhistory.org

Printed in Canada
Designed by Percolator Graphic Design

12 11 10 09 08   1 2 3 4 5

Library of Congress Cataloging-in-Publication Data
Bilen, Wendy, 1969–
    Finding Josie / Wendy Bilen.
        p. cm.
    ISBN 978-0-87020-391-6 (hardcover : alk. paper) 1. Broadhead, Josie, 1911–1994.
2. Bilen, Wendy, 1969—Family. 3. Middle West—Biography. I. Title.
    CT275.B7354B55 2008
    977.033092—dc22
    [B]

                                                                2007037330

For all the Josies whose stories remain untold

Contents

Acknowledgments

So many people helped me to tell this story. I could not have gone far without my mother, Mary Bilen, and my aunts, Beverly Ranis and Karen Broadhead. My gratitude to them knows no bounds. I also thank the numerous others—whether mentioned in these pages or not—who generously shared their time and allowed me to probe for memories long since blurred. The individuals and resources at the Library of Congress as well as public libraries, government archives, and historical societies in La Crosse, Wisconsin; Viroqua, Wisconsin; Bismarck, North Dakota; Carson, North Dakota; Minneapolis, Minnesota; and Caledonia, Minnesota, provided invaluable assistance. Advice from professors and fellow students at George Mason University enabled me to shape this narrative into something closer to an actual book; the vision, encouragement, and skillful judgment of my editors, Kate Thompson, Stephen Schenkenberg, and Dawn Shoemaker, carried the story the rest of the way. I also extend grateful appreciation to the Wisconsin Historical Society's Amy Louise Hunter fellowship fund for helping to make this book a reality.

I don't know what I would have done without my husband, Paul Thorbjornsen, whose patience and never failing support enabled me to start and keep going on this long and challenging journey, or my dearest friend, Carrie Theisen, who sustained me through many a draft and freely loaned her faith and perseverance. Above all, I thank God for giving me Josie, this story, and the indelible effect they both have had on my life.

Author's Note

In the interest of privacy, I have used the following pseudonyms: Edward and Irene (Miller) Broadhead; Susan, Michael, Curt, Allison, Eric, Jill, Nancy, and Bobby Broadhead; Aaron Will Broadhead; Frank, Marge, and Kimberly Christine (Broadhead) Patterson; and Don, Dorothy, and Mark David (Broadhead) Miller. For the same reason, I have omitted photos of these individuals.

I pieced together this narrative from scores of sources with the intention of presenting an accurate portrait. Some stories could be verified; some could not. Where accounts conflicted, I noted the disparity or chose the most likely version. Any scenes I have created remain true to actual events; although I have taken creative license with description in some cases, what appears here has roots in research, family accounts, or personal observation.

Lost

Carson, North Dakota
2003

NOT QUITE A MILE OFF ROUTE 21 in south central North Dakota sits the town of Carson. It doesn't bustle, buzz, or shake—it sits, as if resting on the porch after a Sunday potluck. Carson, pop. 319, is a far hour from Bismarck, in a good year nestled among buttes of electric green dotted with Holsteins and Herefords. The county map runs bloodshot blue with creeks leading to the Heart and Cannonball Rivers, which lie underneath a grid of narrow two-lane roads peppered with wild sage or leafy spurge, the soil near their roots slowly burying chunks of petrified wood.

Deep ditches show where the Northern Pacific once ran, long since rerouted. Now the town is quiet, and old grain elevators lean in as if listening hard, tornado damage from years ago still unfixed even though the insurance company paid out. Main Street leads into and slices through town like a spine. On one side a blue and yellow sign by the Future Farmers of America welcomes visitors,

1

while across the street the Carson Flour Mill, once producing seventy-five barrels a day, stands empty and gray as it has for nearly half a century. In the center of town, storefronts resemble the Old West, vertical slats of dark wood in boxy arrangements, a renovation courtesy of a benefactor thirty years ago. Those who explore the other roads in town will find a grocery, a post office, and a nine-room motel but come up short looking for streetlights, movie theaters, and libraries. A blond-bricked county courthouse calls Carson home, too, but that is hard to miss—it's at the dead end of Main.

I have come to Carson because I'm looking for my grandmother.

I am her youngest daughter's daughter, and though I knew her for the first twenty-five years of my life, it took me another ten to realize that I never knew her at all. She was, I now understand, a woman proud and humble, loving and unaffectionate, strict and visionary, joyful and troubled—a woman held together by contradictions like an arch and its capstone. I didn't know any of this when as a child I visited her and my grandfather on their farm outside La Crosse, Wisconsin, and I held down a squeaky mattress on their upstairs landing, well past bedtime, staring at strips of ugly flowered wallpaper rebelling in curls and tears. The ceiling hung low, also pasted in flowers, and slanting toward me so that I could almost touch it with my head on the pillow. On many of these nights the landing door was open to the roof and cricket song, and I fell asleep to voices murmuring at the kitchen table downstairs, the smell of coffee still fresh, waking only at the noise of the creaking stairs when my parents came to bed. In the early morning I awoke to the sounds of voices, mismatched dishes clanging, and containers of milk and butter and unknown sauces or spreads coming out of the refrigerator. I didn't think about the wonder sitting downstairs on a vinyl chair, kneading dough or peeling boiled eggs with a paring knife. I just knew I wanted to be at the table.

My mother was the child who moved away, so I saw my grandmother only a few times a year. We always loved going to visit, my brother and I, and even now in his thirties when he returns he still gets giddy about twenty miles away, even though my grandmother has been gone for many years. The farm on which she and my grandfather lived was another world to us, a couple of kids from suburban Chicago; it was exciting and smelly and scary and exhilarating. We could disappear for hours, and no one would mind. It was hard to get into trouble, though my brother managed a few times. Because almost nothing was off-limits to touch or eat or try, we milked cows and drove tractors and baled hay in short sleeves and thought we were big shots. Our cousins laughed quietly.

You'd think after spending time with her over a quarter century I'd have abundant memories, but most of what's in my head are impressions—like a Monet painting instead of the scenery itself. I remember the way the creek (pronounced *crick*) silt felt between my toes when I waded in it, and how the cow pies rippled underwater, spaced out like mines. The air hummed—a far-off combine harmonizing with the cicadas and the asthmatic breathing of the milking machine. Because we city kids didn't understand these things, I once tried to care for a three-legged runt pig that was destined for an early death. When we were tearing down an old barn I stepped on a rusty nail that went straight through my sneaker and left a blood spot the size of a silver dollar forming on the heel of my sock. I limped home to Grandma, who cleaned and bandaged it. Then I went back to the barn and stepped on another nail.

I remember her kitchen, hazy with grease as she made her "nothings," fried pieces of sweet dough smeared with icing. One time I thought her saltshaker was sugar and when no one was looking took a big swallow.

Sometimes I burned their garbage out back in a steel drum, the smoke and rot mixing with the manure and hay already in the air. When I was in kindergarten she let me dig up one of her peanut plants and take it home for show-and-tell. Without looking I would find in her house mysterious old school books and pieces of toys and stickers on mirrors that tattled on unnamed ghosts.

The last time I saw my grandparents alive together, they had pushed the kitchen table against the counter and were frying up some doughnuts. The cord of the electric frypan was stretched taught, the oil crackling as she cut the dough with a biscuit cutter and he stuck each O in with a fork. The sweet rings bobbed like life preservers, browning and filling with oil, coming out onto paper towels for breakfast. If I concentrate I can still see their faces.

My grandmother is, by some standards, not a hard woman to find. The very fact of her existence littered her trail with evidence: she was born, she attended school, and she was confirmed. She fought off illness. She married, bore children, owned property. She acted as a foster parent, a church leader, a writer. Nearly each step produced a document: birth, school, and church. She left traces in clinic and hospital notes. Marriage licenses and land transactions. Photographs, letters, journals. People. I can find these papers and individuals, and they can tell me what she did, but I am not easily satisfied. I'm after who she was, and that's not something I can find bound in a book at the back of a courthouse. What I want involves retracing her steps—seeing what she saw, going where she went, knowing who she knew—because I want to know why she did things people talk about still.

The number of people my grandmother Josie Broadhead and her husband, Lee, took in—including children, adults, and those who should have known better—changes with the seasons. The family tends to stop counting around twenty. Some asked to come, some didn't, and some had no choice. She wouldn't have opened her home without Lee's permission, though it's hard to believe he would have tried to cross her. (Once she wanted a laundry chute, but Lee wouldn't build one, so she knocked a hole in the wall so dangerous he had to fix it, and since he was at it, he might as well make a drop for the dirty clothes.)

They started coming soon after she married, and even near the end they still flowed in a steady stream. When all was said and done, there had been beggars and drunks and children of drunks, mentally ill children and children with mentally ill parents. Brothers and cousins and sisters and in-laws and strangers. Babies. Boys on the brink of manhood and vagrants walking the side of the road and others who no longer have faces or names. What drew so many people to Josie is probably as much a matter of pragmatics as anything else. When they were in a bind, they knew she would take them or their kids; everyone knew she was more reliable than food stamps, the welfare department, and all other forms of government aid put together.

She attributed her openness to a promise she made to God that she would do whatever He asked. Because they started coming way before the holy conversation in question, I guess that's not really the reason, though it likely helped her make a couple of the difficult choices. There may be something in her childhood that explains part of it, but I also tend to think that God just wires some people differently because He has plans for them, and the rest of us could stand to see something a little extraordinary now and then.

She would have been uneasy with so much fuss over her life. She would have said that all those years she was just doing what any good person would do, what God would want done. The truth is, though, that I'm not doing this for her or my mother or anyone else. I'm doing it for me. I tell myself it is penance for the sin of youthful ignorance, which left me wishing after she was gone that I had watched her eyes, her hands, her smile so that their images would become more real, more tangible, like names etched in a just-poured sidewalk. Ignorance that discouraged me from touching her when we talked, even though it wasn't her way, from asking more questions, from letting her teach me even the small things: making potato salad, growing a garden. And so I am doing the only thing I can do: seeking her story and collecting the details of her life, her marriage, her reach, hoping to know now the woman I failed to know then.

That sounds right, but it's not fully true. I'm looking for my grandmother not because she is lost, but because I am.

My generation has been telling me for years that I deserve to do what I want. That work doesn't define my life. That I should stay true to myself. That everything I do is a stepping-stone to something else. That I can do anything, achieve anything I put my mind to. That I can live fully, make a difference, be happy.

Make a difference.

Be happy.

I believed it. Every word.

Despite my efforts to move smart, move fast, move up, I have spent the past five years wandering in circles, trying to find out why it's not working—in other words, not moving at all. I've always believed that my grandmother and the farm to which she belonged were magical in a way I couldn't articulate, maybe because I came from the city, maybe because I was young. It's that brand of magic that now sifts through my fingers, magic that eludes me though I long for it and look for it at every turn. It's the magic I have yet to find in work and marriage and the trappings of my ripe adulthood, magic I would give almost anything to recapture. If I can have what I want, I want *this:* the wonder and meaning and legacy that I glimpsed too briefly in that woman on a farm.

Until now, I have gone about this all the wrong way.

My grandparents visited us in Illinois sometimes, and when I was home from college during one of these visits I must have started to realize who they were, what I had in them, because I decided I wanted a picture of the three of us. I sat between them on the couch and had someone snap the shot. I don't remember who. None of us is smiling, and all hands are resting in their respective laps, awkward like a first date. I can barely stand to look at it. I should have known better. They weren't the type of people to show their love in arms around shoulders. I've made that mistake again and again, taking pictures of fences and barn doors and lilac bushes and sky in an attempt to capture like a firefly in a mason jar everything that is my childhood and my grandparents and the life I knew, even the little of it, in Breidel Coulee. I know it's pointless. No frame is big enough to hold it all. Never was.

But I have allowed myself to entertain the possibility of another way, which is how I have come to be staring over a barbed wire fence a mile outside Carson three years into the new century.

EVEN WITH ONE HAND PRESSED to my forehead as a visor, I squint. Cumulus clouds line the earth and obscure the midday sun, but they do little to quell the brightness. Slightly sloping hills surround the depression in which I stand; those straight ahead and to the right are speckled with black cattle. Tall grasses carrying the earthy scent of grain ripple and swell as though I am in the middle of the sea and at this moment walking on water. Far off, halfhearted buttes poke up from the horizon: some flat, some rounded. Five enormous cottonwoods stand guard a quarter mile ahead, while a row of smaller trees lines the ridge to the right—the only trees for miles.

Tumbleweeds have caught in the fence like lint on a sweater and are piling up. My husband of nine months, Paul, slams the car door, a sound that interrupts the silence and is carried away by the wind. No rusting metal sign dangles between fence posts telling us not to trespass, so we lift the top wire and slide underneath. An old dirt drive leads into the property, parallel tire grooves worn but still visible. A few feet in, the drive vanishes beneath willowy grasses and weeds, so we veer left, toward the cottonwoods.

A few days ago, we left Chicago and drove a thousand miles on a winding route through Wisconsin and Minnesota. I packed a camera, a laptop, a digital recorder, the wrong clothes. It's early June, and temperatures at night dip into the forties. Because we are willfully unemployed and preparing to move to the East Coast, we have been camping. Even fully dressed and wrapped inside my sleeping bag, which is stitched and padded to withstand far colder temperatures, I shiver most of the night. We had planned to camp last night, but the only campground in the vicinity was missing toilets, leaving us to heat chicken and canned green beans over a propane flame before trying the motel in nearby Elgin, fifteen miles away. The sign in the window read NO VACANCY, but I felt certain someone had erred, as we had seen fewer people in Carson and Elgin combined than we would at our commuter train platform on any given morning. My husband went in to check. Minutes later he returned, assuring me that the sign was indeed correct: nurses helping at the hospital held keys to all thirteen rooms.

Twenty minutes later, we sat in the parking lot of Carson's El Rancho, where a scruffy dog strained his chain just out of reach of the office, barking and snarling almost rabidly. I stared him down as I walked through the open door. The small office was empty. I heard televised laughter somewhere beyond, so I called out, knocked on the inside door, waited. No one came. Noticing a white phone on an end table, I sat down and dialed the number of my grandmother's niece, Evelyn, whom I'd never met, and stuttered out a request to stay the night. I had merely intended to interview her for a couple of hours, but Paul and I had run out of options.

"See," she said, "it was meant to be."

Ten miles back into prairie obscura, we knocked on a door, which opened to a woman wildly swinging a broom. She swatted and scowled at the dog jumping on and around our feet—her son's dog, it turned out—trying to protect "them newborn kittens" in the garage. "Shoo! Shoo!" she shrieked, beating the dog back. When the dog finally got the message and retreated, she warmly showed us in. I liked her immediately.

Evelyn Johnson Skretteberg is a short, rapid woman, or rather she gives the impression of constant motion because words leave her mouth and finish quickly. Born in 1920, she belies her age in youth's favor, nearly bowing as she walks because her mind seems to be ahead of the rest of her body. Her hair, dark gray, softly curls close to her head, and during our visit she wears a black sweatshirt from San Antonio screenprinted with Indian beads and feathers. She flavors her language with humor, pausing for a retort and then snorting at her own lines. The details of her house, which is modest and built for retirement, tell you who she is: mismatched china plates resting in brass holders on the wall, photographs of four generations, collectable and homemade dolls in frilly dresses behind glass. Recliners. Furniture made of real wood and plastic magnets on the refrigerator announcing "Uff-Da," and, "Be kind to me. I married a Norwegian." She lives here with her husband, Morville, a kind-faced gentleman whose eyes, even behind his bifocals, prove shinier than his unassuming smile.

We spent the evening huddled around a small, round kitchen table. Paul and Morville cradled their coffee mugs with both hands while Evelyn shuffled through photographs as though dealing a deck of cards. "I hope you got good eyes," she said, " 'cause these pictures are small. This is Benny's boy that was killed on a motorcycle, and this is the Broadhead reunion, and here's when Old Carl passed away. And here's Benhard when he passed away. And here's Grandma. And this is down at Josie's." Within seconds a whole era spread out on laminate. After only fifteen minutes, she pushed the pile of photographs toward me. "You can have them pictures," she said.

"Oh, no, I don't want to take your pictures."

"No, well, when I'm gone, my kids don't know who they are. They'll go out."

We continued through the pile, swapping stories and pouring black coffee into the night, and when everyone started yawning, Evelyn showed Paul and me to a bedroom in the basement, where we fell asleep under afghans and homemade quilts, the soporific and musty smells of country in our lungs and the cold well out of reach.

* * *

NOW I CAN SEE THE HOUSE peeking out from behind the shorter
clump of trees at the base of a hill. Only the frame remains, and
with whole sections of the roof and walls gone it resembles a lantern awaiting a candle. It supported two stories once, with a long,
slanted roof rolling the rain and snow off both sides. After sizing
up the outside, I carefully scale what's left of the steps and walk
inside, creaking and cracking each time my sneaker touches down.
There I snap a photograph through the window, peer into decay-
ing kitchen cabinets, crane my head around the stairs. My grandma
is not here. This was her brother's house. He built this place after
he took over the family farm, using the wood from their father's
house, which once sat a few yards away. He pried up one board at
a time from that old house, walked it over to this spot, and nailed it
to the new frame.

Just outside Paul and I find a square hole cordoned off by splin-
tering logs: the well. Homestead documents will later tell me that
it goes down fourteen feet, dug by my grandma's father and her
brothers more than ninety years ago. I peer over the edge, where
the air feels cooler and thinner and smells of still water, and hear
my voice echo in the blackness. We then amble to the other side
of the house and find remnants of an outline, probably the barn,
where rotting wooden planks stick out of the ground. Up on the
hill an iron pump pokes the horizon, likely put in after my grandmother was gone; when she was here, they used the creek.

Her story started here, somewhere on this land.

From the map and the road I know the creek flows beyond the
cottonwoods, so I walk that way. Cows have slogged through here
recently, leaving behind dried pies and deep hoofprints in the mud.
I pass a broken gate lying sadly against a post and wonder whose
hands hammered it together. The creek winds through the grass,
but it is dry now, cobblestoned in pebbles. Louse Creek, just as
she said. An image appears and is gone: little girls in dirty cotton
dresses splashing and dipping pails for the livestock. Above, the
trees rustle their papery leaves, whispering.

Large, rough stones form a pile nearby like a grave, or an altar, though I know it's merely a collection of what early residents— maybe my relatives—removed from the yard. I select.two stones from the pile and start toward the car, pausing only to brush off ticks and take one last look, though not for long. The stones propel me, the weight like a healthy baby in my hands.

Departures

I WILL START HER STORY on February 15, 1932, and have her eyes open before first light. She finds her sight quickly—outlines of a bed, a night table, a bureau—though the hazy darkness is more shale than black, diluted through the windows by snow. It's a habit, waking this early, before the cows low and the roosters crow and the horses push up from their knees. Her body knows to rise and dress, to put on the coffee and start the chores. On mornings like this, when the snow seeks entrance at every window, when the fire has long gone out and her breath hangs in the air like a misspoken word, the temptation is to stay put. The longer she burrows under the quilts, the longer she puts off the chill that shoots through her body when her feet touch the bare floor. The longer she inhabits quiet, away from the family and the hired men. The longer she retains the illusion of solitude.

But this morning she is not alone. This is her bed, to be sure, and this is her room. The roof above belongs to her sister, Minnie, and her nieces and nephews are sleeping beyond these walls, no different from any other morning. But if Josie slept at all, she is awakening to the momentary confusion of a broken routine, heart pounding. An instant later comes the rush of relief, of remembrance. A suitcase holding all her clothes and personals waits obediently in a corner. The crack beneath and the iron grille overhead reveal two twins pushed together. And beside her, the quilts gently rise and fall, reminding her that she is no longer Miss Josie Twite.

They were farmers, not romantics, but they wed on Valentine's Day. Lee looked so handsome in his suit, his red hair combed down flat like wheat after hail. Josie wore that dress—oh, if she could have kept it!—the one of dusty silk with gauzy cape-like sleeves weighted by tiny pearls. Where the neckline plunged, a brooch anchored the fabric, and a single strand of pearls encircled her neck. A shining pair of dark pumps scored with white graced her feet. Someone had set her hair so that it crimped and tumbled in waves, brushing her cheeks and shoulders, with a definitive part on the right side. And so she wouldn't miss a thing, her wire-rimmed spectacles lighted on her nose.

So many folks crowded around the ceremony downstairs in the living room—more than twenty, just counting family—that it seemed Reverend Norlie was marrying the whole lot of them. Josie's younger brother, Mort, stood up as groomsman, her friend, Mildred Kamrath, as bridesmaid, so says the marriage license. Afterward, the photographer captured the couple before a canvas backdrop, Lee resting on a wicker seat and Josie perched on the edge of a stool. In the photograph Lee's face expresses a solemnity akin to consternation. His feet cross at the ankles, and one hand nestles in the softness of his bride's leg while the other remains hidden behind her, either gripping the stool or daring to touch her. Josie's face exudes a quiet calm, her lips flat and serene but her eyes unmistakably bright.

Lee and Josie Broadhead on their wedding day, February 14, 1932

Because a girl doesn't kiss and tell, we must imagine.

Where can we find her thoughts, this young woman of twenty? Do they linger on the ceremony: reliving the vows, the clapping, the kiss? Are they hung on the last words she said to her mother and father, her sisters and brothers and their children, or the words they breathed in her ears? Have they fixed on the wedding night, on touching and being touched in ways and places that still make her eyes close and her heart somersault? Or are they simply on the man sleeping beside her and the disbelief that he is hers?

These thoughts provide nourishment she will need, as within the hour she will bundle herself in wool stockings and scarves. Lee will pocket his wallet bulging with forty dollars and brush the snow off his '27 Chevy Coach truck before loading their bags and a shovel into the backseat. Her sister will hand them a basket of food: cold beef, bread, wedding cake, a thermos of fresh black coffee. She will wrap her arms around her nieces and nephews, her sister and brother-in-law. Lee will do the same, interjecting an occasional handshake. Then the two of them will climb into the truck and set out on a six-hundred-mile journey. The destination will be La Crosse, Wisconsin, their purpose to claim a wedding gift from Lee's father: the largest farm in Breidel Coulee.

From North Dakota it will be a trip of several days at best, given the shifting mounds of midwinter white, which on the prairie often require a strung wire just to walk from house to barn. Because Josie has never before left the state or had much reason to set foot outside this county, she will marvel at the scenery, what shapes she can decipher through fogged windows and horizontal snow. She will stare, disbelieving, at the trees. Her world has, until now, been a patchwork quilt of land squares framed by county roads and section lines. The prairie, unapologetically Saharan, is all she has known.

THAT SHE WAS BORN IN NORTH DAKOTA on September 3, 1911, was an act and consequence entirely of her father's doing. Some sixteen months before her birth, Josie's family had been fixed to dandelion roots in the southeast corner of the adjoining North Star State. But Martin Twite—husband, father, failure—folded up the family and hauled his brood six hundred miles. Such a move would have meant exile for nearly anyone, all the more for a Norwegian American family with nine children. But the seductive pursuit of free land had called too loudly to Martin—that and the promise of not just a clean slate but one sanded smooth, a slate pitted by the poor judgment and bitterness that come from alcohol. So he staked a homestead claim on a quarter section a mile outside the new town of Carson, just south and west of central.

Josie had dropped into her sister Manda's wet hands, the tenth child of thirteen. At sixteen, Manda was a capable midwife, having already ushered another Twite child into the world. Several years later she would birth her own baby one morning, clean up, and bring forth a neighbor's that same afternoon. (So says Josie's older brother, Henry, who got himself interested in the family history and recorded ten hours of it on cassette.) Though the birth certificate, not registered until 1942, showed that the baby's name was Teolena Josephine Twite, I know of no one who called her Teolena. She was always Josie, which explains why her given name often appeared incorrectly as Taillina in formal documents—she herself wasn't sure how to spell it. I think it was a good choice, going with the middle name. Not only was Josie easier for the little ones to say, but the name also contained a secret promise: *Josephine* means "God will increase."

The North Dakota prairie in those days was—and by some accounts still is—a place where many folks, especially farmers, needed such an extra measure of God's help, as they lived with an expanse prone to disasters of earth and heaven: droughts, hail, fires, and swarms of grasshoppers that searched for crops to eat away. A sturdy, stubborn man, Martin Twite had not established himself as a particularly skilled farmer before he homesteaded, and it cannot be said that he improved with change of address. As the choice had been made, and he lacked the courage to undo it, the Twites stayed farmers. Even if he had miraculously transformed into a landsman, it wouldn't have mattered because Martin had left the Land of Ten Thousand Lakes for a desert.

The requisite faith for such an undertaking, it was generally understood, germinated within Martin's wife, Martina; his doctrines, more principle than practice, centered on how to farm, how to box, and how to avoid shotgun weddings. A slender and graceful woman people likened, ironically, to a Grecian goddess, she epitomized prudence. Her small eyes pierced but showed kindness, and she fashioned a bun on the back of her head that became tighter with time. Her limbs rarely saw sunlight, mostly covered by wool even in summer, and if photographs tell the truth, she didn't even wear a wedding ring. Martina had spent all her Sundays in church before she married, but then her attendance dwindled; her husband didn't consider it important, and keeping the Sabbath holy is perhaps the toughest commandment for farmers, especially those who are hard up. While a traveler in Minnesota could in some places encounter as many Lutheran churches as barns, in North Dakota Martina had to travel twenty-five miles to Mandan or make do with a Methodist clergyman. Even so, the Lutheranism of Norway was as much a part of Martina as her blood and bone, and it was fused to that which drove her.

Because no one can conceive that Martina would fail to wrap her children in the same religious conviction, I see no reason not to believe that Josie started out the way her mother intended—with Noah and Joseph and Jesus. The Twite house rang with hymns in English and Norwegian verse. Household routine included stories from the Bible, as well as prayer at meals and before bed. The youngest Twite child, Tina, can still recite this Norwegian prayer:

J Jesu naun gaar vi til bord an spise, drikke paa vit ord
In Jesus' name we go to the table to eat, drink at thy word
Gud til ære os til gaun, saa faar vi mad, j Jesu naun, amen
God honors us to be gifted, so we receive our food, in Jesus' name,
amen

Despite their crowded conditions, they always found room to put up the itinerant minister when he passed through, and studying a year of Lutheran catechism with Martina was a rite of passage, though most, if not all, of the children were formally confirmed in a Lutheran church, however far they had to travel.

The only known photograph of Josie as a young child, taken in approximately 1916, shows her standing on the tattered grass near their house with her father and two of her sisters. The house, finished one year earlier, reveals the clean lines of purchased lumber, paid for with who knows what. Josie's brother later used this house as raw material to build the successor I walked through taking photographs. Function divided it into two sections, one for eating and one for sleeping, each with an outside door (one gabled), plate glass windows, and a chimney. A square door on the hillside just out back, nestled against a ridge of waving saplings, led to the cellar. In the photograph, the girls' white dresses glow against the dusty backdrop, great bows keeping longer hairs from their faces, hairs like corn silk. Josie's older sister, known as the second Clara— the first one had died choking on a kernel of corn—sits against a box of vegetables, her feet straight out in front of her like those of a rag doll. Josie stands to the side, head cocked, index finger in her mouth as if deep in thought. Her hair, cropped, rests on her shoulders, while her dress bellows out around her bare knees. Martin holds an infant, Josie's younger sister Emma Lillian, a towel across his lap. The photographer stood behind Martin and captured only his profile. He looks younger than his forty-eight years, with a hat tilted far back on his head, arms and face darkened by the sun, and the shadow of the next day's shave on his jaw. His head turns toward Josie, suspenders tight against his back, and even from the side it's clear that a grin has pushed his cheeks wide.

Josie didn't yet know how to be angry, to resent her circumstances, unlike her older brothers and sisters, who had known a better, if not easier, life in Minnesota—who had at least known *rain*. But the anger came soon enough, when her father sent her to herd cattle. She wasn't special, just six years old and next in line. The children saw herding as quite possibly the most boring and cruel job anyone could imagine: sitting for eight to ten hours a day in the field, alone, watching beef cattle that someone else would eat. Because herding cost less than building fences, herders worked from sowing to threshing—May into September or even October—as hungry cattle wandered into the long, green rows to graze on sweet

Martin Twite and his daughters Emma Lillian (with Martin),
Clara Matilda (center), and Josie (right) at the second Twite home
on the Carson, North Dakota, homestead, circa 1916

shoots of wheat. Josie's team included Mayflower, her horse, who
would veer left on "yee" and right on "haw," and a border collie
named Carlo trained in hand signals like all Twite dogs. The three
of them had an easy job unless the bulls were breeding, mean, and
likely to attack, with or without a warning snort. Carlo earned his
supper on those days, charging the bull and nipping at the tender
part of the leg, aptly substituting flight for fight.

It would be just like Martina to draw connections between
David, the shepherd king, and Josie's job in the fields. But even
hearing tenfold the importance of the shepherds in the Christ
story couldn't soothe the growing bitterness she felt toward her
father, not merely because she had to pass her days in the fields,
but because she had to miss out on something she wanted more
than Christmas: school. When Morton County split in 1916, Carson
became the seat for the western half, new Grant County—an initia-
tive, some family members say, that was partly Martin Twite's doing. Validating Martin's choice of settlement, the town now boasted
a flour mill and two grain elevators—which I've seen, telephone

connections, a doctor, a Presbyterian church, a couple of pool halls, and a brand-new school.

Thain Consolidated School stood on a hill like something out of Jesus' parables. The front section of the cubed white structure jutted out beneath a symmetrical triangular roof, and two Corinthian columns supported a portico beneath an arched window. I doubt that anyone knew or minded that the architecture mixed Greek Revival, Colonial, and Italianate styles, and in fact residents were probably pleased that it just looked nice. With four rooms, Thain offered primary grades on the first floor and two years of high school on the second, and its library held a couple hundred books—a dramatic departure from one-room schoolhouses. Even so, what people remember is not its tomes or building or teachers; what they mention before anything else is the school bus.

Thain's school bus ran every morning and afternoon; a couple of horses provided its engine, wooden benches inside a covered wagon its seats. This bus supplied the reason Josie went to school as much as she did; because Thain was a mile and a half from the Twite homestead and the lone school in the township, Martin not only helped to develop the school and joined the school board, he also volunteered his children, as they came of age, to hitch the wagon and drive the ten- to fifteen-mile route. (The older Twite children must have laughed cynically upon learning of their father's role. He did not oppose education in principle, they knew, and he had sent each of them off to first grade. But this they also knew: whether their father needed the help or was just plain threatened by the idea of a smart kid, he got itchy when anyone reached age ten or eleven, and relief came only through yanking that child from school.) The driver's job was fraught with the perils that a concoction of children, weather, and horses can present, but even runaway broncs, accidental stabbings from a covert game of mumblety-peg, or wagons stuck in ice or mud or hoppers were welcome alternatives to herding cattle.

Sometimes the school year started late to accommodate thresh-ing, but more often Martin Twite kept his children out long enough for them to be sufficiently behind. Original school records expose the truth: Josie missed an average of thirty-eight days a year, the worst run being 1926–1927, when she missed more than seventy-two days—40 percent of class time. Sitting on the hill as the hori-zon pushed away from the sun, Josie could clearly watch the school bus on its route. "I often thought my father thought more of the cows," Josie later wrote, "than he did us kids."

Though Josie hated the fields for their manacles, they granted her more freedom than anywhere else. There she could be and do almost whatever she wanted, and her imagination and courage grew fat on time. She held her own school: lessons required building cas-tles and cathedrals from stones, acting out stories from the books her brothers brought or left at home, and singing hymns in operatic falsetto. On some days she gave great speeches through a mouthful of pebbles to improve her diction; on others she solved the problems of neighboring farmers (or so she thought). The hills represented her vast stage, the beasts her only audience, and she built a fantasy world that chased away the monotony and its acrid taste.

Even so, Josie claimed that she was not an outgoing child, that people scared her, and that she hid behind chairs when they came to visit. Certainly weeks upon weeks in the wild bred into her a savage inwardness, a fierce possession of her world that had no-where to go when the cows came home. All her imagination and dramatic revelry simply served to fill the hole where confidence should have been, and even then the fit wasn't right. Not know-ing things—being kept from school—might have siphoned her self-reliance, and it didn't help that she often learned through humilia-tion, which kicked her right toward an unflinching integrity. That first year in school her teacher caught her copying someone else's answers during a test and placed a sign around her neck that said CHEATED IN SPELLING—a lesson, it would turn out, with claws.

Probably she was just lonely.

When Martin told Josie to take the cattle to the north range, he might as well have told her that the hills were made of sugar, because her best friend, Ruth Keierleber, herded there. Their homesteads touched at the corner. The girls passed the long days by collecting polished stones, splashing after water bugs, and forming mud mounds, usually coming home wet or dirty and almost without exception a disheveled mess. Once in a while things got rough between the herds or the girls—as when Ruth threw a snake at Josie—and they parted ways, but mostly they played. In the afternoon, they'd hoist themselves up onto their horses and guide their herds home, Josie riding bareback because her father couldn't afford a saddle.

Threshing almost compensated for the rest of the year, and not only because it meant no more herding. When the steam engine rolled in, adrenaline revived tired limbs, and even the most resistant found reasons to help. Most farmers couldn't afford their own threshing machines, so they pooled their money and rented one, complete with four or more operators. Each paying man had a turn and, what's more, a full crew to shoulder the work; the men traveled from farm to farm with the thresher. The process, though simple, taxed man and horse alike: before the engine arrived, they mowed, gathered, bundled, tied, stacked, and dried the wheat. Then they fed the brittle shocks into the separator, which, after sending the wheat high into the air, spit the straw onto the ground and piled the grain in a wagon. Shiny levers, chains, and cogs spurted great noises and unknown smells of oil and smoke. Josie, her brothers and sisters, and the neighbor children scurried nearly all day bringing water and coffee and food to the men, looking for reasons to linger by the strange machine. With twelve or fifteen people in a threshing crew, the wives, red-faced and damp, worked all day in the kitchen preparing the biggest meals of the year: meat and potatoes, bread and pie. When it was all over, each farmer's yearly income was heaped in bushels and needed only to be taken to market. Josie's brother Henry explained that on the Twite farm, "The grain was shoveled into granaries and stored until such time that the price was right or you had bills to pay, which usually was the case."

Perhaps Christmas showed the children the state of their parents' finances more clearly than any other time of the year. One Christmas morning, Josie raced to the fireplace, pulled her stocking from the mantle, reached inside, and drew out a school tablet. A disappointment. She reached in a second and third time and found one piece of hard candy each. The fourth time in, her hand felt only yarn, so she turned the sock upside down and shook it, but nothing came out. She threw the stocking down, ran upstairs, leapt into bed, and cried.

Martina, on finding Josie muffled by quilts, told her why the stockings were so empty. "Santa is very poor this year," she told her young daughter, "and he couldn't afford any more." Josie sulked, thinking only of returning to school and having to hear about the gifts her classmates had received: baby dolls and hair bows and other dreams from the Sears, Roebuck catalog. Her first day back, she quietly asked a friend what she had gotten for Christmas. The other little girl nearly wept, embarrassed, and whispered, "A tablet." Josie then knew her mother was right: Santa was having a hard year.

North Dakota fared no better than the North Pole. Even if Martin was shrewd and savvy with money, which he wasn't, the Dakota climate couldn't keep up with the demands that farmers and crops and livestock placed on it. While 1908 and 1909 had continued a long trend of higher wheat crops, right after the Twites arrived the pattern broke sharply, and it stayed broken the following year. Then the yields shot up again before plunging. These inconsistencies could have resulted from any number of factors, but the reasons didn't matter as much as the impact: they made planning nearly impossible and could swing a farmer from prosperity to crippling debt in a matter of months, weeks, days, or even minutes.

Plan A: raise crops and cattle.

Plan B: sell anything you can.

Though farmers worked where they lived, they juggled the farm and family as they would a snake in hand. Ideally, most of what a farm produced would be income, but because reality tended toward insufficiency, means of filling their own stomachs and covering their own skin usually came from other sources. Martin and Martina each tended a garden. They reared a few sheep for wool, hogs and chickens for meat and eggs. The family churned butter and molded "stinky cheese" (similar to limburger) from the milk they kept for themselves, and the mill in town ground some of their grain into flour for bread. Girls plucked and canned; boys hunted, trapped, sheared, tanned, and smoked. With all their work, and if heaven cooperated, they had enough to feed and dress themselves and still some for market. Barely.

Apart from the beef cattle and standard crops—wheat, oats, flax, corn, peas, and potatoes—Martina traded eggs, onions, cabbage, and turkeys for cash or store credit. The turkeys paid for most of the clothes and the peanut butter, which came mail order from Savage and Co. The onions provided for coal from Pederson's mine, which was only a dollar a load if they shoveled it themselves. Cabbage bought oatmeal, sugar, and sometimes—if a sale was on—molasses for ginger cookies. Cream checks took care of salt and saltpeter, kerosene, school tablets, spices, and other necessities.

Because the Twites sold their milk, when Josie wasn't in the field, she was ridding the barn of birds. If they were left to nest, careless wings or droppings could wind up in the milk and spoil an entire bucket. Josie and her younger brother, Mort, tried to catch those barn swallows, which led her to amble up into the rafters and hop from beam to beam. It became a game. When she unretractably lost her footing, as she did on one particular day, the fall was a good fifteen feet onto packed dirt, and only providence ensured that she just missed the horses and sure death from a retaliatory kick in the head. Josie crawled toward the house until her mother saw and ran to help. Martina applied the usual medicine—Watkins liniment and skunk oil—to the stunned girl, washed her up, and helped her to bed, but by the next morning one leg had swollen to twice its size and marbled black and red. A fever brewed. Martina begged her husband, who had no time for doctors or their bills, to go for help, but like numerous times before, her pleas did as much good as that smelly old ointment. So with uncharacteristic asser-tiveness, Martina hitched up the wagon and took Josie herself, by-passing Carson's Dr. Leavitt and driving out of town to Dr. William Shortridge at Flasher Hospital, more than fifteen miles away. "The doctor took one look at my leg and demanded to know why I hadn't been brought in before," Josie later wrote. "He shook his head and said he didn't know if he could save the leg." Martina muttered un-der her breath.

The doctor laid the weak girl on a long wooden table, removed her clothes, and wrapped her in a sheet. After rubbing her leg with disinfectant, he set it, grunting with each pull and twist. Josie screamed until she passed out. A week of delirium went by. When she came to for good, she found herself connected to a web of ropes and pulleys anchored by a milk bucket, her leg white as wool and thick with plaster. There she lay for several weeks until the leg had healed strong and straight. The injury stayed with her, contribut-ing to an almost deforming and crippling hunchback effect in later years that no one could fully explain; still, the day her cast came off she thanked God for the medicines and the doctor just as surely as her mother did, even if her father begrudged the bill. (Ninety years later, though she didn't live to see it, her great-grandson David repeated this episode, falling through the second story of a barn and severely breaking his leg.) This incident could have shifted Josie's life dramatically if her mother hadn't intervened. She not only would have been crippled, but she would have known that no one—God included—cared enough to advocate for her. Instead, she witnessed the risk and sacrifice of love, and it restored her, and her faith grew.

The mother Josie knew in those years was the same one her older brothers and sisters had grown up with—filled with faith and virtue, endless fortitude and energy—but her father was not. Since leaving Minnesota, he had stayed dry—a character good and raw and unburdened by the drive to meanness that alcohol once fostered. To those he begat on the prairie, he had always been the giver of hard candies, which he tucked up in the kitchen rafters. He had been the cutter of men's hair, a man who barbered tobacco-spitting neighbors for good conversation or a little help in the fields. Even if he emanated sternness at times, he also remained a fixture at the almost weekly house parties, where—if he wasn't playing the popular Norwegian card game whist—he glided bow against fiddle as the whole family danced the one-step or polka long into the next morning. Martin represented an important someone in the community who helped convert wagon trails into roads, built schools, and promoted 4-H clubs (head! heart! hands! health!). Josie's face often dripped pink from his watermelons as she and the other children paged through the Sears, Roebuck or Montgomery Ward catalogs at night—before the books were relegated to the outhouse—looking at hair combs and books and phonographs, even if they ordered only winter clothes and shoes. I don't think calling him her hero would be overstating the case. This is the father she first knew, but it would not be long before she saw the other one.

Just after Josie started school, any threads left on the Twites' thin string of plenty began to strain, fray, and unravel altogether. In October 1917, Josie's sister, Emma Lillian, who had lived only nineteen months, developed a flulike illness bad enough to call in Dr. Leavitt an unknown number of times between October 12 and October 30. A week into November the illness still raged, and because Martin would not fetch the doctor again, the younger children stood by the crib with their mother and watched Emma's tiny body violently convulse and at last be still. "I happened to be there with Mother," Josie wrote, "and saw the sadness and sorrow that can come to you when a loved one is gone." Emma died from those convulsions, but Dr. Leavitt wrote on the death certificate that a contributing element was exhaustion; she had been ill for at least twenty-six days.

After they buried Emma, ten-year-old sister Clara told her mother, "I'm not gonna live either." Boils from the tuberculosis she'd been fighting for most of a year covered her body, and she'd say, "Set me down, Mama, set me down," because it hurt too badly to be held. As with Emma, Dr. Leavitt had attended Clara throughout her illness but hadn't been to the house specifically to treat her since early September. On December 10, with a mound still fresh in Community Cemetery, the second Clara died of multiple tubercular abscesses, just as she predicted. *The Carson Press* listed the obituary under "News Items of Town and Country" on an inner page: "This is the second time the grim reaper has visited the home of Mr. and Mrs. Twite in the past few weeks, which is very lamentable." The family buried Clara next to her sister, and as they couldn't afford a proper grave, a grieving Martina drew stones from the creek for markers, using a hammer and chisel to carve her daughters' names.

While Martina, carrying her last baby, believed that losing her daughters was God's will, some of her grown children shook their heads and blamed their father. They continued to assume that if their sisters had received proper medical care, the two girls would not have died. Josie, having a leg spared but two sisters not, must have seen even then that denying a child help was close to unforgivable, and she couldn't be that kind of person and live with herself. Her parents had unknowingly begun to hold themselves up as her two choices: mercy or self-serving coldness of heart. Though at times her nature vacillated between them, one would have to win, and her conscience screamed to her which one it would be.

Martina never recognized cruelty in the loss, nor did she blame. She instead spoke openly of clinging to faith, of holding her face to the light so that the ever-darkening shadows would fall behind. And years afterward she told her grandchildren about the day she saw Clara fly to heaven. In perhaps his own sort of faith or atonement, Martin wanted to name the coming child Clara, but Martina protested—not unreasonably—until they decided on Tina Advina Twite. More than sixty years passed before Tina applied for Social Security and learned the truth: although they had called her Tina, her father had named her Clara after all.

After illness had taken two of Josie's sisters, the government threatened to take her two oldest brothers. When the boys received their draft summonses for the war, twenty-one-year-old Benhard (pronounced *Bennerd*) enlisted first, but the navy rejected him for being too slight. Clarence, then nearing twenty-five, had by some accounts moved from working the Montana beet fields to the West Coast the year before, so he wrote to his draft board and asked if he could report to Fort Lewis outside Seattle, a shorter and less expensive trip than the one to Iowa. "Son," they told him, "this is the army, and you go where we tell you to go." Their response set off Clarence, who had a penchant for doing the opposite of what others expected of him, a privilege the oldest son wasn't supposed to get. Norwegians didn't much like Swedes then, so it was Swedes with whom he associated and worked. Instead of hunting, playing sports, or wooing women, he gambled in back rooms, traveled alone, frequented whorehouses, and discovered what his father liked about drinking. The folks in and around Carson learned right quick to keep Clarence away from parties if liquor was being served. To his younger brothers and sisters he could be a tyrant, someone who had mastered not delegation but domination, but the right circumstances exposed a tenderness: before leaving home, he had given Josie a doll for her sixth birthday.

Clarence, Minnie, Manda, and Benhard Twite, likely taken in Minnesota circa 1910

The Twites on the North Dakota prairie, circa 1918, from left: Manda Twite Johnson, Josie Twite, Minnie Twite, Martin Twite, Martina Twite, Mort Twite, Charlie Johnson holding son Clarence, Carl Twite, Benhard Twite, and Henry Twite

The most telling photograph of Clarence shows him facing a friend, his head turned toward the camera, cigarette dangling from a smirk. A dark cap turns his hair into shadow. He wears a turtleneck and jacket, and side-hooked boots poke out from short pants, right hand mysteriously digging into his pocket. His features, almost handsome, and a soaring heft bring his father to mind. Two mismatched chairs slant askew behind the men; perhaps they were supposed to sit, posed, but couldn't make themselves do it. Clarence's friend betrays the reason: he stares directly at the camera, holding a cigarette in one hand and a flask in the other, inviting the photographer to join them.

Clarence did not show up at Fort Lewis or travel to Iowa. Instead he did something the draft board would have anticipated if they had known him: he disappeared. And not just for the rest of the war. Forever. (He might have been scheming even when he completed his draft registration card a year earlier; he initially wrote "married" but crossed it out and penned "single" atop the scribble.) Stories that he had gone north circulated—stories of cryptic notes jotted on cigarette paper and postmarked Canada. Rumors and names were whispered. Relatives spoke of sightings, but when they confronted the man they believed to be Clarence, he said only, "I don't know what you're talking about. My name's Merry Christmas." Then he vanished again. "Ma kept saying [he was] a God-praying boy and would do the right thing," Josie recalled, "but I could tell Ma was worried too. Pa took to walking down the road." Josie also claimed that someone found a letter in a ditch, one Clarence wrote while waiting to hop a train. I have been unable to locate the original; I have only Josie's retyped version. It is addressed to their mother, but most of it sounds too humble and self-deprecating for a rebel son. It also refers to Montana, not Washington, so one of two things is likely fiction: the letter itself or the persona Clarence wanted his mother to see.

I'm sorry I haven't written before . . . but, believe me, I couldn't. I was too ashamed—let me explain.

The draft board sent me a letter that said I was ordered to ship out from Carson. But Ma, how could I? I had just gotten the job in the beet fields and hadn't been paid. I wrote back to the draft board and told them I didn't have the money to get back home. They wrote back and ordered me to be in Carson on September first. I had told them that I was willing to ship out from Butte, but they paid no attention to me. I had orders to ship out from Carson.

I knew you and Pa didn't have the money, and the feller I came up here with didn't have any money. I went to the bank and they wouldn't listen to me either—so what was I supposed to do? I tried to pray on it, but I don't seem to get an answer.

I've decided to take off to Canada. I don't know what else to do. I'm writing this letter on some scrap paper that I had.

I'm not taking violin. The people I board with said I could leave anything I wanted, so I haven't got much and I would like to take along my violin, but I don't know where I would pack it so it would be safe. The violin has good memories. Remember how we used to gather around the kitchen table and sing. I remember your singing. I miss our singing. The people I stay with don't do any singing.

There is a lot of arguing—sometimes even fighting . . . the man of the house drinks worse than Pa. How is Pa? If you could get Pa to swear off drinking, I think you'd have money to pay off the debts. If I get work up in Canada, I'll send you some money.

This isn't the best paper to write on but it's the best I have. My sock has a hole in it. I'm not very good at darning, so I wear my socks until they wear out and throw them. I know that's not the way you do it Ma, but I'm too clumsy. I can't handle a needle like you.

How's the sheep? I was pretty good at shearing sheep. They have lots of sheep here on this ranch, and big fields of beets. This part of Montana looks a lot like North Dakota. I didn't get in on the sheep shearing, but the beets are ready to be harvested and it's all hard work. At the end of a day, my back is feeling kinda rough. Don't worry, Ma, it's nothing serious.

I do a lot of thinking. How are Minnie and Manda and Peter? I wonder if Pete got the barbering job. Is Ben still fiddling around inventing things? I liked that little windmill he made, and the square bolts, and that turn-table. He used them square bolts on that table. I know because I helped Ben install them.

A cricket just crawled over my shoe. That reminds me of home too. Not so much the crickets but the grasshoppers. I see the train coming. I'm going to jump on the train. Don't worry, it's just barely going as they have so many cars on.

The Clarence who surfaced through that letter—a man with good intentions and a longing for home—was the one that Martina hoped to see coming up the road for years afterward, though I expect she would have settled for her boy in any condition. She chose not to believe it then, or ever, but with the coming of the draft notice, she had said good-bye to a fourth child. Josie, if she ever mentioned or wrote about her oldest brother in later years, did so only in wondering. Where he would be, how old, if he was

Clarence Twite (left) and a friend, circa 1917

still alive. Decades later, she drafted a book of embellished letters to him, hoping that she could reach him through "the mass media," but the messages failed to leave her notebook. She never said she missed him, though she kept wondering for seventy-five years. I wanted to find him for her, but Clarence has eluded me, too.

As Clarence mentioned in the letter, around this time Martin remembered the allure of the bottle and Josie began to experience the depths of her father's darkness. Maybe building two tiny coffins sent him spinning toward forgetfulness. Or, it could have been his son's gradual disappearance that renewed Martin's failure as a father. Possibly it was just one too many days of searing work he didn't like in a place he couldn't win for a life that wouldn't end. After eight years divorced from liquor, Josie's father started coming home drunk, introducing her to the father she had yet to meet, the father she had only heard about, one she didn't want any more than she wanted to drop out of school. Josie's childhood melted away, and in learning to hide from him and his curses she learned a lot of other things as well, namely, that alcohol is godless—to a child of seven, that meant a scary man who stayed out late, yelled mean words, and threw good shoes in the fire. She found that the more her father drank, the more she had to work and the more her mother cried. Mostly she learned how to watch someone to whom she was inextricably tied teeter on the edge of hell. This is the father she would remember, the one who would inspire in her as much strength as he did fear.

IN AN HOUR JOSIE AND HER NEW HUSBAND will leave the prairie for a life she must still pinch herself to believe. If she thinks she is shedding her past like an old rattler skin, she's wrong. It will follow her, just as sure as night chases day. It will haunt her, threaten her, forge her. It is in her. If I were Mrs. Lee Broadhead, I would draw close to my dreaming lover, and, for the moment, try to forget everything but him.

Kinship

Burke, Virginia
2004

THE USUAL TRAPPINGS LITTER MY DESK: things to write on, write with, fasten together. I have also placed here a kaleidoscope, green, a slate coaster, square, and a lamp, burnished. Two photographs float in clear rectangular frames, the light from the windows illuminating them from behind like an old View-Master: Josie and Lee in the shyness of courtship, Josie standing in the ocean. I hadn't thought to put them there until I heard several other writers describe their desks as shrines of evidence. Research. Inspiration. I removed the pictures from the box next to my desk and placed them on display, many months ago now, and I must say that I at last see the logic. I stare at them often; they do, in a sense, communicate.

I also stare at the two paperweights over near the pencil cup, both medallions. One is brass. The other, pewter, feels heavier than it looks and strangely soothes the fingers—the weight, the cool texture. I often run my thumb over the molded image of a right hand, which grasps a feather pen above an open book. The other side reveals an etching:

1st

Plays

J. Broadhead

No one had to tell me to put that out.

My grandmother was a writer—at least she wanted to be for the last thirty years of her life, making her and me the only aspiring writers in this family line. Ours is a family of teachers; counting daughters-in-law there are seven. Need, not want, first drew Josie—somebody had to write and direct the kids' Christmas plays at church and 4-H—but in time the need became a monopoly: "Josie did *all* the programs at church," says Jean Schmaltz Henderson, who can still picture Josie corralling her and the other children for rehearsal. Then the monopoly became a need: Josie simply could not stop writing. She had, at last, an outlet for her imagination, a place to let loose the ideas and stories that had trailed her since her days of herding cattle. She had, at last, something that belonged entirely to her.

Writing for church was day work; writing for herself remained an indulgence relegated to minutes eked out late at night after everyone else had gone to sleep. When the typewriter instead of children's voices called her in the afternoons, she allowed herself to draw near and hunch, frenetically pecking away. Classes—made just for her!—such as the partnership between Western Wisconsin Technical College and the Harry J. Olson Senior Center, eventually introduced her to plot, character, and dialogue.

Josie convinced Lorraine Leske, then the church choir director, to join her for one of these workshops. A short, heavyset woman, Lorraine Leske wears her hair long and streaked. A fierce pride commands her face and her voice, almost humorous in its earnestness. She lives in Mormon Coulee on Leske Road, a couple of miles from the farm. "I don't know if I should use the word," Lorraine confides, "but we fancied ourselves as writers. I think she sucked me into it a little bit for the transportation sometimes."

That is probably true. The state of Wisconsin issued Josie her first driver's license after she turned fifty-five, but she stopped driving outside the coulee soon after because she blacked out once on a trip back from town. So Lorraine would pick Josie up, and they'd tool off to class at the old Northern States building on Green Bay Street, talking about writing all the way there and all the way back. Their discussions continued in Josie's driveway until darkness precluded them from reading their work or one of them said, "Well, I s'pose I should get on inside and get something done."

The front-seat workshops centered on Josie's plays, mostly because that's what Josie wrote. Plays had use; she could see them working on multiple levels as her stories and their morals did their jobs with the children and the audience. But she had some problems with character movement, so more than once Lorraine pulled out a sheet of paper, drew a stage, sighed, and said to Josie, "Okay. You have this here character leaving through this door one minute, but then you have him over there saying something the next. That just won't work." Josie would nod and take it all in.

If the teacher had returned their work with comments, many of which were far from praise, the two women discussed those, too. "That didn't seem to slow 'er down a whole lot, though," Lorraine remembers. "She studied that a little bit and then, 'Well, okay,' and she'd rip the page in half, [put a] new one in the typewriter, and away we go again. She spent more time typing than the law allows. I don't think she gave one diddly darn if she ever published anything or ever produced anything outside of the 4-H. She just liked the exercise of doing the work."

I've since thought about this remark. My mom has always talked about Grandma Josie's writing in an unapologetically pedestrian manner—that it served merely as *something for her to do*. But if ever one woman lived who could do without an extra item on the checklist, it was Josie. She might have enjoyed writing for the challenge—unearthing just the right word, painting a scene, communicating goodness and rightness and truth—but she wanted everything she did to matter. My cousin, Paul, I think, has it right: "She wanted to write something that would be published or people would see and accept and read." She sought not the prizes of pewter medallions and jade rings and flawless report cards; she sought impact: *That was powerful. You touched me. I am changed.*

I think she probably surmised later on that writing should have been her life's work, or at least a bigger part of it. Writing suited her in the way that farming suited Lee; it allowed her imagination to flourish, her mind to sharpen, and her conscience to rest a little more often. Writing gave her a sense of accomplishment and fulfillment, because for Josie it transformed from an activity into another tool for helping people—not only the words on the page or in a young actor's mouth but also the process of putting those words there. Josie wielded the pen as she would a hoe or a wooden spoon, using it to draw in those who lived among the fringe, women such as Hilda First.

On May 25, 1967, Josie sat at the kitchen table, the *La Crosse Tribune* spread out before her, when she came across a photograph of a smiling young girl in a pageboy haircut and Peter Pan collar. The child attended third grade at Washington School, the Broadhead kids' alma mater, but the photograph's placement captured Josie's attention: it appeared beneath "TRI-STATE DEATHS."

"Services have been arranged for Julia Kay First, 8, who died in a La Crosse hospital Wednesday, May 24, of injuries she received when struck by a vehicle near her home Tuesday evening. . . ."

Josie hadn't met the Firsts, a rather new and still unfamiliar family in Mormon Coulee, but after the funeral she drove—herself—over to their home a few miles away. She walked up to the door and knocked on it, and seconds later the dead girl's mother, Hilda, answered. Josie introduced herself, most likely with food in hand, and said she was so very sorry about Julia. Hilda, now an ample, gap-toothed woman with a sleepy voice and short reddish hair, still remembers the gesture with fondness. "Some of [the neighbors] sent stuff and I never saw their face. She was the first neighbor who bothered to come talk to me," she says. "We got to be friends that way."

Hilda's grief poured out in spiritual journaling and poetry, ways to release the rawness but contain it enough for her to keep functioning. She had other children to care for; a husband, too. When Josie checked in on Hilda and learned of the writing, a prompt and enthusiastic invitation to writing class followed. Not only did Hilda become a valuable writing partner, but she earned her GED, finished a two-year program in food management, and began a career she had longed for but thought she could never have with only seven years of school.

Like Lorraine, Hilda served as a counterpoint to the idealism Josie inevitably funneled into her work. "She wrote a lot of stuff," Hilda says, "but she didn't write much bad stuff, you know. She'd write a high school play. And I remember one where she had some kids in the park that were breaking bottles or doing something and the cops turned around and caught 'em and they just turned around and turned out really good, you know. And I'd try to say, 'Well, Josie, you've gotta, you know, do some bad stuff and then some good stuff and then some more bad stuff and then some good stuff.' She wouldn't do that. That doesn't make an exciting story."

Josie's two friends laugh now at her naïveté even as it warms them to remember. They knew she sought not only to tell but also to redeem the stories she had gathered about the people coming in and out of the farm, about her childhood on the prairie, about the black stove. They knew, too, that she changed names because she didn't want to hurt anyone. Oddly enough, she changed significant details as well: farmhouses became mansions landscaped with swans and birdbaths; blue-collar workers evolved into surgeons. I suspect she crafted on paper the life she thought people should have, the life she felt they deserved.

She carted her manuscripts back and forth in a black vinyl briefcase that she patched with electrical tape. She affixed to the side a piece of scrap paper with *Josephine Broadhead* written in black marker. When she didn't have any staples, or her manuscript grew too thick, she sewed it together with a zigzag stitch or poked holes with an awl and used safety pins. No matter what, she kept writing, even when she could no longer type and her pen wobbled her letters into illegibility. It was, it seems to me, her salvation.

I, HOWEVER, AM AN IMPOSTER.

A tourist, a pilgrim, a voyeur, a wanderer.

I came to writing under false pretenses, and it's sure to find me out any day now. Perhaps that will be a relief, as the work is far from easy. What I really want has nothing to do with words.

For as long as I can remember, I've felt compelled to do something extraordinary with my life. My husband, Paul, believes that significance is broadly interpretive and can mean helping a single person, but I tend to think in terms of size, volume, numbers, originality. I never formally embarked on a search for What I'm Supposed To Do with My Life, or my calling, as it's sometimes known. Purpose, passion, path, impact, contribution—whatever you want to call it—I simply can't remember a time when I wasn't looking for it. But it has evaded me. All the while, the clock cartoonishly spins, reminding me that a considerable portion of my life has slid away.

This is what started the whole Josie business.

Not two years ago I lived just north of Chicago in a treetop vintage condominium a few blocks from Lake Michigan. Five days a week, at 7:16 a.m., I rushed down the back stairs, through the gangway and alley, across Kedzie and Chicago Streets, and up to the platform to catch the 7:21. After a sixteen-minute train ride and a twelve-minute walk to the financial district, I wound up in the lobby of the Federal Reserve, where I rode the elevator to the twelfth floor and walked to my desk. I wore heels and skirts. I drafted proposals. I managed projects. I attended meetings. I had business cards.

The job was temporary, I knew, until I could claim that which would one day unfold before me in a glowing Joycean epiphany—that which would propel me from then on. I'm talking about a driving force that thrusts my life forward all the way to the end, not time carved out here and there, not volunteer work, and certainly not leftovers. The problem is, I'm terribly impatient and get tired of waiting for meaning to show up; it tends to travel in the far-right lane. Me, I have to go out and make a life, find a purpose, and create my significance, even though I have a belief in God, and this should all be settled.

After a few years of false starts and outright hallucinations, I persuaded my new husband to migrate eight hundred miles from Chicago to Washington, DC, with me and my dog, Lewis, and all of our stuff. I had orchestrated change for the sake of change, cushioned in the hope that it would elicit more change.

I tripped into writing because a university accepted me into its graduate program after I failed to find a job. Until then I had been in the habit of discounting writing as an impossibility, because I assumed my life's work would involve a profession through which I could measure and quantify my accomplishments. But I could not ignore the facts: a master's degree and dozens of possibilities lay in my wake, possibilities I had sampled and evaluated without hearing the click of fit. I knew that my corporate job would end up with the rest, so, with nothing else brewing and a solid decade of noncommittal dabbling behind me, I became convinced that writing, along with moving, offered the change I had so long sought and very possibly entry into what I'd been born to do. Even so, stripping away the years of trying to become something I'm not for reasons that belong to someone else requires strong turpentine.

So I see. Part of me expected that because I showed a natural inclination toward writing, narratives would gush forth in long days of prolificity, internal motivation would compel me, and I would recognize my calling not only by skill and satisfaction but by ease. Writing has exposed the fault in this thinking, baring its ignorance. On most days, I rise when my eyes stay open, usually about 9:00, find the path of least resistance for taking Lewis out—sweatshirt? trench coat?—and read *The Washington Post* over a bowl of cereal. I may shower, or I may stay in my pajamas. (I can go up to two days without showering or leaving the vicinity of my house and sometimes do.) Then I grade papers for the junior college where I teach part-time, or I write, or I simply stare at my computer screen, which gives me a headache and an excuse to watch television. Every so often I get up and do something neurotically concrete and fulfilling, such as organizing the linen closet. Around noon the mail comes, but inconsistently, so I may make two or three trips to the mailbox before I get it right. Then I go back and write some more and obsess over single paragraphs for hours.

Like a hiker who finds her surroundings suddenly darkened by the dense brush of an unfamiliar wood, I have wandered into a profession known for its mental illnesses and derangements. Because I have chosen late, in my mid-thirties, I study mostly with writers ten years younger than I, who, though I already have a graduate degree and have been teaching since they were memorizing their multiplication tables, seem to receive the assistantships, stipends, and fellowships. The work is solitary; its siren song draws me in and encourages seclusion, and I don't need any help being melancholy. As in my life before, I draft proposals, but they disappear in the mail to strangers—people who return in my self-addressed stamped envelopes comments and decisions on form letters where, if the souls are particularly thoughtful, they've scratched my name into the blank after *Dear* above phrases such as "isn't quite right," "does not fit," and "doesn't meet our current needs." This year alone I have received twenty such letters. I sent out twenty-one. I have no business cards. I attend no meetings. I receive no regular pay-check, and my earnings total less than one-sixth of what I grossed as a corporate consultant, which would place me at the poverty level were I not married to someone employed. I feel constantly guilty that I contribute so little to the household. Whenever I cry and moan and complain about how hard it is, as doubt gnaws at what's left of my rational mind, debating whether this truly fills the void my life whistled with not long ago, I pull the string on my husband, and he tells me exactly what I need to hear: "Just write your book."

WHEN I TOLD MY AUNT BEV that I wanted to write a book on Josie, she hauled out three large cardboard boxes and said, "Here you go." I lifted the flaps, and inside I found a collage of papers and files and photographs and driver's licenses—all the documents Josie had when she died. I began sorting through each box, piling bills here, medical records there, but I was unprepared for the number of manuscripts—first, second, third drafts—the research, the lists of ideas jotted on the back of scrap paper I recognized from Bev's classroom and my dad's office. Notes from teachers scribbled in red pen busied some copies (*A ballad must read better than this, dear. This needs much work!*). I stumbled across a few letters as well, all too familiar by their content: *Dear Author: Thanks for writing us about your manuscript. We've considered it, but it's not what we're currently looking for. Each publishing company has to set its own priorities, and sometimes the choice of what to publish can be very difficult. We sincerely hope you'll be able to place your work with someone else.*

I hauled one box home and began reading her papers and scan-ning them into my computer. Her work, though raw and undeveloped, showed promise, and her mistakes were those of an amateur, which she was. Telling, not showing. Too many adjectives. Lack of dramatic tension. Melodrama. More than one letter, though, such as this one from a professor at the University of Wisconsin, contained unusual support and encouragement: *Dear Ms. Broad-head: [The play]* <u>*Him*</u> *does have possibilities. I see what you mean when you indicate that the real life story of this boy was a poignantly heart-wrenching one. There is in fact the basis for a fine play in this material. But while your present draft does give evidence of promise, I'm afraid it doesn't probe anywhere nearly deep enough into the motivations and drive of the chief characters. They are by and large shadowy, and therefore the play itself still seems sketchy . . . I hope you will persist with this play.*

What I keep coming back to is not the fact that she could have been a good writer, given enough time, although I have come to believe that. What I keep coming back to is her choice to be wrapped in words—her stories, her writings—during those last months, days, and minutes of her life. But instead of comfort, the stacks of manuscripts pinned her with guilt and regret. She didn't get what she wanted. She didn't become good. She didn't get published. Her passion never became her vocation, but it did become her sacrifice. Something else—or someone else—always came first.

Was this her secret? Giving up her loves? I don't yet know, but I do know it scares the hell out of me.

Neither of us set out to be writers. And maybe in some sense neither of us is yet. But some things happen in spite of ourselves, and, well, here we are. Because of the work she did long ago, and the work I'm doing now, it's come to where it should be and perhaps should have been from the beginning: she extends the left hand, I the right, and together we will tell this story.

Bearings

La Crosse, Wisconsin
2004

When I was a kid and living in suburban Chicago, driving to the farm where my mother grew up in La Crosse, Wisconsin, was not unlike unscrambling an anagram. The official designation was and still is "going over the hill," which refers to leaving Interstate 90 in favor of a back route for the last leg of the trip—the point at which we encounter roads known only by letters: YY, M, B, O. Those who live there would claim it's just a bunch of farms not all that different from the ones in Illinois, but for my brother and me, going over the hill was like entering a secret valley. Strapped into the backseat of our station wagon, once we took the exit toward West Salem we put down our books, our crayons, and our crude electronic games to look out the windows with a sort of reverence. A departure from aluminum siding and half-acre lots, every curve held green fields billowing like blankets on a clothesline—corn and oats, soybeans, wheat, and alfalfa all waving hello. Men driving tractors bejeweled with reflective triangles and wheels big as our plastic swimming pool chugged along. Spotted pigs, horses, and the occasional chickens spilled out of red and white clapboard barns, and if we were fortunate, we spied babies: calves, foals, piglets. The very sight of Holsteins caused my mom to coo with a sadness that could make our eyes water even if we were mad at her. We knew when we'd reached the hill; the car told us with its panting and straining, and gravity pulled us back toward our seats. Guardrails also appeared: rounded posts painted black and white, resembling a row of little jockeys. We went up, up to the tops of rustling birches and walnuts, which obscured the view to the striped fields below. Up we went, snaking around layers of sandstone sticking out its many tongues until it seemed the car would take flight and the road spit us out on the ridge, on top of the world.

Though I've probably gone that way a hundred times, if you asked me to drive you on pure instinct, we would surely end up at a hog farm in Neverland. My parents, who drove us that hundred times, would possibly get you no closer. "I know you exit I-90," my mom said when I asked her for directions last week, "and you take that to, uh . . ."

"It's a frontage road, and uh, it's difficult to say," added my dad. "I have to be there to tell you."

"There's three roads—"

"Yes, there's three roads—"

"And then it takes you to Highway 14," she said definitively. "One might be 33."

"Did someone say TT?" I asked, trying to get everything down.

"One *is* 33, by whatchamacallit," offered my dad.

"The next one is YY."

A pause, and then the final word from both: "Ask your aunt."

WE ALL TAKE THE HIGHWAY NOW, and I wish we didn't. The new way, "going through town," means that we exit at Route 16, which hugs the shopping mall and fast-food chains and office supply stores before it narrows into Losey Boulevard, where little houses with perfectly spaced lots line the drive like lace trim. On the left looms Grandad Bluff (though we've always said "Granddad's Bluff"), its American flag waving high on top. If we turn right on any of the cross streets, such as Cass, we'll end up at the Mississippi, and if we keep going, in Minnesota. A University of Wisconsin campus is down there, as is the site of the old Heileman's brewery, which once boasted the world's largest six pack: towering tanks painted to look like cans of Old Style beer.

If we're early, we turn on Market and drive until we meet Sixteenth, where Ranison Ice Cream and Candy peeks out from behind the bungalows and townie farmhouses, an upended rectangle with a striped awning and, in any given season, two or three people licking pastel cones out front. My mom's only sister, Beverly, lives with her husband in the pale yellow house next door. Bev and Bruce Ranis owned this store for many years but eventually sold it to one of their employees. Bruce intended for one of his two sons to take over just as he had taken over for his father—hence, the name Ranison—but the boys have settled into nonentrepreneurial arrangements.

Quiet streets surround the neighborhood store, and although the store isn't quaint, it is comforting. Neighbors can get quick dinners and forgotten items from the row of groceries against the right wall, and they can replenish their coolers with the beer and pop waiting at the back, in refrigerators partially obscured by shiny posters from Coke, Miller, Mountain Dew. For purely hedonistic needs, customers only need lean to the left. Lining the front wall, at child's eye level, is the popcorn and penny candy counter, where my brother and I filled little brown bags with Bottle Caps, Bazooka, and candy cigarettes before our trips home in the station wagon. The chocolate counter comes next: shiny glass cases lined with dark and milk chocolate hiding almonds and peanut butter, mints and fudge, candied orange and lovefood, a crunchy concoction of hardened bubbled syrup. When we were young and unrestrained, my brother and I followed our cousins through the back of the store, where grown-ups dipped those sweet-smelling chocolates and winked as we nibbled on ten-pound bars. But most stop by for the ice cream in the back corner. My mom once said she could eat ice cream three meals a day, and I believed her. Our family considers it a staple. Ranison flavors, none of them low-fat, include Grape Nut and brownie, blue moon and pumpkin. I had forgotten about pumpkin until my most recent visit to La Crosse, but once someone reminded me, I made a special stop to get some.

At 8:00 on that October Wednesday I walk into the store, which I find empty of people, including help. I scan the board and see that pumpkin is available. A minute passes, and no employee appears, so I sing a long hello, like a piano key that's stuck. A petite blonde teenager emerges, scuffing her way from the back in an oversized green T-shirt and braided choker, her hair in an unfinished ponytail. I tell her I'd like a small pumpkin milkshake, please. She sleepily goes to work scooping pale orange into a cup, packing every scoop for several seconds.

"So," she says, staring into the freezer and pausing for emphasis, "how was your day?"

"It was fine," I reply, half smiling. "How was yours?"

"Oh, fine," she sighs.

Silence, another scoop.

"Whad'ya do?"

"I did some research for a book I'm working on, so I went to a county courthouse and collected some records."

"What's your book about?"

"It's about a woman who lived on a farm just outside of town."

She stops, ice cream scoop in hand, and looks at me, her eyes wide. "You're like one of those people on PBS, a detective—what do you call them?"

"A history detective?" I offer.

"Yeah, that's it!" She slowly pours milk into the cup, nodding her head. "So, you're a history detective."

"Something like that."

"I want to be either a history professor or a kindergarten teacher," she says.

"Good for you."

More silence as she inserts the cup into the mixer.

"So. What do you think of La Crosse?"

"I like it," I say.

"Yeah, you know people say that it's boring, that there's nothing to do here, but I think they're not looking hard enough. If I was gonna live anywhere, I'd probably live here, or in Jackson County, but I don't wanna move just to move. I wanna have a reason and not just be one of those people who contribute to urban sprawl."

She mixes my milkshake for a long time.

"Where ya staying?"

"I'm staying with my aunt, on her farm."

"The *same* farm?"

"That's the one."

"Ohhh." More nodding.

I don't tell her that I used to stand where she's standing, that my cousins once locked me in the freezer where they store the extra pumpkin, that I am related to the people next door whose name still decorates the candy boxes. I withhold the fact that the peanut brittle my uncle slathered onto the marble counter out back with a wooden paddle and broke like glass melted on my tongue even before she was born. She doesn't realize that two old ladies, my grandmother and her sister Tina, spent many hours on stools in the back room dipping chocolates, paid with good company and free samples for their men. She has no way of knowing that this place, in a way, belongs to me.

She hands me the cup and a straw, and I pay.

"Good luck with your book," she says.

I raise my pumpkin milkshake and wish her well.

OVER THE HILL OR THROUGH TOWN, we end up at the same place: winding along Mormon Coulee on Route 14. Hills lean in on both sides as if eavesdropping, exposing some farms and hiding others. The farm, our farm, is shy, waiting until the last minute to appear. Just before the turnoff, we see it—the house, the barns, the fields— welcoming us to Breidel Coulee. And though I was neither born nor grew up here, I can't help feeling that it's welcoming me home.

A narrow patchwork of tar and old asphalt, Breidel Coulee Road burrows into a gentle valley like a long ribbon. As far as the road runs straight, about a mile, it flirts with the farm boundary, dipping at the first bridge and leveling out in front of the white house. It remains flat past Heslips' place, rising and cresting at the eastern bend near the hickory trees, uncurling for another two miles into the back of the coulee.

Almost without exception my family's station wagon bypassed the cluster of farm buildings and went straight to my grandparents' house, which, for nearly my entire life, was that white farmhouse a half mile in. I didn't know until recently that the house originally sheltered hired help, then my uncle and his wife, and finally my grandparents. It had been modernized by the time I showed up, so I remember only the aluminum siding, the screened porch, the one-car garage. A large oak shaded the front yard until lightning struck and killed it, leaving a big, flat stump behind the mailbox that someone eventually blasted out.

The yard backed up to the cow path at the base of a hill, or, as everyone still refers to it, "*the* hill," which is different from the hill just gone over. Generous lengths of grass framed the house, the rest of the yard being garden: a smaller one out back and a larger one, which continued a good half acre, to the left. They supplied enough strawberries to warrant the word *patch*. Between the two gardens a rusting steel drum waited for burning garbage near a small shed, where I one night witnessed my grandfather killing a gunnysack's worth of squawking chickens. Truth be told, I only saw his silhouette raise the ax against the spotlight. I closed my eyes for the rest.

Theirs was a house of doors. I count fourteen, seven of which opened to the outside—a terrifically practical arrangement. The front door hinged on the side of the house, a step above a drenched and useless doormat that begged for wiping but was sufficiently ignored, so the tile and old linoleum squares just inside could not seem to stay dry or clean. Here the familiar coulee smell of dirt, iron, mildew, and hay lingered, saturating the wood.

Upon entering, folks had a choice: down to the basement or up to the rest of the house. Few chose down, because two stairs and three steps in, past the narrow inlet for coats and work boots on the left, sat the heart of the house: the kitchen. The table made it so. It was the kind with stainless steel legs and a laminate top, a 1950s model—later replaced by wood—rimmed with mismatched chairs. Everything a person needed was within reach of this table, and folks gathered here not simply for the obvious—food, water, rest—but for the things they would never ask for out loud: connection, comfort, acceptance. On the far wall, set off by wallpapered orange gingham flowers the size of dinner plates, metal brackets from counter to ceiling supported plywood shelves, a repository for photographs of grandchildren, miniature tractors, and a thirteen-inch black-and-white television set that received only channel 8. A working cuckoo clock hung high on that wall, a gift from their oldest daughter, Beverly, when she lived in Germany.

From the kitchen, you could directly access four other rooms. If you walked counterclockwise through the first floor, you'd pass the sliding glass doors to the screened porch and enter the dining room through a gently arched opening. From there you'd cut through the master bedroom, walk by a second basement stairwell, and emerge in a long living room. Stepping back into the kitchen, you could then visit the bathroom, which was nestled between the sink and stovetop.

The dining and living rooms had several things in common: carpet, formal sets of furniture, outside doors, and because the residents were kitchen people, low visitation. In the living room, where bright blue dominated, a sad clown hung framed on the wall. I think now that a relative painted it. An organ anchored one end, a color console television the other. The dining room boasted a four-footed stereo, featuring singles such as "I'm in Love with a Boy from the F.F.A.," and a dark walnut sideboard, which now houses my T-shirts instead of unwrapped linens. On the wall a single nail supported a framed picture of the Dali *Last Supper,* with Jesus presiding over the disciples and the dining room table covered in protective plastic. In the fall, when the heat first came on, to my great disgust, blasts of warm air shot dozens of box elder bugs up from the floor like popcorn, leaving them to crawl and die at the base of the picture window overlooking the farm.

The master bedroom, functional and modest and tiled in dark brown, provided a place for clothes, sleep, and business; the standard furniture lined the walls, and a collage of papers weighted down by a manual Smith-Corona covered a small desk, which snugly fit underneath a narrow window facing the farm. The three upstairs bedrooms waited at the top of a steep staircase carpeted in something not unlike a Brillo pad: the first, my favorite, an iron-railed landing with an outside door to the roof, which was, for some reason, fenced; the second, a rectangular collection of dressers; the third, a long strip with closets that seemed to recede into the next county. In each hung a single bulb accompanied by a pull chain and very high expectations.

The one bathroom, in the kitchen, contained no shower, and the window above the tub always seemed to be open, raising paranoia that certain boy cousins were spying. One mirror hung over the sink and another over the toilet, so not only could you see your front and back at the same time, but you could see reflections of your reflections. To shower, you descended to the laundry and sewing area of the basement, which, because it lacked doors, hurried folks along. People might be lurking beyond the furnace in the shadowy tool corner, where everything seemed to be black and coated in an oily film. Or they might be anywhere in the rest of the musty basement, which appeared even darker for its coat of storm-cloud gray paint, save one feature: a tiny closet that hid bottles of sugary pop and sealed jars behind a sheet nailed to the wall.

For years I imagined how I would redecorate the house if it belonged to me—paint, wood, trendy furniture—but a couple of young teachers bought the place for sixty thousand and change in 1995 and did it instead. I've seen it since, and their changes were remarkable, in line with what I would have done. I know that they replaced the wallpaper with creamy shades of paint, put in new carpeting, added a bathroom, but even so, I can't much remember what they did. Seems what's stuck in my mind is what was there before.

I REMEMBER GRANDMA JOSIE in these places as she was in the later years, when her hair was white, her glasses wire-rimmed, and her skin the texture of bread dough. By then she had perfected the hawkish screech that came out when she was yelling for or at Grandpa Lee; it was meant to sound intimidating but resulted only in making anyone who might be standing around—including her husband—laugh under his breath. She hunched over from back pain, which she believed resulted from that rafter fall and too much hoeing. A fashionista she was not, in her polyester pants and blouses, and though I don't remember ever seeing her in makeup, she painted on the cheapest, reddest nail polish she could find, the only thing that would cover up the dirt wedged underneath. She had plenty to paint; she always kept her thumbnails long enough. Her friend Lorraine Leske says, "Those two thumbs were like a spade and a shovel."

She didn't look all that unlike other grandmothers, though if you expected a plump woman in an apron to meet you at the door with a plate of cookies, I'd have advised you to move on. All the elements existed, just in a different order. She baked, but if it couldn't be fried or dropped in a pressure cooker, it generally didn't get any attention. My dad still says that woman knew how to ruin a good steak. But just try to keep a plate of her sizzling "nothings" or cake doughnuts sitting around. She might boil up some water for cocoa after sledding, or you could get yourself something to drink by venturing down into her basement for a glass bottle of Crush—orange, grape, strawberry. She sent cards on birthdays, too, often with a short typed message. She typed everything, in capital letters.

HAPPY BIRTHDAY. LOVE GRANDMA B.

She wasn't the kind of woman who lived for her grandchildren, whose life midway through started circling her children's children, even though four of them lived up the road and another two in town. She wasn't a cheerleader, nor one to greet you with her arms open for a hug, even if you had good news. A distance surrounded her; something about her always remained apart. In the past I might have thought that she was holding back. Now I know that she just treated everyone the same.

Reasoning with the woman, however, proved near impossible, though enough people tried. (I once discussed the idea of the occult with her, and she couldn't see how anyone would want to worship the devil. I kept telling her I knew that but people did it anyway, and she kept saying that couldn't possibly be because it made no sense.) The smarter ones recognized the futility earlier than the rest and learned to work around it. If she saw on the rare occasion that you'd outsmarted her, she'd pull her chin down and laugh a bit, and all was forgiven.

This was the woman I wanted to be, even before I could articulate why. I've always felt a little guilty about that, as if I cherish a stolen desire or an undeserved taste, because in some ways Josie wasn't my grandmother at all. My cousins, who saw her every day, had a grandma, someone they could tell about their test grades and invite to their choral concerts and ask what she would do about those mean kids at school. I had a woman I saw a few times a year, someone I patched together from cards and visits. Geography and personality forged this relationship, and I blame no one; my parents built a life the best they could in another state, and Josie could not have been any other way. I might have earned the right, like the others, to capture and preserve her in my mind, but how could I presume the arrogance of loving and wanting to be like someone I don't even know?

I was keenly aware that the farm wasn't my home, as much as I wanted it to be or thought it so. I was out of my element, out of place, regularly reminded by ignorance, by hesitancy and the fact that I had to ask questions that startled everyone with their simplicity: *How does that machine work? What's that smell? Why do I have to wear long sleeves when it's so hot? What are you feeding those animals? What's a clutch?* My clothes differed, as did my posture, making it painfully obvious that I lacked the informality my relatives shared. Caught between what I knew and what I wanted, I couldn't let either side go.

I knew enough to understand that Josie was the queen, and this was her kingdom; I bowed down in awe, but I needed the farm to help me approach her. Businesspeople might call her *task-oriented,* someone who worked on what she could measure, accomplish, see—what was immediate or very close by. Because the farm always presented a thousand things to do, jobs with which I could help, processes I could watch, and questions I could ask, I had a language with which I could speak to her and begin to understand not only how this place operated but also who she was. It was a language of dirt and seeds and breath, one of simplicity and completion. So I peeled eggs and picked berries and did what I was told so I could be near.

Not that she didn't care about people. In fact, people entwined with her biggest and most important tasks, and often they became tasks themselves—in ones, twos, eights, or larger groupings. There was always something to be done with someone, a change or a generosity with which she either could or couldn't help. And once her effort had spent itself, the moment had passed, or the transformation had come, there just wasn't much else to talk about. It may sound cold to those who don't work this way, but it's merely a way of thinking, of preventing the chaos of the mind from taking over. I think most people fail to understand that for women like Josie, compassion and love take the form of action, not affection.

I understand this because I'm the same way.

The farm alone did not unearth my awkwardness. It happened at our home in Illinois and later in Florida, too. When she and Grandpa Lee came to our house to visit for days at a time, they sat. We sat. Unless my mom found them a project—something to stir, something to hammer—they were lost, I knew, as if we had disconnected them from oxygen, and they were struggling for air. Certainly seeing us gladdened them—spending time with their daughter and her family—but they didn't know my language, the dialect of the suburbs: car pools and televisions, Brownie troops and play time. They also didn't know how to *be*; they knew only how to *do*. And because I didn't quite have a grasp on either, that left me wondering what to do with these people sitting in our family room.

CONSPIRING, MY HEART AND MIND transformed Josie into a mythic figure when I wasn't looking. It happens to some extent with all family stories, I suppose; with time, fact blurs into legend. Characters exaggerate, events rearrange, and morals amplify, but the result is no less true. The myth that is Josie has served me well, but I don't remember wishing for someone larger than life. I wanted what my cousins had all along: a grandmother.

The heart has its reasons.

Intersections

Carson, North Dakota, and La Crosse, Wisconsin
1890–1932

MARTIN TWITE AND GEORGE BROADHEAD were in-laws and peers, but if Martin was gravel, George was Gibraltar. Like Martin, George farmed, though he should have worked Wall Street. Instead of collecting almanacs and horses, George collected land. He must have learned of the North Dakota homesteading opportunities when Martin did, because during the same period George got his hands on more than fourteen hundred acres in Grant County, shrewdly registering various lots in the names of brothers and sons. He also owned at least six hundred acres on the hilltops of Vernon County, Wisconsin, where he farmed until 1922, but legend says that he once owned everything from his hometown of Retreat west to the Mississippi—a good ten miles—though I haven't been able to prove that's more than just talk. He had been buying up property in La Crosse as rental investments; his name appears regularly in the county record books. He used his profits to create loans for the less fortunate, most certainly applying what he had learned from serving as a director of the DeSoto State Bank or from his brother, Albert, who ran the bank in Retreat. (The family still believes that George Broadhead alone kept one or both of those banks open during the Depression. "What they did when they left the bank at night," his grandson Richard chuckles, "I think they put it in their pocket and carried it home.") When he died, George had twelve existing loans and mortgages out worth over twenty-five thousand dollars. His cash net worth equaled today's figure of three quarters of a million, not including five lots and seven farms totaling more than fifteen hundred acres. He didn't run a farm operation; he ran a dynasty.

The oldest of three sons and a short man, petite really, George often sported a white fedora, tilted forward to shield his eyes. What he lacked in stature, he made up for in grit. He held tight to his money, never letting on how much he actually had. With room for spending but not waste, quality but not excess, his philosophy crossed somewhere between the Rockefellers and the Quakers. He issued nonnegotiable orders to his family and employees, and thus he garnered more fear than respect so that his persona lingered and morphed into a threat his children and grandchildren have seen fit to use on each succeeding generation: "You're just lucky Grandpa George isn't here."

When George and his wife, Maud, retired from farming, they transferred management of their primary farm to a son or hired help and moved into La Crosse, building one of the city's first prominent houses at 2502 Cass Street. More than eighty years later, the house still anchors the southeast corner of Cass and Losey, its prairie architecture standing out like an orchid accidentally planted with the daisies: three stately stories with a square foundation of dark brick, an arched porch, and wide dormers. Because George could afford these kinds of luxuries, he hired his grandson, Richard Broadhead, as a chauffer. One time Richard drove George out of town in a new '34 Ford with suicide doors. George liked his tobacco, and the first time he opened the door of the moving car to spit, the door swung around and hit the back wheel. "Turn this thing around, Rich," George grumbled. Right then they returned to La Crosse, got rid of that car, and traded it for one with doors that opened the way doors should.

With their father's English blood and their mother's Irish, every one of George Broadhead's kids was a heartbreaker. As the story goes, each of George and Maud's five daughters received an education, each of his six sons a farm—except that the sons received an education, too, some of them. George intended equity and pride in his giving, a sign of good breeding and prudent spending, but that wasn't always the case: each year all the grandsons got a tie for Christmas, but no shirts or pants to match, and not all of the families had funds to complete the outfit. "We looked good with a T-shirt and a necktie and a pair of overalls," Richard says.

George Broadhead picking tobacco, 1927

George and his brother Albert married the McClurg twins. Albert's wife, Mabel, never had children, but her sister Maud bore fourteen, including two sets of twins, though three of those four died at birth. When the only surviving twin and oldest son, Wallace, reached his early twenties, George sent him to North Dakota to run a farm in Leith, near Carson, a prospect that no doubt sounded appealing to begin with. The operation represented a business venture between George and his other brother, Edwin Broadhead, who had purchased the farm on the return train from a prizefight in San Francisco and subsequently sold half of the eight hundred acres to George. Off Wallace went to run the place, to raise dairy cattle and wheat, his future signed and sealed by his father, his uncles, and the recorder of deeds. After he had proved himself, Uncle Edwin purchased Wallace his own farm in 1915, two miles straight south of the land he had managed and two miles northwest of section twenty-eight, the home of his future wife, Minnie Twite.

If Josie's oldest sister, Minnie, had had her way, she wouldn't have married Wallace at all. A pretty girl with crystalline eyes and delicate features, Minnie didn't have to wait for a man—many takers would have gladly eliminated that inconvenience—but she wanted to. A fiddle player named Homer had stolen her heart and would have kept it if the war hadn't interrupted. Theirs became a courtship of letters that stretched across the country, across the Atlantic, and into France. There, at the front lines, Homer lost hope and told Minnie that he did not expect to come back alive. Minnie kept asking the postmaster was there anything today, but after that, no more letters came. Several weeks later an envelope arrived by train for Homer's mother, but the United States government had sent it, and it carried the words no mother wants to read.

In despondency, so the story goes, Minnie blindly turned to Wallace Broadhead, looking for security and stability, if not love, proved by the fact that while he farmed just fine, folks said he drank too much. Wallace drank with the Twite boys, especially Carl, who frequented Carson's beverage establishments on Saturday nights. Minnie knew as much as anybody how alcohol could ruin a man, and when coupled with the ruthless prairie, it could take down everyone in sight, but what did it matter now? Some people, like Reuben Zeller, a lifelong resident of Carson, don't see drinking as anything to wrinkle a forehead over. "He helped himself to a little booze once in a while. Hell, who didn't? What else was there to do?" But if Minnie and Josie heard Reuben say that, they would be quick to ask, perhaps not begging his pardon, whether Mr. Zeller had grown up with an alcoholic.

Wallace and Minnie most likely met across heads and shoulders in town or at a house party when she was home from Mandan, where she kept house for the well-to-do Cummins family of the Cummins, Thorberg, Theis Co. Department Store. A mutual connection linked them, too: her brother Benhard Twite worked for Wallace. After a courtship long enough to woo and short enough to fool, Minnie and Wallace married on December 26, 1918, well before the war ended. Minnie moved those two miles to live with her new husband, who accepted her with or without the knowledge that he had taken second place.

Not until after the wedding did Minnie learn that the War Department had erred: Homer was alive and coming home. Before she could fret too much over how to face him, and what to do with herself and her husband, Homer developed pneumonia on the ship and died while still at sea. She received news of the second—real—death, and she grieved a second time. It was painful and sad then—still is—but if all of this hadn't happened, Minnie wouldn't have married Wallace, and Josie wouldn't have gone to live with them, and then she probably wouldn't have met Lee, and I wouldn't be here to tell this story.

Lee Walter Broadhead was George and Maud's youngest son, born on August 8, 1909. The Irish features of his mother's side graced his head, down to the thick red hair, fashioning a gentler version of his father's face. Of the Broadhead boys, he worked hardest, it's easily said; folks saw him as soft-spoken, uncomfortable in the spotlight, passive to a fault. They often misread his shyness as arrogance, and the half smile he usually wore didn't help matters. When he stepped out of Central High School in La Crosse in July of 1927, he probably had a different graduation gift in mind than a trip to the prairie, but Lee made the mistake of loving or even just liking a local girl from a family not up to George's standards, so after a time George sent Lee off to Wallace's farm in hopes of the romance fading. Lee didn't think of not going, even as a man. George's plan worked, though he might not have anticipated what he would get in exchange.

Lee Broadhead's senior portrait, taken in La Crosse, Wisconsin, in July 1927

NECESSITY STENCILED JOSIE'S ROUTE to Wallace and Minnie's. The years following World War I showed no mercy toward Dakota wheat farmers who had become accustomed to war prices. Taxes shot up over 70 percent in 1919. Price drops over the next two years turned the payment of debts and taxes into a mirage that kept moving farther down the road. Land in Grant County declined and hit less than half of its value within five years. Folks realized that North Dakota farming had become a loveless marriage, and they wanted a divorce. Droves of them. The Twites stayed, though between the economic conditions and Martin's drinking, they couldn't pay their bills. They had officially owned the land since March 1914, when they received their patent, but that piece of paper couldn't pay the taxes. Family accounts say that Martin borrowed money, but whether he did or not, eventually the change in his pockets could not balance his obligation, and the county threatened to repossess the property. The Twites needed a miracle worker, fast.

On December 17, 1923, Josie's second-oldest brother, Benhard Twite, accepted the role when he paid the taxes, purchased the farm from his parents for four thousand dollars, and moved home. At twenty-six, though he would have rather done something else, he was the only son who could. Clarence was gone. Peter was in the military and headed toward barbering, and Carl was following a similar path. Henry was enrolled in business college in Missouri, and Mort was too young. As it turned out, Benhard was the best person for the awkward and humiliating situation—and not only because he had the money.

Benhard had inherited his mother's face and build: sloping shoulders and an oval face on a short and delicate body. The way his dark eyebrows framed his eyes suggested an earnestness about him, and in the pictures I've seen he always seems to be looking at something far off. Folks recall his even temper, one that could navigate around the infuriating, cool and smooth like a windless lake. His small stature provided reason to sharpen his brain; Benhard had learned, in a home with many limits, to improvise, which had developed in him a keen creativity. As such, most people couldn't tell that he had little schooling and learned slowly. He could fix nearly anything with bale wire. He constructed tiny architectural replicas. He patented devices for early automobiles. One fall he disassembled an entire Ford engine to see how it worked, but he didn't finish before the first snow, so the parts sat frozen and buried all winter. Once spring chased away the drifts, he found every last piece, by then rusty and waterlogged, and put the car back together. It ran.

Not counting his father, he had worked for at least three farmers before—the Templetons, the Hammerstedts, and the Broadheads—which is where, in addition to hunting and trapping, he earned his money. Now in charge of his own place, he still worked hard and expected others to do the same. He maintained tight control of family finances and took out double insurance. When a storm blew in, he climbed to the top of the hill and gazed west for a long minute before scrambling down to give a report. He granted a day of rest on Sunday and is remembered as standing beneath the eaves of the house, calmly issuing his challenge to the wind: "Let it come." He was not his father.

Benhard let his family—father, mother, two younger sisters and a brother, and an uncle—continue living on what was now his farm, a mixed blessing if ever one existed. Most show gratitude over his saving the farm, but the 1930 census hints at how Martin took this change of events: it lists two heads of household on the property. The family had to know life couldn't continue in the same way, and it didn't; on August 16, 1927, Benhard brought home a bride. Though Nettie was quite possibly the sweetest girl any of them had ever met, barely eighteen and too kind for them to resent, she could not be expected to share her new home or husband with her in-laws, let alone his three younger siblings. Rather than evicting his kin, Benhard got himself thinking and soon churned out another of his ideas: converting the granary into a house. The family said yes, and they helped with the conversion, but then what else could they do? Benhard had saved them once already; could they begrudge him a second time?

Staked above a dirt cellar, the granary house consisted of two rooms and a shanty entrance. The first room served as a kitchen and eating area. Immediately inside the door stood a washing machine, which Martina had purchased with her egg money in 1920. The first corner held a washbasin and mirror, the second, Martina's cast-iron stove with its wood and coal boxes nearby. The other side of the room netted a hutch and cabinet, a round table and chairs, and hooks for coats and hats. A mantel clock poised almost daintily on a shelf near the second door, which led to the bedroom. Six

Benhard and Nettie Twite on their wedding day
(Josie Twite is at back right), August 16, 1927

people slept here, sometimes more: Martina, Josie, and Tina in one bed, Martin in another, Morty in a fold-up cot between a dresser and a wardrobe. New boarder Uncle Carl, Martina's younger brother, squeezed in where he could, not to mention extra guests that continually appeared at the door, such as the roaming Reverend Norlie.

It's not hard to understand why the transition invoked difficulty. Tensions that inevitably arose from too many people and too few rooms—familiar territory—coupled now with the unspoken humiliation of stepping backward, of having to be rescued. The arrangement required them to carry water from what was now Benhard's well. It also required sixteen-year-old Josie and eleven-year-old Tina to share a bed with their ever-frigid mother and a room with their brother, uncle, and drunken father. The new residence smelled dank, of wood and dirt long exposed. The roof leaked. Manda's oldest girl, Evelyn Johnson Skretteberg, who later lived in the granary house while attending Carson High School, says, "When it rained, I mean that leaked like a *sieve*. We had these here straw helmets that we wore 'cause it was drippin' all the time. We couldn't mop and throw it out fast enough, so I drilled a hole in the floor so the water run down that old drip basement." Mice nibbled on elbows and knees in the night, perhaps looking for the former tenants. Of course they did. The building that had once housed feed and grain now housed people.

The situation forced the granary residents to choose between blessing and burden. Josie's only related comments simply recount the facts and imply she leaned toward the latter: "Eventually, my father lost the 160 acres he'd gotten by homesteading it. My brother Ben was grown by then and paid the taxes and took over the farm. He let my parents live there. Ben was not cut out to be a farmer." But Martina planted morning glories around the door.

Here Josie lived for one year before moving to sister Minnie's in 1928, just shy of seventeen. Any of several factors could have prompted the decision: Uncle Carl's permanent visit; Josie's persistence in wanting a full four years of high school, which Thain Consolidated School couldn't offer her; or Minnie's need, which included three young children (one having died), a very large farm, and a demanding father-in-law. Whatever the reason, Josie moved the couple of miles to work for Minnie and Wallace Broadhead. There she continued her education at Leith High School and once again lived in a real house. There she became one of them.

AND SO IT WAS THAT BY 1930 both Lee and Josie lived and worked with her sister and his brother. On the eve of the Dust Bowl, Wallace needed all the help he could get. Even then, every year George sent horses and grain for spring crop to his son because Wallace's accounts had worn too thin. Josie certainly knew some of this, but she was, after all, nineteen, and plenty of other more fascinating things tugged at her attention. She helped Minnie with the new baby, yes, but she also studied literature and democracy, Bible and economic geography. She competed with the Leith High School debate team and the women's basketball team. She had gotten what she wanted, what she had longed for through all those years of herding cattle, a chance to learn and stretch, and she threw herself at every opportunity the school gave her. Maybe because her fingertips began to touch the edges of an extraordinary life, drawn in by magnetic possibilities. Maybe because she began to see herself as an individual who could do something in this world.

Who would.

Yet her attentions divided no less here than they had at home. If Minnie needed help canning, watching the children, or doing laundry, Josie put her books aside or stayed home from school, eventually creating a jagged attendance pattern that threatened her graduation. Minnie argued with the school, an inconvenience for all parties involved, especially the family, where a girl's education fell behind getting wagons to the grain elevator. Minnie, after all, had left school before she could get half as far as her sister.

Josie Twite holding her niece, one of Wallace and
Minnie Broadhead's children, circa 1930

The Leith High School women's basketball team (Josie is at far right), 1930

Lee worked the fields with his brother and the other hands, appearing only to eat and sleep, just one employee among many. "When I first met Lee," Josie later wrote, "I wasn't particularly attracted to him. His arrogant and intimidating ways turned me off." He didn't seem to mind. He had this way, without trying, of looking sure of himself, as though he knew the ending of the story so he could just sit back and enjoy the telling of it. She soon saw that he was quiet, not aloof, and that he farmed like he breathed, easy. He held no contempt for the land, something Josie had seen so often, and revealed no traces of the complaining or the worry. You can see this, almost feel it, if you study the photograph of him pitching oats that hangs in my hall. Knee-deep in straw, he grips the fork handle with hands as large as softballs, each knuckle and nail outlined in black. Along with the collared work shirt and striped overalls, he wears a matching cap bent up boyishly. The long arm of the combine spits out chaff above him, which fills the horizon like thousands of snowflakes. He looks down at the straw, smiling, and the sun seems to be all around him at once, causing him to glow.

Josie watched him for a while, which normally would have been problematic with her being the talking sort, but Lee was magnetic, cool before people even knew what that meant. In the early days he smoked Camels or Lucky Strikes, or rolled his own—a pack a day—and he often wore a Greek fisherman's cap, tilted on his head without intention. His small eyes, full lips, and giant braided arms gave him a dreamy quality, and he felt at ease sitting on a fence post or in a shirt and tie, though he tended to roll the sleeves of collared shirts up past his elbows. Josie started looking for reasons to run into him in the barn, not realizing he was doing the same.

There had been other boys for Josie, though not because of her beauty. Some would not describe her as pretty, with her round face and short, colicky hair. Nothing about her was dainty. She took on her mother's features and her father's girth, and though she didn't have unusually broad or high shoulders, her body implied that she would have no trouble lifting a fifty-pound sack of grain without breaking a sweat. She always said she didn't know what a hairbrush was (her daughter, Beverly, still jokes that "she probably used a twig on the prairie"), but she certainly did not try to be unfeminine. Photographs chronicle collars and stockings, heeled shoes and plaited tresses. Her coloring matched the other Twites—light hair and eyes—and she shared their thick eyebrows and thin lips, but a toughness surrounded her. Though neither oldest nor youngest, prettiest nor smartest, she might well have been the feistiest. Maybe her stubbornness and vision resulted from splashing around in the whirlpool of a large family and being overlooked.

It's another mystery who started it, but Lee and Josie began courting, an experiment both exciting and unusual since their address, employer, and family already overlapped. Josie had never before seen such goodness and gentleness as Lee lavished on her. "I enjoyed being treated so graciously," she recalled, "so unlike many of the rough and rugged farm hands that would often time get into brawls after a few drinks. I would get angry and refuse to go home with them. This never happened while dating Lee." They were photographic negatives of each other, except that they both danced with life in a way that kept them untouchable, distant. That they had an understanding became clear soon enough, and they respected in each other what they saw in themselves. "Lee's attentiveness and warmth was so genuine," she wrote, "I learned to love him."

Josie graduated from Leith during their courtship. For the ceremony she wore a new chiffon dress and rayon slip, gifts from Minnie. Something new underneath, where folks couldn't see, now that was a luxury. The palest pink showed through her dress, like a rose just coming to bloom. In a classroom before the ceremony, she twirled, showing off her layers to envious girlfriends. To her surprise, one of the other graduates started to cry, pulling at a faded torn red scrap that looked like a brothel's castoff. The girl begged Josie to wear the new slip, since she probably had a sliver of pride left. Josie, simply happy to be graduating, wriggled out of her new lace and rayon and handed it to the girl. Then she pulled on the red slip and finally her dress, which couldn't hide the ugliness and didn't even try. It didn't matter to Josie because the diploma meant so much more; she was only the second child in the family to graduate—the first girl—and it had taken her fourteen years. She didn't realize then that it was her first major lesson in not caring about what others thought.

Lee Broadhead and Josie Twite (left) courting, likely taken in North Dakota, circa 1931

Josie Twite's senior portrait (above), taken in Leith, North Dakota, 1931

She walked the ceremony and hugged her girlfriends afterward, clutching her diploma as if the wind would blow it away. Someone gave her a ride home, and when she walked into the yard, Minnie met her, grabbing her by the arm with a force she had seldom seen. Minnie, bull-furious over the slip, demanded an explanation, which she got but didn't like, and then slapped Josie clean across the cheek. Everyone who knew Minnie remembers her sweetness, her gentle demeanor and refined ways, which makes her response either a shock or a fabrication. But considering all the pieces—a short childhood, a father and now a husband who drank more than she wanted, a lost love, a dead baby, and a thirsty farm—it's not difficult to see how Minnie could resent her young sister right then. Josie went off to bed, still grasping her diploma, fading off to sleep praying for Minnie, whom she knew hurt over something much deeper than an old red slip.

Forgiveness came easily with Minnie, perhaps because the hurt affected the private and personal. But the choice proved more difficult when Josie's friend spread rumors that Josie was sleeping with the new redhead. The spite of it, the meanness and the lies sorely wounded Josie, damaging the reputation she had worked so hard to create. The night she found out she cried herself to sleep. When she awoke, calmer, unaware for a second or two, her mother was sitting on the edge of the bed. "I relayed the whole story to her and told her that I was not a 'bad' girl," remembered Josie. "My mother, who was very understanding, counseled me and said that I had nothing to fear. She told me to pray for the girl. I couldn't believe what my mother was saying. *Pray* for her! Why, that was the last thing on my mind. She owed me an apology and I was not going to forgive her, either. My mother began to tell me that there was a lesson to be learned from this incident. She took my arm, and sat me down, and told me that we have to forgive those who hurt us."

Though a friend's jealousy lay buried underneath the dramatic plot, and she knew it, Josie could think of no other way to mend her reputation than to stop seeing Lee. Words and reasons passed between them. He didn't want to lose her, he would help her, they would dispel the rumors. But he could not convince her; she felt the relationship must end.

End it did, and the breakup flattened Lee. He walked the farm, low and heavy, pained at the sight of Josie several times a day. She watched him, aware that she felt just as pained. It might have taken her some time to sort out her feelings since she hadn't grown up in a place that acknowledged, recognized, or named emotions. The heart came second after what needed to be done, and she followed the same protocol here as she always had. With enough of her mother's compassion in her, she couldn't simply ignore Lee's hurt, and that triggered the realization that she felt the same way he did, and if she didn't do something, she was about to lose the love of her life. So, she dug around inside herself and found a way to apologize, and they reconciled, and to her surprise he proposed right then. She said yes.

Which places our newlyweds on Highway 14, just coming around Mormon Coulee.

MR. AND MRS. LEE BROADHEAD, their backs stiff and their truck tired, do not drive over the hill. They come from the west and ford the river into La Crosse, wheels spattering and spinning on the slushy roads leading up from the bank. I have to believe that as the truck trudged through town, passing the familiar—Dr. Skemp's clinic, Central High School, his folks' place—Lee cracked a smile. Though he has likely not been home in the two years since he left for North Dakota, here lies everything he knows: land, people, sky, all of which work in tandem with an effect that is soulful.

They see it before they turn onto Breidel Coulee Road: a constellation of white slat buildings lining a circular drive that begins and ends on the road. The first is an open machine shed with four oversized mouse holes for cars or tractors, a granary and storage room upstairs, and a hog house at the east end. Next door stands a cow barn, which eclipses the long, high tobacco shed out back with its bulk: fifty-four stalls, indoor silos, a hayloft, a feed mixing room, and an attached chicken coop. A horse barn follows, with front and rear ramps and capacity for thirty-two horses. Another tobacco shed hides behind the stable, and a lone corncrib anchors the flat across the way. The drive corrals a smaller cluster inside the loop: a second machine shed, a garage with nearby gas pump, and a two-holer privy. A quarter mile down the road and across the first bridge, the windows of a white two-story house for married and midwinter help stand out against the snow like postage stamps on an envelope.

The farm started as a homestead plot at the intersection of Breidel and Mormon Coulees in 1851, only seven years after Mormons settled the coulee following the Nauvoo massacre in Illinois. The settlers voted to name the area the Valley of Loami, a derivation of Lo-Ammi ("not my people") and the creeks the waters of Helaman. According to one Mormon account, they stayed only half a year, forced out by bigotry. Though most hopped the flat boats and burned what they left behind, the few that the winter had claimed they buried in unmarked graves up on the hill behind the farm.

The farm passed through the generations until it found its way to George Broadhead, who bought it from Joseph Linse in 1927 and readied it for his youngest son, hiring a man named Burris to run it until Lee could take over. That the place is a beauty farmers and other folks would agree: a good three hundred sixty-five acres cushioned with tree-topped hills and tickled by two undecided creeks on their way to the Mississippi.

Lee and Josie pull into the circular drive and get out of the truck, careful of the icy gravel at their feet. Josie stands in the cold, staring at her new home between the fog of her breaths. Resting in the shade of four large pines, the farmhouse looms before her, square and studded with two porches, one connected to a stone milk house on the east side and another paired with the front door facing south toward a small apple orchard. Few ever use the front door, but for the occasion, Lee might do just that for his bride. They walk inside to a staircase, the walnut banister smooth and dark and molded to the feel of a hand, pooling at the bottom in concentric circles, as if someone had just dropped a stone in water. To the left they find their bedroom, and to their right a long living room, nearly the length of the house, with retractable doors to divide the space. Down the hall waits the dining room, which opens to the far end of the living room and offers stairs to the basement, where cool stone rooms harbor a wood stove and await next summer's fruit and vegetables. Beyond the dining and living room walls lies a roomy kitchen and pantry with a second stairway tucked into the corner. Here, too, a door leads to the side porch and a laundry room, both stacked on top of an old icehouse. The house creaks with bitter cold, an icicle hanging from the kitchen pump.

He has been here before, but he walks the rooms with his bride, their shoes knocking on empty wooden floors. As he shows her each detail, each feature, the blue air warms with her girlish joy, and she follows agape, stuttering, unbelieving. They open each door, peer out each window, fingering the walls, the switches, the trim.

Upstairs the ceiling hangs low and angled, the windows one-foot square and no higher than a milk stool. Two bedrooms line each side, and one sprawls across the north end, the hall between fashioned into a bureau with immense drawers hidden in the wall. Through the east windows the couple can see some stunted oaks reaching their bony arms high in the yard, while a stone fireplace loosely hugs one corner.

They sleep that night in their house, though the chill and the waking dream make it difficult. Josie now inhabits, for a girl of few means and even fewer travels, a blessing unsurpassed—husband, house, farm. She is not accustomed to such greatness, nor such quietness. But such a blessing is too much for one person, even two. It is meant, she knows, to be shared.

Revisitation

La Crosse, Wisconsin
2004

THE FIRST TIME I VISIT my great-aunt Tina in the nursing home she doesn't seem to know who I am. The second time is better, or she's learned to pretend. I walk into the room just after dinner, where I find her sitting in the stuffed recliner next to the bed, where she was when I last saw her. A plastic cup half filled with milk rests on the tray in front of her, a bent straw leaning sadly against the edge. She smiles. I take her hand and lean down to put my face to her cheek, which feels soft and cold. I sit on the edge of the bed; she has nowhere else to entertain visitors.

Tina is the last living child of Martin and Martina Twite, my grandma's sister, a woman who proves that real beauty doesn't age. Her years number eighty-seven, and her roommate's ninety-six. She came here less than a year ago, when someone decided it was time. Like a hospital room, the space accommodates two beds, separated by a table, one television, and a bathroom. Only

Tina Twite Tangen at the Ranis cottage in Winona, Minnesota, 2000

a couple of magazines and papers decorate her side. Her bulletin board is empty. No plants, no framed prints of pastoral scenes, no knickknacks grace the walls or dressers. The room desperately needs balloons. Curtains can be pulled: over the window, around the beds. The window looks out onto a shallow lawn with a tree, and every time her son and daughter-in-law leave her, they wave through that window before going to their car. If someone happened to remove her from this room, it would be very difficult to tell that she lives here.

She has recently fallen again and struck her face in the bathroom, though I can't tell looking at her. Last time it was her arm—broken. The doctors ordered hand exercises, which she didn't do, and we all chided her about it. She looks the same as I remember—white cottony hair, glasses, and the semblance of joy etched on her face—but frailer, sadder. But then she has lost a child and a grandchild, her parents, and all of her brothers and sisters, and now she no longer lives in her house or sleeps next to the warmth of her man.

I'm the one making statements, asking questions, but this isn't an interview.

"I went to see your dad's farm," I tell her.

"Oh," she says with the melody of Norwegian inflection, nodding and smiling.

"Actually, both farms. I drove out and went to the courthouse in Caledonia today for that book I'm writing on the Twites."

"That's so wonderful," she says, patting my hand. "Wonderful."

She leans over to her roommate and her roommate's daughter, who is visiting from Montana. "How are you related to the Twites?"

I don't correct her, but they do. She wrinkles her eyebrows.

THIS TRIP I'M STAYING AT THE FARM with Aunt Karen. I awoke early this morning, my face nearly level with the western windows, which frost had framed during the night. The last week has introduced clear signs of fall, and again I have brought a camera, a laptop, a digital recorder, the wrong clothes. I loaded up my backpack, slid into my jean jacket, and ate a quick breakfast with Karen before getting into my rental car and heading for town.

I took the reverse route Lee and Josie would have taken when they first arrived in La Crosse: down 14 and in past Shopko, by Bethany St. Joe's nursing home. Then down South and right on West, beyond St. John's, where my parents married forty years ago, to Cass. Left, toward the river, and up over the steel aqua bridge into Minnesota. Immersed in a land of apple stands and fields aglow with the copper of unharvested cornstalks, I let the little car guide me through La Crescent, Hokah, and finally into Caledonia. It's only thirty miles from the farm, but it takes a good hour because of all the hills, delivery trucks, and people in no hurry.

An unremarkable small town on a hill, Caledonia prides itself as being the wild turkey capital of Minnesota, though I have yet to see any of its namesake nearby. I drove toward the spires poking above the rest of the buildings and found myself at the base of a church-like structure made from large sandy bricks. Brown wood dots where a clock used to be, and just below, these words confirmed that I had found my destination:

1883

HOUSTON COUNTY

COURT HOUSE

I parked and went inside, looking for the recorder's office. The absence of security guards and metal detectors momentarily confused me; someone noticed and directed me to the second floor, where a bottle blonde woman escorted me past the desk and into an empty paneled room striped with old books. Records. Land records. I nearly felt my heart race. I removed my jacket, opened my notebook to a list of questions, and began searching indexes.

Most of these records, which date back one hundred fifty years to 1854, are handwritten and organized by either plat coordinates or last name, though the latter are alphabetized only by first letter. So if you don't come with something to go on and don't have several weeks to spend, you could really be in trouble. I was in good shape: I had names, dates, section numbers, townships. I also had all morning, and I was determined to find Martin Twite. Before he moved his family to North Dakota and begat Josie, he lived here, in Houston County. He was born a few miles from this courthouse, and married. Had his first two farms. Spent a lot of time in this town, and even a little bit of it in this very building, though generally for less acceptable reasons than searching through records.

I pulled out the index for the end of the nineteenth century and flipped to T. The books weighed more than I expected, bound in woven cloth or leather with metal spines or hinges, delightfully tangy with dust and tanning. Dragging my finger from top to bottom of each page, I stopped at Twites, Tweits, Tveits, and Tvedts every few seconds, noting the location for each record. Soon my list spread over two pages. I paused, told myself to focus, find what I was looking for: Martin Twite. Martina's father, Fredrick Hanson. Her brothers, Martin and Carl Hanson. Farms in Winnebago Township, Caledonia Township. Peder and John and Iver and James and the others would have to wait.

After I identified the first record, I ran to the copy machine, thrilled to check off one of my questions. The room started to fill, and I realized my jacket, open purse, notebook, and papers were still spread out over the counter. *Look at me: I'm part of history.* I reluctantly returned to my corner and resumed my work: scanning books, making copies. Several books later I glanced at the clock: 10:30. My aunts expected me in La Crosse at noon, and I still wanted to drive to some of these sites. I paid for the copies on the honor system; I'd racked up a twenty even with the bargain price of fifty cents per page (most places charge two dollars). Then I stared for a good minute at the 2004 map on the wall. Who needs to pay four dollars for a copy when the roads haven't changed all that much in the past hundred years?

Back in the car, I followed the geese in search of Martin's first farm. For five minutes I drove, then ten, fifteen, twenty, unable to find the turnoff; every road looked like the one before, and I was driving way too fast while hopelessly trying to match my 1896 map to the roads on my left and right. Frustrated and nearly out of gas, I returned to town, where I made two stops: the service station and the courthouse.

Winding through the bowels of the courthouse in search of the auditor and his map supply, I ran my hand along the jagged stone walls, which felt chilled even through the white paint. For an instant I became my great-grandfather, walking these narrow corridors in shame. I lost my way. An employee directed me upstairs, and when I found the right window, I gladly handed over four dollars. When I turned around, map in hand, I noticed framed and hanging on the wall a large plat of Houston County—the same one I had in the car. I hesitated long enough to locate Winnebago Township, toward the bottom, and find two squares: Martin Twite, Carl and Martin Hanson. *Look at me: I'm part of history*. I smiled all the way to the parking lot.

The second attempt went markedly better, and I found Martin's first farm off Route 76 and, I think, Camp Winnebago Kruse Ranch Road. (It was hard to tell because there weren't any dotted lines.) Because someone else now owns that land, trespassing was required. I got out of the car, took a picture on either side, stood for a moment out of respect. No great revelation presented itself, simply a lot of mowed field stubbled with the remains of the harvest— what I'd been looking at through the windshield all morning. Off in the distance, before the telephone wires on the next ridge, the land plunged into a valley where a creek ran—a valley that, at least for now, would remain only a fictional image represented by pen and ink on my copy of the plat map.

Time had run too short for me to visit Martin's second farm, but I had to see what he moved to next, measure his upward mobility. This square now lined up with Beaver Creek Valley State Park, so I passed back through Caledonia and picked up Highway 1 going west. The speedometer bounced up, and I hated myself for rushing through this.

Driving into the park, I flew by a sign that said I must have a permit in my windshield to proceed. I pulled over at the ranger station and ran inside. "Hi," I said to the ranger and his assistant, a little man working at a computer. "I saw the sign about the permit, but I was wondering if I could just drive into the park. I just want to drive in and take a look and then leave."

"You just want to drive in?" the ranger said, his eyebrows raised. The assistant looked on with interest.

"Yes. You see, my great-grandfather had a farm here on this land, and I just want to see where it was, take a few pictures. That's it."

"Where was the farm?"

"Shoot. I left the thing in the car. I'll be right back." I ran outside to my car, my heeled boots banging on the wooden ramp, and grabbed the entire stack of papers on the passenger seat. Back inside, I scanned the legal-sized copy for the location, breathing a little heavier than I wanted. I spread out my four-dollar map, and we began to sketch in the quarters. "Um, it was section seventeen—the southeast quarter of the northwest quarter and the northeast quarter of the southwest quarter and the southwest quarter of the northeast quarter and the northwest quarter of the southeast quarter."

"Oh, you can't get to there from here," the ranger said. My shoulders dropped. "That's up on the ridge. You have to drive up and around here." He used the tip of his yellow highlighter to show me that although I was less than a mile from the farm site, I needed to backtrack and make a giant loop at least ten miles long.

"Can't I see the ridge from down here?"

"Nope. Too many trees. Who owns that place up there now?" the ranger asked his assistant. "Is that the Oeseths?"

"Could be," the assistant said. "The Kochs and the Lees are up there, too." The ranger penciled the names on the park map in front of him.

"Okay," I said, repeating his directions. "Can I still drive into the park just to see it?"

"Sure," the ranger said. "Are you going to hike? If you're going to hike, I have to charge you."

"No, I just want to drive in and out."

He uncapped his highlighter and began marking key spots. "This is Big Spring. We're fed by fresh water springs. This here is a blue ribbon trout stream. Some of the best in the state."

"Okay," I said impatiently, picturing Josie's older brothers, then little boys, wading in the creek and casting for dinner. The ranger finally handed me a little pink square, which landed on the passenger seat, along with the maps and papers, though the ranger specifically said it must be on the dashboard. Into the park, past a few campers and through that honest-to-God trout stream, I looked up, trying to find the ridge, but the ranger was right: the trees camouflaged it. When I reached the loop at the end of the road, less than a mile in, I turned around without getting out. Back at the entrance, I grabbed the permit and darted into the ranger station. This time I left the engine running.

"Thank you so much," I said, laying the permit on the counter. "You have a very nice park."

"Good luck," they both said, and I waved good-bye.

Minutes later I was atop the ridge, looking out over Martin's second farm, congratulating myself on finding it, though it looked in every way like his first.

"WHERE DO YOU LIVE NOW?" Tina asks.

"We live in Virginia."

"Oh, that's nice." We sit in silence for a few moments. "How did you get in? Did Waldo let you in?"

"No, the girls in the front let me in. Waldo's at home."

She puckers her face again, almost imperceptibly, never one to be rude.

"Where are you living now?"

A YEAR AGO TINA ACCOMPANIED ME on my first visit to Caledonia at the start of my research. I had spoken to my mom on the phone, let her know how things were going, told her we were driving to Houston County for the day. "Oh, you ought to take Tina. She would just *love* that." I should have thought of it, but I lack my mom's sensitivities. All were game, and Waldo even offered to drive his new Buick, a bus big enough to also accommodate my husband and Bev.

First stop: the Houston County Historical Society, a tent peg on the fairgrounds. Staffed only by volunteers Monday through Wednesday, the society offers a tiny museum and even tinier room with a microfilm cache of old newspapers, vital records, cemetery indexes, and other county documents. Our party of five immediately overcrowded both. While Paul and Waldo spoke of hardware and *Norskedalen* in the museum area, I sat and looked up anyone I could find with the last name of Twite or Tvedt. Hands cradled in her lap, Tina smiled and watched Bev peruse the file on people who have previously studied the Twites.

"Now look here," Bev said, "a *Julie Twite* has been doing some research. Do you know a Julie Twite? I don't know a Julie Twite. I'm going to write her e-mail address down, and we can contact her." The two volunteers and other researcher looked at us as if we had pushed a full cart into the express checkout.

Before long, Martin and Martina's marriage certificate lit up the viewer, along with the announcement in the *Caledonia Journal*. Then came a story about Peder Twite, Martin's father, nearly losing his life in a fire, the first Clara's death record, plat maps from 1878 and 1896 showing the Twite and Hanson farms. Bev leaned in, while Tina sat, still watching, still smiling.

"Look at that," Bev whispered.

"That's just wonderful," Tina said. I reminded myself that it was her sister, father, mother we had dusted off and were squinting at on the dark screen.

With several copies in hand, we reloaded the Buick and zoomed over to the Redwood Café for a bite, Dairy Queen being voted out. On full stomachs, we then zigzagged the county, finding clues everywhere we went. Waldo readily chauffeured us to all the key sites: land, churches, cemeteries. He didn't need a map from this century or the last. At Blackhammer Lutheran Church, we let ourselves in and examined the confirmation photos on the wall, hands passing over black-and-white heads, lists of names typed in capital letters. My husband found a Twite—Minnie—and I found two more: Clarence and Manda. At the Wilmington Lutheran churches and cemeteries old and new (*burials since 1883*), we walked each row, looking for Twites, Hansons, Smestads, Tosteruds, photographing each family stone, recording each date, name, place. Here lay Mathildas and Kirstis and Ivers and Margits and Marens and Ostens and Peders. It became a game, with much pointing and snapping and scribbling. Wedged in the backseat and zipping back to La Crosse, Bev and I filled in my ratty old family tree, or tried to. Tina didn't say much—Waldo handled most of the direction and commentary—but my mom was right: she loved every minute of it.

THE MILK SITS, UNTOUCHED.

"You're so pretty," Tina says again and again. I tell her I'll have to come here more often. I rarely get that compliment. I have Josie's genes, which are far stockier than Tina's and get rather attached to extra sags and pouches.

She has few girls in her life. Her only daughter, Joan (pronounced *Jo-ann*), a blonde with Grace Kelly looks, learned at age eighteen that she had no uterus and would never have children. The emotional problems started then, and in 1969, she walked into a train. Tina and her husband believe with all that is in them that their daughter simply failed to look where she was going. Almost thirty years later, Tina's seventeen-year-old granddaughter, Amy, mysteriously died of a seizure. Her parents found her on the floor after school, and a good explanation has never materialized. That was the summer of my divorce from my first husband. I didn't go to the funeral because my own pain clawed at me, and I've always regretted my selfishness.

As we talk, a hunched-over woman propelling a wheelchair with her feet heel-toe-heel-toe pulls up outside the door. She begins an oration about her mother, how her mother called her for dinner, how her mother had such a beautiful voice. After a time she rolls away. When Tina tells me that's her friend, I wrinkle my eyebrows.

"Did you get my birthday card?" I ask a moment later.

She mutters and fumbles. I hadn't seen it on the board with the others the last time I visited, which was just as well since I, of all people, after researching the family for over a year, got her age wrong in the card. Still, I wanted to make sure she was getting the mail. I know Evelyn Skretteberg writes her regularly. They have been good friends for seventy years, but Evelyn can't call anymore. Tina gets too confused on the phone.

"Can you get phone calls? Is there even a phone in here?" I ask the roommate's daughter. She doesn't think so. Leaning back I accidentally bump Tina's tray table with my boots. She looks down.

"Are those comfortable?" she asks.

"No," I sigh.

"They just look good, huh?"

"Yes," I laugh, caught and surprised at her wit.

I miss her lefse, the thin Norwegian pancakes made with many pounds of riced potatoes. She makes the best lefse I've ever had—almost paper-thin and floury, and smeared with butter. Three years ago at our family reunion I suggested we make some of the traditional recipes, including lefse and krumkake, except it turned out to be about ninety degrees that day, and no one wanted to cook, so Tina stooped over her lefse iron and made it all. Then all the lefse got ruined when the ice melted in the cooler.

WHEN I INTERVIEWED HER a year and a half ago, in her house, Tina could still tell stories about North Dakota, about her dad and her horses, about grasshoppers and school and the homestead. Tina, Waldo, my mom, my aunts Bev and Karen, and I sat in her living room where a painting of the granary house tilts on the wall. (Downstairs, just outside Waldo's fruit cellar, hangs a framed picture of the first dead Clara.) She did pretty well, considering four women fired questions at her in rapid succession and switched topics without notice; but then she is a Twite. The entire party stopped and cooperated only once, when we talked about a song Martina used to sing. The song is formally titled, "I Have a Father in the Promised Land," though everyone knows it as "I'll Away" because they can remember only the chorus:

I'll away, I'll away to the promised land,
I'll away, I'll away to the promised land,
My Father calls me, I must go
To meet him in the promised land.

If I so much as mention the song to Tina, my mom, or Beverly, they immediately break out singing, though no one can ever remember the third line. It comes out as *When ah-da-ohhhh, I will go, to meet Him in the promised land,* sounding more like a bar song at closing time than a Sunday school staple. On a recording Josie made about her family a few years before her death, she listed some of her mother's favorite songs. One of them was "I'll Away," and almost as soon as she started reciting the lyrics, she, like everyone else, began to sing.

Other than that, I found myself frustrated because every time I asked a question, Waldo charged in and answered before Tina could get much out. Later, when I mentioned it to my mom and aunts, they said, "Yes, but Waldo is probably right. He's her memory now."

THE LAST TIME I VISITED TINA, we filled the room: her son and daughter-in-law, my parents, my brother and his family, my husband, and me. We had come after a Twite reunion she so badly wanted to attend but couldn't. We brought cake for her birthday. I opened my laptop and showed her some of the old family photographs I had scanned in. Some of us stayed well over an hour. But today, after forty-five minutes, I say I should probably be going. For no good reason. I could reappear with pumpkin ice cream, or a fist of balloons, or both, but I know I won't. Even as I say good-bye, I feel the right kind of guilt that I can't find it in myself to stay longer. Simply to sit a spot while I still can.

Rough Passage

La Crosse, Wisconsin
1932

JUNE 15, 1932, A WEDNESDAY. I see Josie bustling about the kitchen as usual, making supper, facing south to keep the late afternoon sun out of her eyes. Chicken again, potatoes and fresh bread, perhaps some early peas or green beans. I place her here, the spot where all things important are discussed and chewed over, because she is about to receive news. I don't know whether the farmhouse has a telephone yet, but I'm inclined to believe it does because of George. I also don't know whether the Twites back in Carson have one, but folks talk about having to lift phone wires with fence gates, so maybe that's not so far off. Even if the granary house doesn't, Benhard probably does, and the post office or general store is certainly connected. Today, one reason makes a phone call worth the ride, the expense, the time: Josie's father has died.

THIS KITCHEN HAS BEEN A CRUCIBLE for Josie during the past four months, the place where will and pride have battled, bloody, with

New bride Josie Broadhead on her farm in La Crosse, circa 1932

casualties on both sides. It started right off, in February, with her standing in her new kitchen, bolted to the floor by horror. If I have it right, she hadn't bothered to peel off her coat, on which lingered the midwinter chill, or put down her handbag. It was all she could do to keep from screaming. Her face flushed, a smoldering crimson, and of all the words, only one eclipsed all others—and there were others—No. No, no, no, no, *no*. Fists clenched and shoulders tensed as she stared down her adversary, the one she thought she had beaten when she left the Dakotas. Her behemoth opponent stared back, unflinching, dwarfing the kitchen like a giant shadow. Its matte black cast reflected the color of despair, and there, right on the front like the eye of a Cyclops, its insult stamped in iron: "The Kalamazoo Stove Company."

Josie approached it, the familiar and noxious smell of blacking filling her nose. She needed no instruction booklet; everything was exactly where it should be: warming compartments overhead; an oven, firebox, and ashpan below; a range between. She bent toward the burners, each iron circle notched and awaiting the lid lifter. Catching something amiss on the stovetop, she leaned in closer.

What she saw evoked a gasp and raised her seething anger to another level: one of the plates had a hole in it.

The newlyweds had expected a new stove as part of their wedding gift, but this was 1932, the era of nickel-plated shine. Josie had figured on modernity, thinking, perhaps not unreasonably, that she had left behind the days of ugly stoves that smelled of blacking. Companies like Kalamazoo and Glenwood had experimented with shades of key lime and peach ambrosia, but George must have gotten himself a deal on an older model, possibly because of what the dealer had assured him was a tiny flaw in a burner. A well-connected man like George had to have known that his purchase was outdated at best; even the one Josie's penniless mother now owned on the prairie had more advanced features, which might explain why he had it delivered to an empty house—an act of deception, or cowardice, or both. In this case, the present was small, the underlying message large: *I decide*. The thoughts swirling inside entertained all possible insults about her worth and upbringing. She wouldn't say it, but she knew she deserved better, especially from people who could afford ten new stoves.

Enter Lee, a man, by most accounts, not keyed into the emotional ramifications of the gift, before or after. The exchange was brief:

"What do you think?" he said.

She started to cry, which he mistook for joy until she wailed, "I hate it! That's not my idea of a stove. I hate it!" Lee was too newly married to fully understand. The stove was the problem, so the stove they must fix. A man accustomed to frugal finery, he nonetheless offered a solution, which he failed to recognize as total defeat: "I'm sorry. Tomorrow we'll go and buy the model you want."

"Really?" she sniffed.

"If that's what you want. We'll put this in the garage, and we'll look at your kind tomorrow." The chill tapped on his shoulder, reminding him that the deliverymen had removed the small cook stove, so he disappeared out the side door, returning with arms full of corncobs, wood chips, and newspaper, which he stuffed into the firebox and lit. The paper blackened and curled, igniting the wood and cobs, the fire crackling as it grew. A caustic odor rose from the stove and enveloped the room as the newness burned off. Lee forced up a window.

"You all right?"

Josie nodded silently.

"Then I'd better finish the chores." He came close to place a quick kiss on her wet cheek and was gone, wood and then screen slamming behind him.

Appeased but still under the spell of her anger, Josie plodded off to the living room to escape the smell, sulk, and finish an earlier project, hanging drapes. Pieces of floral and gingham fabric lay scattered on the floor in sad little heaps like wilted haystacks. "Nobody will make me use that awful blacking," she muttered to herself, stooping to select a red and white valance for ironing. "If people would buy the right kind of stove in the first place it wouldn't be necessary." The iron, now cold, balanced where she had left it. She lifted it, paused, and set it down again. Her hands swiftly grabbed the valance and hurled it to the floor, and then her legs marched her back into the kitchen. There she stared at the monster before her, loathing it anew. It was not a stove; it was a sentence. This marriage and this farm were supposed to be an escape from the prairie, from being poor. The years of giving up her dreams, of being tied to her father's erraticisms—all of that was supposed to die when she climbed into that truck. She didn't count on finding herself under the whims of her husband's father, confronting the possibility of a new lyric with the same old tune.

What happened to the gratitude she felt just weeks before?

Josie stood as the injustices weighed themselves in her mind: the unfairness, the insensitivity, the control. WE THE JURY FIND THE DEFENDANT, GEORGE BROADHEAD, GUILTY ON ALL COUNTS. She laughed bitterly. No one ever convicted George because no one could summon enough courage or strength. Instead they bore his blame and carried his fault, and they expected her to do the same. But this was not only about George, and she knew it. It was about being a person of gratitude, not one of insistence. It was about finding within herself the ability to accept what she is dealt, to handle it with grace.

She knew her options did not include confronting Lee's parents, but purchasing a replacement stove would deplete a good deal of the remaining dollars in his wallet. If they spent the money there, they wouldn't have enough left over to buy the tractor they needed. "He said he would buy me a new one, and I don't care if we can't afford it. What do we need with an old tractor anyway," she grumbled to herself, knowing as the words formed that they weren't true. But she had to say them, to release them and deflate their power over her. Only once the steam had escaped could she make the hard choice, the one she had recognized she must make from the beginning, the first in a long line: keeping the stove.

It was the right thing to do, this she knew, but it didn't make her dislike it any less. But Lee—now that was another matter. Lee had been willing to give up his tractor for her, a gesture highly romantic and worthy of appreciation. Out came her dime store bowl, wooden spoon, butter knife. Dump, mix, cut, and flour, water, and lard assembled into tiny balls. The dough stuck to her fingers, to her wedding ring, becoming one big ball, heavy and dense. A sprinkle of flour on the counter welcomed the dough, blowing white onto Josie's dress. The ball became tapestry, rolled into parchment. She pressed it into the pie pan, molding it to the edges, running a knife around the circle. A jar of canned apples became the filling, leftover dough the top. She crimped the seam, slit the top, and, grinning over her handiwork, walked to the oven, determined to give it a chance. Dishtowel in hand, she opened the oven door, but instead of being greeted by a blast of dry heat, she felt nothing. Perplexed, she set the pie atop the range and opened the firebox where Lee had built his fire an hour or so ago. There was no heat, there was no wood, and to her great disgust there was no fire.

Josie growled and kicked the stove—a move she regretted at once—and ran from the house. Lee noticed her wandering and stomping about the yard.

"What's wrong?" he said, his boots crunching underneath as they sunk through the crusted snow.

"Lee," she said sharply, "that stove is *no good*. It's absolutely worthless."

Lee walked deliberately back into the kitchen, Josie following, a smug defiance on her face and arms folded into a knot. He then leaned over and peered into the firebox, the snow already puddling around his feet. There lay his answer: a fire left to die, untouched, by his bride. It had seemed perfectly sensible to Josie to label the stove the culprit because oven fires don't just smother themselves. They burn for a while, and then you simply add more fuel. But this was prairie reasoning, which might have applied to coal or cow chips, but not to wood. In North Dakota, wood was scarce and using it for cooking or heating akin to burning money. So Josie had never learned how to burn it—she never needed to. With a stifled chuckle, Lee showed her, patiently, how to layer the wood in the box, how to stoke the fire to blaze, and how to feed it like spooning meal into the mouth of a baby.

History has never revealed how she handled the black stove with her in-laws—was she gracious or unsparing?—but it certainly didn't end the in-laws' gifts or the newlyweds' dependence as the house and garage contained only an old table and chairs, not nearly enough to stop the house from echoing. They now had a stove, but they still lacked an icebox, so Lee's parents provided one, to be kept cold with chiseled chunks from the frozen creek. The newlyweds also borrowed an iron bed frame. Surely Lee's mother couldn't bear to see her youngest son suffer and brought out a few more items with each visit. But the hand-me-downs would have to do until they could harvest that fall and afford their own furniture. For the time being, Josie worked at building fires until she was as good as Lee, which was important, because it would be ten years before they got another stove—won in a raffle through Rural Electric—but it would be electric, and it would shine like a jar of mercury on a windowsill.

THE BLACK STOVE UNWITTINGLY became an actor in the kitchen drama. Josie was, of course, our protagonist, and George the antagonist. In his presence, tension created itself; in his absence, his rules—sometimes unspoken but nonetheless expected—did it for him:

> Thou shalt attend the family church in town.
> Thou shalt not kill any cattle or swine for food.
> Thou shalt shelter, feed, and employ anyone thy father-in-law
>   brings to thy door.
> Thou shalt discuss any decision pertaining to the farm with thy
>   father-in-law.
> Thou shalt not question any of the above, and thou shalt be grateful.

Josie that summer secured a victory in the church department and left the Broadheads' Methodist congregation in town for Trinity Church just up the road. Swiss immigrants had planted the tiny fellowship in 1865, and though it had seen its share of preachers, it still called the Reformed tradition its own. The saying that hung just to the right of the pulpit, framed in dark walnut (and that still hangs in the sanctuary today), vouched enough for her: *Gott ist die liebe*—God is love.

She fared less well with the other rules, especially the one pertaining to slaughter. The farm crawled with beef and pork, but George prohibited Lee from butchering any of the livestock, perhaps because he saw it as blurring professional lines, or he just plain considered it indulgent. Fishing, hunting, and trapping were not viable alternatives for this farmer's wife, so Josie started raising chickens to accompany the staple milk, bread, and homegrown potatoes. They ate chicken every single day because of George, and Josie fixed it in all possible ways—fried, braised, broiled, boiled, smoked, in soup, stew, and sandwiches. This monotony caused Lee and Josie's son to refuse to eat chicken his entire adult life, and Josie herself at one point, fed up with poultry, and, no doubt, George, went and sawed the outhouse in half. (To everyone's relief, once pacified, she nailed it back together.)

A houseful of men to feed three times a day complicated matters. At peak operation, the farm had thirteen or fourteen men on the payroll, all working for room, board, and a modest salary of one or two dollars per day. The bachelors took straw mattresses in the upstairs bedrooms, and workers with families filled out the house down the road. Most of the time Lee and Josie selected their own employees, but not often enough for Josie's taste. She learned before planting season that George had his hands in that, too. Maybe he saw it as his Christian duty, but he seemed to pick up all the out-of-work vagrants he noticed along the side of the road, bring them to the farm, and add them to the crew without asking Lee. That meant Josie must cook for them and invite them into her house. I imagine words flew, and she kicked and screamed her way into a scowling submission.

She started breakfast shortly after dawn: eggs, potatoes, bread, pancakes, and, in season, berries from the garden. Preparations for dinner—the biggest meal of the day—began almost as soon as breakfast ended: chicken, bread, potatoes, canned or fresh vegetables and fruit. Supper came at dusk, after milking, and included much of the same fare as lunch, only more of it was cold. The help wasn't always gracious: a fat hired man named Carl, emboldened by the red handkerchief he wore to ward off evil spirits, once tossed a cut of chicken back at Josie telling her she should learn to fix it properly.

Even with the hired hands, Lee rose at half past five in the morning and often worked until at least 10:30 at night, sometimes seven days a week. Josie worked just as hard, cooking and laundering for her mishmash family, as well as mothering them. She really didn't have anyone else in those first two years. With the exception of her brother Peter in town, whom she didn't see much, presumably because of his drinking problem, her family stayed far away. Her relationship with the Broadheads, who didn't care for her blunt ways, warmed no more than a spring creek. Some of the neighbors were still intimidated by the outsiders with six times as much land as they had, and Josie lacked children to buffer the awkwardness. Their first son, Lawrence Lee, wasn't born until March 1934, and Beverly Ann didn't show up until strawberry-picking season in 1937.

Lee Broadhead (above) on his farm in La Crosse, Wisconsin, in the late 1930s

Lawrence and Beverly Broadhead (right) on neighbor Herb Kramer's farm, circa 1940

Anytime George decided to pay a visit, which was often, the hired help scurried like field mice, looking busy, not wanting to incur any harsh words from their real employer. And they made up quite a crew in those early years, a motley gang of has-beens and wannabes who are remembered mostly for their idiosyncrasies and mistakes. Ernest cultivated every other row of corn and worked alongside his brother; Arnold stole everything from razors to money. Phillip bit off the heads of sparrows while stripping tobacco. Ole told good stories, and when he broke his leg, Lee and Josie gave him their bedroom so he wouldn't have to climb stairs. Clarence, a former circus worker, wore his old clown shoes until his feet reeked, infected and rotting, and Josie got him a doctor and new shoes. Mac fed his four children week-old rolls and milk. One man greased the door hinges so he could slip out at night, and another stole into young Beverly's bedroom and tried to pull down her pajamas. There were the brothers, too—Carl and Mort Twite came, as did Leonard, Ralph, Earl, and Joe Broadhead—who seemed to show up when they ran out of money, couldn't make a way on their own, or got orders from George.

More people meant more accidents. Lee himself lost the tip of one finger all the way to the joint. Trees fell on him; cows kicked him. He tumbled off wagons and cracked his head open. Fires burned dried crops. Workhorses kicked and trampled, crushing and bruising bodies. Machinery shaved off slices of skin or bone. Axes chopping wood missed the block, and splinters the size of pencils lodged in shins. Tractors tipped or stuck in the brown swirling flooded creek, and much, much worse: the drowning of a hired man's two little boys.

Nothing was ever mentioned after the saying and doing of things gone wrong, of stupid or careless mistakes, but you can believe that there was a lot of saying at the time. Josie had a predisposition toward justice that went back to getting caught cheating in the first grade, and she had no respect for silence in the name of propriety because she wasn't raised to be a lady. Although these men worked for her and Lee, she no doubt saw it partly as a favor on her part. She fully expected those she helped to get up and start moving in the right direction, probably because she knew she couldn't do it for them. She took it personally when they yanked on the strings she attached to her generosity, or broke them, and it saddened her for a time, but only for a time.

Even so, there was no talk of feelings, of how a grown man trying to pull down your pants made you feel scared or violated. There was only action, of telling a man what-for, of getting him off your land and yelling how could you and then forgiving and moving on. Genuine sorrow existed, but then it was all about getting the grieving back to work right away because it doesn't help anything to wallow. If Josie had ever learned to identify and monitor her feelings as she did the weather, she'd never have made it out of North Dakota. Not only because feelings are fickle and egocentric, but because they would have been so out of balance from all the misery that they would have ensnared her, wrapping her tight as a winch does a cable, and they would have gnawed at her already-low confidence until she slowed down and eventually stopped, no longer believing that she could do much of anything.

Besides, she couldn't afford the luxury of lingering feelings, because her husband was a pleaser, partly by default, partly because of his father. Years later Lee's grown son said that George's strength only served to make his kids weaker, which is probably true. Lee didn't stand up when his father intervened in his Romeo affair, and he didn't grouse when shipped off to North Dakota. He didn't argue about getting the farm, the stove, or any of the other accoutrements. But hearing Josie in the house and George in the barn, Lee must have realized that he had married himself into the middle of two oncoming trains. His wife's will flexed just as much strength as his father's, but maybe somewhere inside he knew that already. Maybe he married her because he feared making his own decisions—or because he just didn't know how. Regardless, the blood between Josie and her father-in-law remained septic, as it had been even before she arrived in Wisconsin. She had seen how he operated, manipulated, and dominated, even two states away, and now knew for certain that she had married two men: the heart of one and the will of another.

As THE STOCKPOT SPITS onto the black iron like rain on a summer sidewalk and dough rises in a ceramic bowl on the counter, a towel draped atop, Josie stands with an eight-inch knife in her right hand, a chicken leg in the other, sawing through still-warm cartilage and bone. Having just grabbed the headless body spewing blood on the grass, having plucked the feathers and pinfeathers, having cooled the body in water, it is time to cut. Chop, chop, drumsticks. Chop, chop, wings. Chop, chop, thighs, breast, gizzards. The pieces slide in the Dutch oven, finding their places. The back and ribs drop into the crate at her feet, the unlaid eggs reserved for breakfast. The temperature coaxes sweat from the chicken, from Josie. She wipes her forehead with her upper arm.

The phone rings: two longs and a short—it's their call. She wipes her hands on her apron as she walks toward the phone, but when she lifts the black receiver it still feels greasy, bits of chicken fat and skin between her fingers, beneath her nails, creeping up her arms. Leaning against the doorframe, she can see through the porch to the yard, which always looks a bit like a storm's coming the way the milk house crowds it so.

Hello, hello, Josie? Pa's dead.

Benhard most likely reports the death, calling his brothers and sisters, now spread throughout the upper Midwest, to tell them that although the death certificate will record something else, their father died from excitement.

Martin went into town yesterday, June 14, 1932, for new clothes in anticipation of his son Peter's visit. He hasn't seen his son in years, and everyone likes to look better than the last time, even poor fathers. The ride, easy and familiar, a couple of miles by wagon and road, meant that he should have returned well before supper. Martina, Mort, Tina, and Uncle Carl ate in the granary house, cleared the dishes, went about their evening reading and mending. They changed into their nightclothes, turned down the lamps, slithered under the sheets. Still no Martin. Martina instructed her children to pray; it wasn't unusual for Martin to return late, but it was unusual for him not to return at all.

They slept, the best they could, and this morning, to everyone's horror, Maude and Topsy, Martin's team, wandered into the yard. Neighing and frothy, the horses dragged their broken harness behind. The Spielman boys trailed them, their heads low, their hats coming off before they reached the door. They knew where Mr. Twite was. They'd been seeding flax and seen him hunched over in his wagon, but they figured Old Mr. Twite was a drunk, and they let him be. But when they seen he hadn't moved, they walked over, and that's when they seen him in the wagon, on the floor, dead.

The editors at *The Carson Press* have already begun typesetting their center headline for tomorrow: "Martin Twite Dies Suddenly of Heart Attack." The reporter, who got what he could, explains it this way: "He evidently had a heart attack while driving and the team kept on going home. In turning a corner they turned short and the front wheel struck a brace wire on a fence corner, stopping the buggy and breaking the double trees to the buggy. He was found about one and one-half miles from home lying in the buggy."

Benhard went and got Pa, brought him home, and laid him on the kitchen table. Sheriff Lackey was called, as was Emanuel Hertz, the coroner over in New Leipzig. Hertz listened to the story, checked the body over, and determined it had not been a heart attack that killed Martin Twite but a stroke. He hasn't scribbled *apoplexy* on the death certificate yet, but he will. Then he and Benhard will sign it, stating the time of death was 11:00 p.m. on June 14, though no one will ever know for sure how long he lay in the wagon before he stopped breathing.

If the yard blurs as Josie listens to her brother, it's because she is thinking of her mother, or she feels sad in spite of herself. She has not mentioned missing the prairie or her pa, and never will, and when she drove away that February morning, my guess is that she hoped she wouldn't see either for a long time. The prairie was ruthless, her father cruel. Together they created a vortex of poverty and abuse of many kinds, a force that would chew up, spit up, or throw up all chances of anything solid or good. All of the Twite children had left the Dakotas except Minnie and Manda, and of course the two still at home. The fact that the rest came back to visit testified only to their love for their mother. Josie might not have hated her pa, but on a rational level she wasn't necessarily sad to see him go, either. She wasn't the only one. Manda's youngest daughter, Bernice Twite Steinley, says that her mother "was probably glad he died." And the word is that he hadn't even been drinking.

Mr. Stegen, a neighbor, will carefully embalm the body soon, right there on the kitchen table. Martina and her youngest children, fourteen-year-old Tina and eighteen-year-old Mort, will watch, and Tina will remember the event with a lingering sadness and distaste for over seventy years, unable to speak about it in complete sentences. Then they will have the funeral and bury Martin near his daughters in the Community Cemetery atop Circle Butte, and his wife will chisel a stone with a screwdriver to match the one at his girls' heads.

The grave will still be there into the next century, when I walk over a bull snake to get to it. But by then Evelyn and Morville Skretteberg will have replaced the marker with granite—stone and metal for the little girls—when serving as cemetery caretakers. The fencepost that did Martin in will remain there, too, leaning like the hand on a sundial, weathered and sore, and even though Evelyn and Morville insist it can't be the same one, I believe with all my heart that it is.

Wrong Way

Burke, Virginia
2004

A PHOTOGRAPH:

I am seven, standing outside Josie's house, in dirty sneakers, too-long purple Toughskins, and a pink polyester shirt my mom made in Stretch-and-Sew class. The wind blows my ponytails back toward the garden, which looks slightly overgrown. Raspberries are ripe. My brother Matt, three, stands next to and just in front of me, also in Stretch-and-Sew, though appropriate blue stripes span his chest. His growing tanned legs peek out from shorts and end in bunched tube socks—with matching blue rings—and blue sneakers. His hair shines nearly blond, though the wind rebelliously musses the top layer. Though the shadow of maple leaves and branches cross his face, chest, arms, and legs, his shadow falls on me. He squints in the sunlight that manages to get through to his eyes, and his two forming buckteeth dig into his lower lip, which has pulled tight in a wide smile. He holds his right arm up, clutching a stringer

101

of fish, bluegills and crappies, their scales reflecting a silvery white. I help him with both hands on the string. My face grins too, as wide as it knows how.

A memory:

My dad wakes me while it is still dark. We're going fishing with my grandfather and cousins. I've never been fishing, so I invited myself—the only girl. I pull on my purple jeans and T-shirt, and my mom yawns as she brushes my hair into two ponytails.

By the time we reach the Mississippi, the sun has risen high enough for lessons in baiting and casting. The worms squirm in the coffee can, but the mosquitoes aren't too bad. I step onto a big rock, which wobbles a bit in the muddy clay underneath, and toss my line out into the water. The red and white bobber dips and bobbles, staccato, and everyone watches as I reel and hoist a thrashing bluegill from the river. My dad and Grandpa are smiling, and we all have trouble grabbing the fish as it swings like a piñata at the end of my pole.

When we drive back to Grandpa and Grandma's house later, sunburned just enough to warm our skin, the stringer is full of small catch, all of them mine.

I'VE LOOKED AT THAT PHOTOGRAPH many times and wondered how I made the men take me along. How I demanded a place. I certainly hadn't grown up with a sense of entitlement. Ours was the middle-class Protestant tradition: you work hard and do your best at whatever needs to be done, and what you want comes second, maybe. You can't always have what you want. Be grateful for what you have. Live by the Golden Rule. Be practical. Be good. Be kind.

If it wasn't entitlement, and it wasn't expectation, where did I get the nerve?

Self-consciousness had found me early; I cared what people thought because they told me, and it didn't sound at all good. Other children and even adults toyed with me because my belly pulled at the stitches in my polyester pantsuits, because my arms plumped like hot dogs, because I never lost my baby fat. My parents taught me that sticks and stones may break my bones, but names will never hurt me. But I did hurt. So how did I keep taking risks when every time I put myself out there, I became a big fat target? Was I stubborn or simply stupid? Had self-consciousness not yet metamorphosed into self-doubt? Or perhaps something clicked early on and prodded me to prove myself, to show them, to be good enough to like, love, keep. I'd like to believe in the latter so I can have something to blame this obsession on, this obsession to make my life extraordinary, to avoid the average at all costs. I'd like to believe that when the school placed me in advanced reading classes, in drama and math and art enrichment courses, and when I performed on the piano before large audiences beginning at age five, dressed as Little Bo Peep and playing "It's a Small World," I formed the driving need that haunts me still; I formed it by overcompensating. I'd like to believe that because then maybe it can be fixed, cured, erased—or, at the very least, managed. That, and it's better than the alternative: it's in my DNA.

At some point my need for accomplishment fissioned, multiplied, and grew large and bulbous, took on a life. I worked hard and did everything well except look thin and pretty, yet people teased, didn't like me, demanded more. I still didn't get far enough, couldn't stand tall enough, wasn't good enough. But they—classmates and teachers and actors and parents and politicians and pastors—they made me believe if I tried harder, everything would magically happen: success, acceptance, peace. The American Dream. Abundant life. *Jesus loves me, this I know, for the Bible tells me so.* What would Jesus do? They told me, again and again.

Make a difference.

Be happy.

On the farm, animals live and they die. They hurt and they heal. They suffer and they adapt. Life is hard, but you go on. You go on because others need you, even if they're cows and pigs and a litter of barn kittens. Your role is secure, important. In the suburbs, and maybe in the city, you learn that life is hard, too, and you go on, but it's to prove something, to numb yourself, to find a place where you're needed, secure, important.

To matter.

Wendy and Matt Bilen outside Lee and Josie Broadhead's house in Breidel Coulee, La Crosse, Wisconsin, 1976

Guides

HER DAUGHTERS FEEL she was a woman born before her time, and they'll tell you so. When it comes to their mother, it's one of the few things they agree on, one of the few things time and memory haven't corrupted. They can sit at the kitchen table for hours debating the past they share, cheese curds and fresh berries and lefse at their fingertips. Occasionally the oldest of the two will disappear into another room and return with proof—an old church program or creased photographs with the names of the posed written right on their images—or pick up the phone, hung next to the table, to call the neighbor or cousin or friend who will know for sure. In the end the truth doesn't matter much when it comes to these discussions because the sisters know nothing they can dig up now will change what they came to believe long ago.

Toss their sister-in-law into the mix, and you've got a trio that calls itself "the three aunts" and signs joint correspondence like this:

Technically, they're two aunts who rotate since somebody always has a mother in there, but no one minds the designation. Together or separately, they're a force to be reckoned with, fearless and better connected than the underground. I have always known the three aunts, and they remain the strongest link I have to Josie. I tap them for every drop they can give, a process as humorous as it is useful since bizarre tangents occur regularly, as do disagreements, memory lapses, and snack breaks.

Over two April days, the sisters, Beverly and Mary, hunch over Bev's kitchen table as they assemble and salvage their past. They're doing it for me, but I know they would find a way to talk about these things even if I wasn't here. The oldest of the three aunts, Beverly Broadhead Ranis, is a stocky woman with large auburn-gray curls and a nearby smile, one of those people you can't help but like. A former fourth-grade teacher, retired several years now, she collects cow paraphernalia and can often be spotted in appliquéd sweatshirts, sneakers, and bifocals, a uniform suited to her constant movement. The modern art that has lived on her walls for years, a seeming contrast to the Hummels and the Bing and Grondahl plates lining walls and ceiling, exposes her bohemian side. She generally sits with both feet flat on the ground and slightly splayed, as if she might rise any minute. Tears surface nearly as often as laughter, and her voice expands a room with its fullness. She speaks with authority, rarely presenting a caveat, though her retractions sound just as authoritative and unapologetic. Going on seventy, she brags of two sons and seven grandchildren, including a set of twins (a result of those Broadhead genes). She gives the impression of unpuncturable strength, yet she tells the other aunts how it hurts when her husband of almost forty years says intentionally mean things or deliberately forgets their anniversary, both of which he does often.

Bev has five years on her sister, my mother, Mary Broadhead Bilen. She and Bev share the same build—"big boned," is how they like to put it—though Mary stands some inches taller. She, too, wears appliquéd garments in country colors. The sisters sound exactly alike on the telephone, though in person Mary's voice comes across much softer and more hesitant. She is aging well—at sixty-three her short brown hair still fights back the gray, and her hazel eyes still sparkle brightly. She has two speeds—high and off—and rarely goes more than a couple of weeks without having guests in her Florida home for dinner, a party, or a visit of several days. Her husband, my dad, insists he is also an extrovert, and I suppose he has to be to entertain at his wife's request so often. Hospitality fuels her; to watch her at one of her events is to encounter a woman lifted directly off the pages of *Better Homes and Gardens*. (She once won a blue ribbon in their garden contest.) She works in a church office, and after years of not reading, she has recently taken to sprinting through every book Nicholas Sparks has written and then passing them on to Bev.

The three aunts outside the La Crosse farmhouse in 1998, from left:
Beverly Broadhead Ranis, Mary Broadhead Bilen, and Karen Broadhead

I ask the sisters to tell me about life growing up with Josie.

"We took piano lessons," Bev says, laughing.

"She used to—now Lawrence didn't—but they used to send us on a bus, the old Winnishiek bus. We'd get out of school at 3:30?" says Mary. "We'd catch the bus, at something like five after three? We'd take it into town—I don't remember how much the bus cost—but we'd take it into town, and walk—what, two, three miles?"

"Oh, yeah. We had to *walk*," adds Bev.

"We had to walk to Mrs. Sayles's house, who taught both of us," Mary continues. "It was seventy-five cents a half an hour for one, or two for a dollar." They chuckle, knowing their mother was always one for a bargain, as are they. "So we got lessons, both of us, for a dollar. And then we would walk back to the bus station and take the bus home."

They tell me that Josie gave them each a nickel to get ice cream at a place across from the bus station, a place they would now classify as a *dive*. "We didn't know that," Bev says. "We were too dumb." I later learn that they went to town not just for piano lessons but just about every weekend, too. On Friday and Saturday mornings the farmers drove in and parked behind Bonsack's bar. The kids ran over to Kresge's dime store or maybe McClellan's. If they happened to be buying new clothes they went to reasonably priced Spurgeon's, and Arenz shoe store at J and Fourth Streets, kitty-corner from the bus station. There they tried on shoes and stepped into a machine where a green light illuminated their toes, Martian-like, and revealed whether they had on the right size. On Sundays after church—still Trinity, though now Evangelical and Reformed—Lee would pull into Galster's market and buy two pints of ice cream to split five ways. So no one complained, Josie cut the two pints into six slices: one for each of them and one to be divided five more times. Then they went to the country to go visiting. Beverly says, "I always thought that was the funniest thing, we'd go to the country, 'cause we lived in the country." Sometimes they went to see their aunt Mabel, when she still lived in Vernon County. If you recall, twins Mabel and Maud married the Broadhead boys, Albert and George. After Mabel lost Albert in 1949, she moved from her lavish farmhouse to her daughter Mildred's apartment in La Crosse.

"When I was continuing to go to piano lessons, I would stop and visit Aunt Mabel," Mary says.

"She had a dog," Bev adds.

"McGee."

"McGee! Yes, that's right, that's right."

"Did we ever have McGee? Maybe that was the one that lived with us." Apparently the farm took in dogs, too.

"No, never got the dog," Bev insists, her lips tight, her head swinging back and forth.

"I'm not sure," Mary says slowly, as Bev continues to negate the point. "What was the dog that was deaf?"

Bev pauses for a second, looking off to the left. "That coulda been McGee." They giggle.

"Remember Anita Kreutz? She had this big horn—"

"But we didn't have McGee, Mary."

"It was our horn."

"Probably got it at the fair."

"Anita would take this thing up to this dog, put it up to the dog's ear and blow this horn, and the dog just sat there because the dog was deaf."

Bev doesn't find it funny because she can't remember it. They get to talking about one of their brother's dogs, Tammy, a cocker spaniel, who used to lie at the top of the stairs and growl when Bev came in late.

"You *could not* walk upstairs, that dog'd be up there g-rrr-rrr-rrr. 'LAWRENCE! GET YOUR DOG!'"

"It was a little cocker spaniel!" Mary says.

"It was *not* little," Bev counters, "and I tell you, I'd stay away from that dog. Lawrence was the only one who had—*communication* with it."

Watching Bev and Mary, I can tell they are their mother's daughters. Despite their pitted memories, each exudes a boldness in her own way, in the same manner I know Josie did. They care just as little as she did about what people think. Their chaotic speech patterns ring familiar, though they laugh more readily than their mother. Life was serious for Josie; there was much important work to do. Bev and Mary may be just as busy, but they tend to accept what they've gotten done instead of condemning themselves for what they have not. I laugh with them, even as I turn a pale green inside because I know I'm more like Josie in that regard than I am like them.

"I remember Mom used to make us practice. She'd make us practice—" Mary starts, displaying the well-established family trait of veering into a different topic—or one that has been previously discussed minutes or even hours ago—without notice.

"Bless her heart," says Bev.

"—and she'd give us those cod-liver oil pills."

Bev gasps.

"And I used to hate those things—"

"Oh, I hated those!" shrieks Bev. Their faces contort in mirror images. They continue without apology, as they are used to talking over and interrupting each other. Somewhere a clock moos.

"—and I'd hide those in the back of the piano."

"Is *that right?* Oh, yeah." Bev pauses, trying to find the memory. "See, she was a good mother."

"She was. She was a good mother."

Bev gets up and disappears behind the refrigerator door, her arm jutting out with a bowl of grapes and a mottled chunk of white and yellow cheese. I know she bought the cheese at a plain old grocery store, but I hear my mind say, *Now that's good cheese.* My mom's voice. She has indoctrinated me about Wisconsin dairy products.

"You never heard her say, 'You need to do this,'" Bev continues. "You never heard her say that kind of stuff. 'Get in there and practice.'"

"Ohhhh yeah, oh I had to practice," Mary argues. "She made me practice."

"She'd never rationalize anything. No way. She'd just tell you to do something, and we did it. 'Get down in the garden.' We'd never say, 'Why?'"

"But I have to tell you, when it came time for doing chores in the morning—"

"Oh, yeah," Bev laughs, knowing she's been had.

"'Bevvverlyyyyy! It's time to get up!'" Mary cries in a mock holler, her hand a crescent around her mouth.

"No, not in the morning," counters Bev. "We never did chores in the morning. We did them after school."

"Well, right, most of the time, but there were a few times—"

"Lawrence did mornings. We did afternoons."

"Must have been weekends."

"Okay."

"'Bevvverlyyyyy and Lawrence! Get up!'"

"I'd get lost. Know where I'd get lost?"

"Ten minutes later. 'Bevvverlyyyyy!' she'd holler," Mary continues, hacking slightly at this third imitation.

"I'd go to the bathroom. I'd go to the outside toilet. We had an outside toilet."

"*Anything* to get out." Mary says, still coughing on the way to refill her Charlie Brown glass at the sink. Cartoon characters decorate many of Bev's glasses, remnants of old fast-food promotions. These glasses were one of the reasons I grew up thinking Bev so cool—not just because she had them, but because she kept them. Now I realize it's the Josie in her, the free, the good enough.

"Mary's out there working. Where am I? Upstairs. 'I'm changing clothes! Yeah, I'm comin,' I'm comin'!' And I don't remember, but yeah, we had an old upright piano, and I'm sure she had that tuned."

"Think so?" Mary says, following the topic shift without question.

"Yeah, I'm sure she did."

It doesn't strike me immediately, but the content of their conversation is telling: piano lessons, ice cream, pups, visiting relatives, trying to get out of chores. It all sounds so *normal*. They will talk about the frequent visitors and the folks taking up the extra rooms, sure, but those discussions come from someplace farther away. Bev and Mary don't describe themselves as players in those dramas, so they're unable to say too much. In those instances, the daughters take on the role of spectator, with their mother being the producer, director, and lead actress. Somehow amid all the unusualness of the farm, Josie managed to run a regular home, and her kids participated in the things that most kids do. Conversations like this one reflect the fact that Bev and Mary knew Josie and Lee as Mom and Dad; that's how the girls and their brother related to them, and that's how they remember them.

They tell me that each day they took their lunch to school in Karo syrup pails, a peanut butter or jelly sandwich on homemade bread, a wormy apple, and maybe a cookie. They remember that on a morning when the counter held no bread for sandwiches, Josie told the girls she'd bring their lunches by later. At lunchtime, because they weren't sure what their mother had brought or where she had left it, the girls waited until the rest of the students had grabbed their lunches and gone outside to eat. Two paper bags sat lonely on the shelf. When Bev and Mary peered inside the mouth of the bags, they gasped: resting on top of each sandwich was a shiny candy bar. They looked at each other, figuring the lunches couldn't be theirs since they never had candy bars. They waited around until their hunger won out and sheepishly ate the lunches anyway. When the girls asked their mother about it after school, they learned that she had surprised them with the sweets. They told her what had happened, how they couldn't believe the lunches were theirs, and to their surprise, Josie cried. She cried because she hadn't been able to give her children much more than her parents had given her, and every time someone retold that story, even decades later, fresh tears found her eyes.

The doorbell rings; Bev lets in Karen, the third aunt. Karen Mullen Broadhead is the only one of us refined enough to ring the doorbell. Most of the time, we walk right in. Sandwiched between Bev and Mary in age, Karen spent thirty-seven years married to their brother, Lawrence, who died in 1999 after ten difficult months with pancreatic cancer. She is a short, quiet woman with dark curly hair and glasses who almost seems to mumble when next to Bev—but then everyone does—and she speaks with greater caution than even Mary. Karen, too, taught in La Crosse, though after she earned her master's degree, she worked as a reading specialist until her recent retirement. She bore four children who now raise her six grandchildren, three of whom are adopted between her two sons. She lives on the farm.

Being around all three aunts at once is like being in, well, an ant colony. Constant motion and prattle breathe life into the kitchen, and then somebody's always pulling something out of the refrigerator because we always sit at the table. It gives us somewhere to lean our elbows and somewhere to set the food. It also gives us a good look at each other.

A few years back—I think after Lawrence died—the aunts started getting together several times a year. They garage sale, scour outlet malls, go to Disney World, swim: activities that allow them to forget their stresses, their losses, and their ages and simply live as girls again. But one of their favorite things to do is talk about the family, which they relish with all the drama of a soap opera. They lean in, hush their voices, and with the banter of an old married couple recount the stories. Bev and Mary forge ahead, and Karen tries to keep up.

"As long as I can remember, people would stop and get milk," Mary says, her words garbled slightly as she chews grapes.

"Yep, oh yeah. Eggs," Bev adds, leaning back in her chair.

"Oh, yeah," says Karen.

"Eggs," Mary repeats, nodding.

"And, you know it, they never left—or at least, yeah, she'd send something else home with them," continues Bev.

"Really?" says Karen.

"Yeah. The garden? Yeah, you know it'd be, 'Lee, go get some potatoes,' or 'We got some tomatoes' if it was in the summer. They never, never left with just—well, not the neighbors, but I mean, if it was relatives or somebody."

"Well, Carl's wife used to bring her jars—" Karen says.

"Oh, *Ann,*" Bev says, her eyebrows raising.

"—and she'd go out and can everything—"

"Can right there," Bev finishes. "Just help herself."

"She never asked. She just did it."

"Ann."

"She was interesting," says Mary.

"Yeah, she *was* interesting," says Bev. "Yep. Ann."

Bev doesn't mention that her son, Steve, and his wife now grow a garden that rivals Josie's for the very same reason: so they can give it away.

"But I think, like I had said earlier," Mary offers, "the kitchen table was a real important part of the house, that was the center. And when people would come, if it would be at breakfast time, and they'd come in, and we'd sit around the table. And Saturday morning I can remember, it was always the later morning, 'cause we'd listen to—never had a TV at that time—but we'd listen to Baby Snooks. Didn't we listen to—or what was the Saturday morning programs?"

"I don't remember," Bev says.

"Weren't those Saturday night?" asks Karen.

Beverly, Mary, and Lawrence Broadhead, 1943

"I remember the PHAN-TOM," says Bev, in her best radio voice. She laughs at herself and raises her open hands in surrender. "Here we go again."

"Fibber Magee," says Karen.

"Yeah!" say Bev and Mary in unison.

"Judy Canova. I remember those on Saturday night," says Karen.

"This would have been—" Mary starts.

"Probably in the fifties," Bev finishes. "You think?"

"Well . . . maybe forties."

"Forties, I'd say forties," adds Karen.

"Forties," says Mary.

"Or maybe early fifties," suggests Karen.

"Fifty, 1950 we got our TV," Mary says.

"Forty-nine we went to Florida. Dad got a new Dynaflow," Bev chuckles.

"Big Buick," says Mary.

"*Big* Buick."

"To hold seven people. Our family, the five of us, plus—I don't know who invited Uncle Ralph and Aunt Marie—"

"*I* didn't," Bev says and laughs.

"Your mother probably," says Karen.

They refer to *the* Florida trip when Lee and Ralph traveled nearly two thousand miles to see their Uncle Reno's place in Homestead, south of Miami. The best anyone can figure, their mother's brother died, and the family had offered his place to relatives before selling it. We know only one thing about Reno McClurg: that he played the violin for a presidential inaugural ceremony. Nobody knows which one. Unfortunately Reno hadn't kept house as well as he had played the fiddle, as his place turned out to be a shack. But Josie wanted that place. Badly. Maybe she saw it as a chance to start over, to get away from farming, or to do something exciting like she'd always wanted. She had been tied to a farm her whole life. Had to fight for her schooling, fight for her men. She couldn't travel or wear fancy clothes. She hadn't become an actress or a singer as she had dreamed on the prairie. She had no time that didn't belong to someone else first. Probably when she looked at the shack she didn't see a clapboard box. Probably she saw one of heaven's mansions, prepared for her.

A photograph of Josie in Florida—the one on my desk, which was likely taken on another family visit within the next few years—shows that she hadn't lost the longing. She wades in the ocean. The water comes just above her ankles, and one leg points in toward the other. She holds her flowered dress up with both hands. The dress looks new, and she fills it out like a woman aging. The wind blows her hair slightly, which lies in fuzzy curls around her face. As she turns toward someone off to the side, the sun puts her cheeks and neck in shadow. The look on her face expresses unencumbered delight, freedom. It is Josie at rest, the Josie who sat on the prairie dreaming. It is Josie without the strain of drinking or farming or poverty. It is Josie at play.

Despite all her pleadings, they didn't purchase Uncle Reno's tropical cabin. They came back to Wisconsin and bought a television instead. They were the first family in the coulee to have one. Maybe because he felt bad about Florida, Lee went into town one day and returned with a set. Despite a screen no bigger than a slice of rye bread, they all considered it the most exciting thing to hit the farm since they could remember. They turned it on at half past four or so, but nothing broadcast at that hour, so they sat and watched the test pattern until milking.

Karen quietly mentions that Aunt Tina and Uncle Waldo expect us in five minutes, so we grab our purses and head for the door, leaving the kitchen table as is: food warming on plates, drinks sweating in glasses, lights shooing the shadows, all waiting for our return. As we scramble into the car, an inarticulate sense nudges me. I revisit it later, realizing only then that I, in some small way, had in those two afternoons spent an hour with Josie.

Trenches

THE PROSPERITY OF LEE AND JOSIE'S farm sometimes made it possible to forget that folks out of work were lining up for bread while farmers plowed fields under and slaughtered whole herds—five million piglets in 1933 alone. The Broadheads' crop stayed reliable, their food plentiful, their house solid, and the climate consistent and gracious. While many of the nation's farmers had already begun accepting government checks under Roosevelt's Agricultural Adjustment Act, Lee was not among them. "Dad never would have done that," his daughter, Mary, insists, and he didn't need to. He remained diversified enough, and although some of his key yield—tobacco, hogs, and milk—met eligibility requirements, he grew the rest of his crops solely for livestock feed and bedding. He and Josie had left North Dakota just in time, and only by a matter of providence did George offer them a Wisconsin farm. Compared to the anemic Dakotas, Wisconsin in the 1930s bulged with veins of iron.

The Dust Bowl wasn't ravaging the Dairy State like it was the prairie, where the land flew about like flour from a mixer on high speed, taxing even the most weathered farmers. When a weary Wallace made a rare visit to see Lee and sat on the porch with his brother and the Kramers from up the road, he said, "I'd sooner wade around in a foot of mud back here than six inches of dust out there."

Even without his father's help, Lee would have made it work, but as it was, he started out with livestock and equipment, buildings and crew. "Grandpa George had a lot of faith in Lee," Lee's nephew, Richard, claims, "which was why he got the big farm." Lee quickly proved he could handle the challenge. He bought his first tractor, known from the start as the Chug-a-Boom, and he made wise and measured purchases until horses, dairy cattle, chickens, pigs, and a few sheep crowded the pens, and the fields waved with oats, hay, alfalfa, peas, and corn—always corn. And on fourteen acres south of the house, he began cultivating rows of leafy green plants, the ones he rolled in little white papers and lit: tobacco.

He had chosen a labor-intensive endeavor; each acre of tobacco could take up to two hundred fifty man-hours compared to wheat, which took three. But every leaf unfurled like a dollar bill—sure money, good money. The season each year went the same way. Two field hands sat on a horse- or tractor-pulled planter. As the machine furrowed and watered a row, one of the hands dropped a plant from the box on his lap and the other spaced them before the machine pushed dirt around the seedling. When summer overtook spring, green worms infested the field, fattening up on the addictive salad, and the help had to pick them off and throw them into a bucket. (Later, Bev and Mary acquired the honor.) Then Lee and his crew pulled the growth off the top, a process known as "topping," before chopping, sorting, spearing, and hanging the plants to dry in the tobacco sheds, which had many thin doors to let in the air. There the leaves shrunk into soft brown leather until January or February, when the crew converted the garage into a stripping

Lee Broadhead spearing tobacco on his farm in La Crosse in 1948

shed and wrapped in newspaper and twine long thin bales weighing about sixty-five pounds each.

That farming was Lee's first love is no secret. That may be why, except for a weakening of the eyes and a few lines on his face, he never really aged. For Lee, the idea of farming the land and everything on it came close to heaven; to own it would be divinity itself. But Lee had to wait, for although George supposedly gave a farm to each of his sons, the truth is that they worked his property and then, maybe, he let them buy it from him after a while.

That chance presented itself when George Broadhead died "after a brief illness" on August 30, 1938. The obituary in the *La Crosse Tribune* says that "he was actively engaged in agriculture all his life"— a gross understatement, if you asked his sons. Six months later Lee paid his mother nineteen thousand dollars for the Breidel Coulee farm; he didn't have this money, so he put down three thousand and promised to make monthly payments of one hundred ten dollars from his milk money, which should have taken about twelve years. Lee did it in six and a half. During the Depression.

Lee got his farm, and Josie got her freedom, or so she believed.

So LEE AND JOSIE SETTLED into the coulee, a slice of which now really belonged to them. That settling involved knowing their neighbors, for better, for worse. It's always been clear that in those days, neighbors and friends came down to the same thing. Generally. They put up with a lot to keep the peace because they never knew when they might need a hand, though not all of the farmers in the coulee earned reputations for kindness, friendliness, or reliability. Some bordered on eccentric; others acted downright cruel. Walter Zielke, who lived at the back of the coulee with his large family, once suckered Herb Kramer into buying an old saggy cow. Herb let it go, but he wouldn't have had a chance to repay the favor even if he had wanted to. When Zielke's boy earned his golden gloves and won twelve hundred dollars in a fight, the old man took the money and ran.

Charles Murphy lived back in the coulee as well, a hot Irishman who had emigrated from town, where he had run a streetcar for many years. Having supposedly been fired when he slapped a woman passenger, Murphy decided to try farming. He traded his house in town for a farm in the coulee, even though he had never before owned a farm or driven a horse and was about as cut out for farming as a snake is for running. Before long, half the floor in his house disappeared to the woodchucks, and piles of wood shavings sat where rugs should have lain. He chopped feed corn with a hatchet, and one time he hurled that same hatchet at Lee and neighbor Sonny Kramer just for passing by. Murphy's team backed the wagon over his leg one time, breaking it clean in half between the knee and ankle. Without a phone or car, he hobbled a good mile down the road using a wooden chair, until the chair broke and Louis Breidel heard him hollering. After they got him into the police car, which doubled as the ambulance service, they realized Murphy had no one to do his chores. So Sonny went home to fetch a lantern. Then he came back, went into the barn, and milked the cows of the man who had tried to kill him with an ax. Lee did the same.

Louis Breidel, son of one of the three boys for whom the coulee was named, farmed a mile back with his brothers Herman and George. The German bachelors just about lived on sauerkraut, which they scooped from a fifty-five-pound barrel behind their front door. Folks could liken stepping onto their property to taking a whiff of smelling salts. How all three of them lived to be near or past ninety years old remains a mystery, the way they ate. Sonny explains that he once watched in horror as the brothers took out a big black frying pan with about a half-inch of lard in it and fried up some unrecognizable clear fatty meat—standard fare for the three.

The brothers also liked their brandy, and even in the nursing home, the afternoon rounds included a daily dose of *die medizin,* one shot. They probably chuckled at the goings-on during Prohibition, when their neighbor, John LeJeune, and his brother brewed hooch. Because the roads leading back to LeJeune's place had established themselves as unreliable, the jugs and still hid beneath the hay in the shed belonging to Sonny's dad, Herb Kramer. Herb didn't like it, but he didn't argue either, in the spirit of being neighborly. On Saturdays the LeJeunes would dust off a gallon, drive into town, and sell it for seven or eight dollars. Then an insurance man called at the Kramers' door, and Sonny's dad mistook the suit for a Prohibition agent. That was the end of that.

Keeping up with these happenings required little effort. To learn the latest news, they needed only to pick up the phone. The party line and the delicious soapbox drama it wired into every house afforded not only a means of communication but also a free source of entertainment. The telephone company hooked up several families together on one line, a cost-effective measure at two dollars per month, but only one person could use it at a time. For years, Broadheads, Kramers, LeJeunes, and Breidels shared a line, and later the Schroeders and some others added on as the phone company worked itself farther back into the coulee.

Everyone knew everyone else's voice, and sometimes they could recognize the breathing. A soft click in the background meant someone had been listening in. Every morning, Mrs. LeJeune called each of her five girls, a constant source of irritation for otherwise steady Lee, who had to call cow breeders at certain times. Eventually he had to interrupt with, "Could I use the phone?" Not everyone demonstrated Lee's patience; some had no problem clicking the switchhook or hanging up for the long-winded who couldn't do it themselves. Even I remember the party line; it stayed around until the 1970s.

This was Josie's community. These were the folks she needed and yet stood apart from. They were the ones who talked about her and wondered at her ways but still called her one of their own. This was the coulee; this was her home.

IN 1941 THE FARMHOUSE ACQUIRED, for a change, another woman: Josie's younger sister, Tina, married and moved to the farm with her new husband, Waldo. They stayed a year, give or take a few months, to give them a good start toward their own place, as Waldo's father was not in the business of handing out farms. Josie found the companionship sweet, the help a relief, and she had plenty for Tina to do: men to feed and children to watch. Little man Lawrence was running around in overalls, a kid with defiant hair, skinny and sporting his dad's smirk. Beverly, three years younger, shared his height, but her body imitated her mother's stockiness. Clothed in smocked dresses her mother made from flour sacks, she had golden hair that had started to find its natural curl, which presented itself in kinky frizz and uncontrollable tufts.

About this time, as Lawrence neared age ten, he rushed into the kitchen holding over his shoulder a snorting, wriggling ball the color of southern soil. "Look, Ma," he said, "I won! Her name is Petunia." Lawrence had won the piglet in the pig club's annual essay contest on how to improve the hog industry. The winner received a purebred gilt with the idea of breeding the female and returning one of the litter for the next year's prize.

Josie hollered. "Get that pig out of the kitchen! Move!"

Lawrence stood there cradling the piglet like a baby being burped, but when Josie looked more closely, she saw that he held a Duroc runt. Its legs jerked and its eyes glazed, both indicators that it might not last the night. "Now I can have my own herd of Durocs!" Lawrence squealed, his words stumbling over themselves. "Ma, can I feed her? Should I use a spoon or get one of those bottles?"

"I didn't want to dampen my son's spirit," Josie wrote later. "[N]either did I want to be overly optimistic." She paused and then suggested Lawrence use something smaller, so he ran out of the room, returning with an eyedropper and a doll bottle.

"Will you help me?" he said.

She hesitated, and he saw it. "Of course I'll help you," she replied at last. "That pig may not make it through the night, but we'll do our very best." Lawrence's eyes welled with tears. "Go get a box and line it with lots of straw. Then make a nest and lay a hot water bottle with the hottest water you can get, put it in the nest and place Petunia on it. You've got to get her circulation going. Then feed her and set the box in the machine shed near the chicken brooder."

"Okay," Lawrence sniffled, running off to follow his mother's instructions. He did as she said, checking in on Petunia every hour and prying her tiny mouth open to squirt in a few drops of milk.

The next morning, Lawrence flung open the screen door during breakfast and slid across the kitchen floor. "Ma, Dad, she's going to make it!" He grabbed a piece of toast and ran out just as quickly, shouting over his shoulder, "She's really going to make it! I know she is." Farm kids are used to death, but Josie probably thanked God that day that it hadn't come to Petunia.

After a week, a stronger and livelier pig trotted around the yard. They transitioned her to dry pig ration with water, not knowing yet that she had discovered the high-protein chicken feed. "All the freedom and special attention she had gotten," Josie wrote, "made this sleek and winsome gilt, with her smart corkscrew tail, a first class pest." Once out of her box, Petunia started following Lawrence everywhere. In the dairy barn she tore up lime sacks or played with the automatic watering machine. She tugged at the drying sheets waving on the clothesline and rooted around paint cans and weed killers and Josie's vegetables, and someone could always be heard yelling, "Get out of here now! Shoo!" Sometimes Petunia showed up in the house.

At six months they washed her and placed her in a clean pen to be bred. Soon after, a litter of eighteen screeched around her, and Lee helped Lawrence set up a rotation for feeding because Petunia had only ten teats. Beverly has a few photographs of Lawrence sitting in the pen with Petunia and the babies, big white stripes down their middles. Because it was a farm, and Petunia was a pig, they eventually sold her, and she weighed in at an impressive eight hundred pounds. Petunia left a hole behind, and Josie talked many times about how the little runt had taught her son integrity and commitment, and, most importantly, to overcome—lessons they would all need very soon.

Josie allowed her kids to simply be kids, and she tried to help them find their way. Beverly worked her mother hard; her routine involved causing trouble at school with someone named Frankie Seebauer. They'd wire their desks together so both tops opened at the same time, or they'd slip outside to the outhouse and play. Normally the teacher required students to sign out on the blackboard before using the outhouse, indicating *one* or *two* for how long they planned to be. Bev used the number two a lot. "You could kinda hide in there," she explains. Their hijinks weren't serious, just enough to show off and distract the teacher. As the only child to acquire her mother's temperament, Beverly also attracted a fair share of her mother's wrath when word reached home. Josie spanked, and she did it as soon as she could, red-faced, using anything that happened to be nearby—a lathe, her hand, a spatula. "That was a common thing for me," Bev says. "I'd get a lot of lickins, 'cause I was pretty mouthy."

Even so, Waldo, remembering those days, tells Beverly, "You was pretty good kids."

"I don't think Dad got after us much," she replies.

"Course, you could hear your mother, couldn't you?"

"I could *feel* her."

True, few things escaped Josie's notice, and she could be harsh, so it's probably no exaggeration that she scolded her adult sister Tina for the tiniest infraction. Emotions ran high anyway; the bellies of the sisters expanded with child, and the war made everyone a little edgy. Lee, still of draft age in his early thirties, received a deferment from the draft board. First classified as 3-A, held back for dependency reasons, he was switched by the government to 3-C and finally to 2-C, agricultural deferment. But Uncle Sam could change his mind at any time. Josie's older brother, Carl Twite, had volunteered, as had nephews Richard Broadhead and his two brothers. Of all the boys on both sides, they were the only ones to go, and, like so many mother's sons, they all came home as radically different men. Though he can't speak for the Twites, Richard insists with a scowl of contempt under his breath that most of the other Broadheads oiled themselves out of their patriotic duty.

With wartime rations on everything from sugar to mileage to rubber, provisions on the farm stretched like winter reaches into spring. Each day the farm had a couple of flat tires, and the hired help fixed them in the garage overnight because they couldn't go out and get new ones. Sonny Kramer, from the farm down the road, who now worked part-time for Lee, remembers a time when Lee bought a wagon with four brand-new tires on it. "Boy," Sonny says, shaking his head even now at the beauty of it. New tires meant a few nights of doing something other than patching rubber. But without a thought, Lee, in a rare gesture of indulgence, took the tires off the wagon and put them somewhere he thought they could be of better use: his car.

Tina and Waldo's move to their own farm in Cashton translated as a long-overdue exit for Lee, since Waldo was the only person on record that Lee had no time for. "Ooooh, Waldo used to get under Dad's skin," my mother says, cringing at the very thought. A spectacled and crew-cutted man, Waldo brought out Lee's well-reserved pride, as he tried to tell Lee how he should milk or bale or, in the later years, golf, and it made Lee mad as a wet cat. Lee probably didn't cry any tears, but Josie did, for she then lost her frontline allies in the war that had started in her own house.

By some measures, it was simple: Lee lived and worked with other men in a community that considered drinking a pastime—the rule, not the exception. By others, it was more complex: he had trouble standing up for himself and had married a woman with a family history in these matters, a wife who didn't let things be. The battle reeked of familiarity, one Josie had seen close up, and though it hadn't been her fight before, she bore enough scars to prove she'd seen combat: the marks of amber and glass, worse than those that come from empty pockets and emptier stomachs, the marks of alcohol. Liquor had followed her to Wisconsin, had crept into her house and into her marriage. Lee was drinking—her Lee! The average person might have had no quarrel with a few beers, but Josie knew what liquor had done to her family, how it had torn up her father and had started in on three of her brothers: Peter and Carl, full alcoholics, and Mort, who just drank too much. For Josie, there was no such thing as moderation when it came to the bottle. She overreacted, and in the wildness of her response Lee lost sight of his increasingly poor choices.

The story piles much of the blame on the hired men. They worked past blistering calluses and numbing exhaustion, and though their employer was fair, their wallets never bulged. They drank because they were worldly and because they could, because it's what they knew how to do. They usually drank to lose their sensibility. Lee, being the kind of man who went along with things, not seeing any immediate reason to object, started to join them, sipping Heileman's during their tobacco stripping, an allowance easily justified by working outside in the cold. The men would routinely strip a row of tobacco, then reward themselves with a round of beers even as Josie hollered inside, "They aren't stripping tobacco *that* long!" Or he would join the men for a few over at the Brown Saddle Inn after chores. (If they tried to sneak small bottles into the house, she usually found them; they learned to use the back stairs to avoid her.) If Lee received glares and words early on, he shrugged them off, pointing out that chores were still getting done, that there was no harm. And for the most part, he was right. But now Josie had another reason to be concerned. On a crisp October day in 1942, Lee and Josie brought home from the hospital their third child, a girl, Mary Beth. My mother.

Lee's behavior worsened with the presence of the baby, and Josie's arguments and demands only enticed shrugs and jeers in return. The neighbors in the largely German community, where drinking was just what men did, mocked her and her old-fashioned views. The coulee threw lots of parties, and they'd be damned if they were going to serve lemonade alone. As such, his decline had been supported and gradual, occurring over several years. However strong the forces, in the end the responsibility landed solely with Lee; the very characteristic that prevented him from standing up to his father allowed him to be sucked into the clawing throes of alcoholism, to be talked or pressured into drinking too much, too hard, too long, by the men who were supposed to be listening to him.

"I don't think Dad was ever an alcoholic," Beverly says, "but Dad followed."

"Ah no, you never want to call him an alcoholic," Sonny Kramer replies sternly. "He was too good a person, but there was bitterness with your mother because she knew what her dad was like. That's all I can say."

By 1944 the men had worn a path to the Brown Saddle Inn, which they drove with their tractors, straight through the field. It was as if they'd paved it for Lee, and he needed only to follow it with the Chug-A-Boom. Though no boss checked time cards, allowing chores to slip was the same as failing to show up at the office. Cows that don't get milked on schedule develop inconsistent milk production, and their risk of infectious mastitis increases. Horses and pigs that go hungry or wallow in their filth get sick and die. Crops left in the field past their due mildew or dry out, or critters eat them. Not only did the men lapse in their labor, but sometimes, proud and swill and sure of their invincibility, they fought. Bickering became wrestling, and then someone threw a punch. Sonny remembers Josie pulling Lee and Mort apart. But it is not her father's absence or the fighting that baby Mary will remember for decades to come; it is this:

Darkness.

Her pudgy legs stumbling along the hard ground, being pulled by the hand more quickly than she can walk.

Entering the dark and smoky Brown Saddle Inn.

Looking up through the haze at her father.

Waiting as her mother confronts her father and then breaks a bottle over the bar.

Being dragged out again, stopping as her mother breaks a bottle from her father's pocket in the doorway.

Darkness.

IT WASN'T THE FIRST TIME, and it wouldn't be the last. "I think she'd even take a stick with her once in a while," friend Lorraine Leske says of Josie's trips to the Brown Saddle Inn. "She'd go up there and raise holy Hannah, and they all had to go home." But her deterrents did no good. Lee drank longer, harder, more often, so Josie began a pattern of her own: she marched into their bedroom, dragged the suitcase out from under their bed, wiped it clean of dust, and opened it. She removed dresses from hangers, undergarments from drawers, and shoes from corners. Then she folded the suitcase in half, buckled it, kissed her children, and hiked resolutely down to Highway 14. There she stood as the cars, trucks, and tractors whizzed by until the bus squealed to a stop in front of her, opened its accordion door, and invited her in. She rode that bus to Cashton, where she then trudged to her sister Tina's house and asked to stay. A few days went by, and then they drove her home.

Josie Broadhead holding her
daughter Mary, circa 1945

Lee Broadhead and Mary on the
La Crosse farm, circa 1944

What happened with the children when she went away remains unclear. Lawrence and Beverly were old enough to understand something about the situation, but they don't recall going with her, and neither does Mary. With all the other evidence pointing to her character and concern for children, I find it hard to believe that her thoughts did not include her own kids. It defies logic why she didn't take them along, unless her logic stemmed from self-absorption, manipulation, or absentmindedness. If you examine one picture of Mary from this period, you might think her neglected, a case for the child welfare people. The photograph shows a toddler walking in the side yard. Ice whitens most of the grass, but her chubby arms, legs, and cheeks bulge from a summer dress some sizes too small. Tights cover her legs, and shoes her feet, but her arms dangle bare. The photographer appears to be the only other person around. No one can explain this photograph or the surrounding questions about the care of Josie's children, but if she had to leave to make a point or keep her sanity, I would guess that she at least made sure they were taken care of by someone, someone dry. The fact that no notable incidents occurred seems to support this conclusion—either that or the grace of God made regular stops in Breidel Coulee. The children might not have said anything, but they had to have noticed she wasn't demonstrating the kind of commitment she had taught them.

After a decade that brought her the Depression and the war, three babies and two funerals, a house full of strange men, drunk brothers, and a withering husband, in the late spring of 1945 Josie played a hand no one expected, not even her.

Barrenness

Burke, Virginia
2004

I REMEMBER TELLING MYSELF—at sixteen? seventeen?—that if I was neither wife nor mother by age thirty-five, I would adopt, an idea inspired by Josie. But that was my backup, the theoretical life one plans to make oneself feel noble. I suppose I wanted to do the kinds of things the woman I most admired did. My adolescent reasoning, surprisingly free from the cynicism I know had already seeped in, was that I would be ready to give back, to nurture and share my life, thinking not altogether untrue. But the actual results disturb me: here I am, thirty-five, married a second time even; there are no children, and I am not too ready to share anything.

Like Josie, the first time I was married, I packed my bags as a threat. But then I told him to pack his, and he did, and he never came back. We had grown up in the same town, gone to high school and college together, so when he slipped away I not only lost my lover and best friend, but I lost my past. I didn't realize it then, but I'd also lost a generous slice of my future. Lopped right off.

I am thirty-five; my body is forty-two. That's the way the doctor puts it, the doctor who draws diagrams of sperm with black ink and narrows my fertility to an L-chart. His office shines. His wife writes humorous books. His children's wedding photographs hang from wooden walls. He will retire soon. His body bends like willow when he's thinking, and he uses terms such as *perimenopause* and *high FSH levels* and *donor eggs*. And *twenty thousand dollars* and *high-risk* and *not likely*. A blood test, a doctor, a percentage: less than one. My eggs have grown old, left in the refrigerator past their expiration date or simply a bad batch.

If I had gotten pregnant, say, in my midtwenties, while married to my first husband, I would likely be a mother now. But that was not to be, since he went and had a baby with somebody else's wife.

I have often thought about the irony of the timing: this news came from the doctor during a season when I spent many hours each day studying and writing about Josie, who made a late-life habit of taking in other people's children, and Martina, who more tragically bore thirteen of her own and lost six before she stopped breathing. It's said that losing a child is the worst grief a person can bear. I can't speak to that, but I do know that it's far worse to have had something taken away than never to have had it at all.

But now that birth as an option has shrunk its way nearly out of integers and adoption become all the more necessary if I want children at all, I haven't been able to bring myself to consider taking in someone else's child. Maybe I'm not ready. Maybe I'm opportunistic in an ambulance-chasing kind of way, and I see my infertility as another barrier removed—legitimately—from the pursuit of doing that really important thing with my life, although I have yet to discover what that is. I keep asking God, and He keeps saying *Hush*. Between the divorce, which left me less committal, and my career change to writing, which left me more reclusive, maybe it's for the best. One less thing to worry about. One less drain on my time, space, and money. One less hindrance as I try to make sense of this life, to find what I'm looking for.

I am not proud of how this sounds, of how this is. I shamefully wonder sometimes if I wanted the experience of birth more than I wanted the child on the other end of it, since people who are parents tell me that a child, in many ways, sucks up anything that comes near. *Before kids. After kids. Do what you want now, while you can.* As soon as I think I might be ready, I consider the cost that a child would exact on my ability to live that life I seek—the extraordinary one—and do nothing at all about it. The truth is, on some days I ache with emptiness when I hear a small child say, "Mommy?" But even that hasn't been enough to propel me out of immobility. Then I look at Josie and wonder how I can be so cold.

Thumbing through Josie's medical records from September of 1951, I discovered a fourth pregnancy. It surprised her daughters when I told them, because they only vaguely and uncertainly recalled it. Josie herself didn't think she was with child until the doctors admitted her to the hospital for vaginal bleeding. Something went wrong, and the baby died inside her. A doctor neatly performed a D & C, and she recovered well, and it was never discussed.

Josie didn't live to see any of my problems with husbands and babies, but I selfishly wish she had. Maybe then we could have talked. Maybe the choices would have been easier, or clearer. Or maybe it would have been enough just to know that she understood.

Two Roads

I SEE JOSIE ROLLING ONTO HER SIDE and staring at the apple or-chard. Her legs ache already. Her back, her arms. The south win-dow's light illuminates the room as a movie projector would a screen, gray and shadowy. On the table beside her a glass of water waits, lukewarm, with a Bible, pencil, paper. She kicks off the sheet, pushing it to the footboard with a pedaling motion, feeling the cool of the breeze on her feet, shins, calves, knees. No one guards the door, and no chains bind her wrists or ankles, but there might as well be for the ones that clank inside her chest.

A tractor sputters out back, and footsteps overhead pound and creak the wooden floors. Josie hears the sound of uneven steps mov-ing up the stairs. She pushes herself up and grabs the pencil and pa-per, and the Bible to write on, and begins a list. MEALS. LAUNDRY. She stops and leans her head against the wall, sighing. She shouldn't be here. There is so much to do. Perhaps Dr. Gundersen overreacted, prescribing bed rest for so long. She doesn't feel sick, just a little tired. No need for all this fuss. What does he know anyway?

It was just a little heart attack.

CONFLICTING ACCOUNTS CLOUD this part of the story. Because the episode precedes the doctor's notes by a year, it's hard to know how bad it was, exactly when it occurred, or what the doctor ordered. Her regimen included a lengthy bed rest, but for such episodes, doctors often pushed rest, physical therapy, heat, a simple diet, and a series of drugs: morphine for immediate pain; phenobarbital for insomnia and nerves; a combination of glucose, quinidine, caffeine, nitroglycerine, digitalis, and iodide of potassium for opening, quieting, strengthening, and healing the heart. The most common side effects from these drugs inflicted the patient and conflicted with each other, leading to crippling constipation, diarrhea, nausea, nervousness, and sedation. It all came down to doctor's choice or trial and error.

Josie's writings mention various medical episodes at various times, all infused with death's closeness and spiritual awakening. Chronic health problems, excessive doctor visits, and hospital admissions prevented her from remembering the pivotal experiences accurately. She always maintained she had had a heart attack, however, and personal accounts from others corroborate that story, including the months of bed rest. Because a heart attack tends to feel like the end of the world, Josie paired it with V-E or V-J Day in her memory, though Bev insists she was the one violently sick with hives on August 6, 1945, a reaction to a penicillin shot. Two reasons confirm why Josie's illness more likely fell in late spring of that year: the earliest medical records in 1946 indicate prior heart trouble, and that's when help arrived.

ABSOLUTE PHYSICAL AND MENTAL REST *are essential for the patient, and are usually obtainable only when tasks are found in some*

other location for the excess number of anxious relatives that usu-
ally crowd the scene. It is far better to engage a capable attendant at
the start.

This is how I picture it: The side door swings open and shut, and
Josie hears Lee's voice, footsteps in the hall. She sits up straighter
and reaches down for the sheet. Lee pokes his head in, and when
he sees she's awake, he walks in. "How're you feeling today?"

"I told you. I'm fine. All this nonsense—"

"The doctor said bed rest, and you have to listen to him. He
knows what's best."

"Is she here?"

"Yes." He motions toward the hallway, and a young girl appears,
smiling politely, a suitcase nervously swaying in her hands. "This
is Ruth Seebauer." The girl's dress indicates a recent growth spurt;
her hem falls at her knees, revealing long, slender shins capped
with folded socks, white, and sneakers, not as white. Her eyes, her
most striking feature, look like two wells in winter, all the more
alluring because her head naturally bows in modesty and shyness.
Her hair parts in the center and descends into braids, a bit of bang
tucked in but fighting. Her innocence is unexpectedly beautiful.

"Hello," Josie says, forcing a smile.

"Nice to meet you, Mrs. Broadhead," Ruth replies in a rolling
voice that gives away her midwestern upbringing and European
heritage.

"Lee, take her out and show her what she has to do."

They leave, and Josie listens as they meander through the house,
their voices muted through the ceilings, walls, and floors. This is
where you'll sleep. This is where the men sleep. This is where the
children sleep. These are our children. This is the kitchen. Down
here is the cellar. There's the outhouse. Ruth follows, staring at the
stacks of dirty dishes, the dried mud outlines of boots on the floor,
and the laundry waiting in piles. "Oh my Lord," Ruth wonders.
"What'd I get myself into?"

Ruth Seebauer, circa 1940

THE NEW HELP, JUST FOURTEEN and days out of eighth grade, had been living over the hill with the Helke family for more than ten years, since her mother entered a tuberculosis sanitarium. Her father lived nearby, a troubled man who eventually took his own life. Ruth thinks maybe Lee got her name from the Hoeths, where she had worked before. He likely secured her employment in haste within the first week or two of Josie's confinement, when doctors made it clear that their patient was not to exert herself for some time. When asked how much Lee paid her, she replies, "Probably next to nothing, but it didn't matter much to me." She did, however, earn enough to buy a bright pink coat from the traveling salesman, an indulgence that she laughs at now.

Despite her age and inexperience, Ruth had many roles to fill. In addition to caring for the children, her responsibilities included cleaning. Ruth probably kept that house cleaner than Josie ever did, not that Josie didn't try. Her house generally stayed as clean as a farmhouse could be, considering all the work boots and dusty bare feet that slapped across its wooden planks. Good friend Hilda First insists that Josie scrubbed the kitchen floor every night on hands and knees, but Dakota relative Rose Twite Gerhart remembers coming to visit and sleeping—or trying to—in gritty sheets. "Gravelly," she calls them, almost embarrassed that the detail has stayed with her. Josie herself told me of the time when she had scrubbed the floor shiny, and one of the farm dogs trotted across it. She didn't much like dogs, but she had an understanding with them: they could stay as long as they chased away snakes while she gardened. She tried to shoo him out, but he crept under the table. When she crouched down and stuck her arm between the chairs to get him, he bit her. Livid, Josie wrapped her arm in a dishtowel, went in again, and grabbed that dog by the tongue. That time he came.

Then there was the sewing. Josie sewed many of the family's clothes and blankets: flour and grain sacks became dresses, old drapes jackets, worn sweaters scarves and mittens. If it could fit underneath the needle, it could be sewn. I wouldn't be surprised if she had Lee rig her sewing machine up next to the bed so she could work from there, but more likely Ruth rocked the pedal, stitching and mending.

It was now up to Ruth to prepare three meals a day, but more than once she looked in the refrigerator only to find it nearly empty. One time Sonny Kramer, by then working full-time at the farm, walked in, and she told him, "I haven't got nothin' to fix. There's no food in the house." He ambled down the road to his folks' place and returned with an arm full of meat and potatoes so she could feed the children and the men and herself. Probably there hadn't been any canning or gardening with Josie in bed, and Lee simply paid no attention.

The laundry, perhaps, proved the most overwhelming. Until the farm went Grade A earlier in the year, Josie had done her wash in the old milk house, setting a fire in the bricks underneath the large kettle sometimes used for scalding hogs. (Later she used a machine with rollers and long skinny legs that stood like an overlayered child in winter, a machine she kept well into the grandchildren decades.) Now that the milk house was obsolete with a new milking parlor in the barn, the laundry moved into the basement—fortunately for Ruth—as the men disassembled the milk house and hauled stone by stone over to Paul Kreutz's place, much in the same way Joseph Linse had built it. When Linse was bringing a load down from the hill to build it the first time, the weight caused the lock on his wagon to snap. He jumped off, but the wagon rushed forward, crushing his brand-new team of Roans, which he had just purchased for six hundred dollars. The stone made it, even if the horses didn't, and now that rock with horse blood on it was destined for the foundation of Kreutz's house, and the bell for his church.

Each night, Ruth collapsed on a cot near the window in one of the upstairs bedrooms, though sometimes she shared a bed with Beverly or Mary if an extra hired man or guest needed that cot. Ruth learned quickly to feel the mattress first because all three children wet the bed—the children whom she now mothered, aged eleven, eight, and three.

No one told Ruth the truth, not only about all the work but about the tension between Lee and Josie, about the drinking. As the weeks hurried by, she learned on her own. Chores didn't get done. Men didn't show for supper, or they staggered in late. When Sonny vomited up the stairs, she was the only one sober or healthy or old enough to mop it up. Another time Richard Broadhead came in drunk with a cut on his forehead, and Ruth tried to clean and bandage the wound when Josie, with a weakened heart but an enduring will, hollered from bed, "You just leave him alone!"

At Christmas Josie still functioned from bed. Ruth knows this for a fact because she had to help Lee play "Santy Claus" for the children. If Josie's bed rest lasted six months, either one of two things caused it: an overly cautious doctor or an unusually severe coronary thrombosis. Josie's "spa regime," the pauper's version, was common for heart attack sufferers—bed rest, massage, supervised exercise, hydrotherapy—but many, if not most, patients stayed down only for a few weeks or a couple of months.

Still, being in bed hadn't protected Josie from the happenings outside. She had heard Lee come in late. She had smelled liquor on his breath. She had recognized the darted responses to her questions. She was losing him, and she could do little about it from that bed.

It must have driven her near mad.

As soon as she could travel, she went to her sister Tina's. "I can still see her walking down the road to catch the bus," Ruth says. "Pretty soon, after a couple of days, maybe it'd be just a weekend she'd go, she'd come back." These visits must have scared Lee something awful, as he depended on her more than he—or she—knew. Because she was far from mum, even at her worst, she most likely threatened in every possible way to leave for good.

Both sides hunkered down for an unfair fight, and during the summer of 1946 the forces broke her. A year after the heart attack, Josie reached the place where she couldn't look away, she couldn't look at what was happening to her family, and she couldn't pack up and go to her sister's anymore. She cried all the time. She jittered with excessive nervousness, and she couldn't sleep. She had choking spells, and stomachaches, and she had lost thirty-five pounds. She hit a bottom she didn't know she had, and it frightened her; she broke down, nervously, despairingly, and inconsolably.

She was thirty-five, the age I am now.

Was there a moment when she knew, one she could pin to a clock and say *then*? Or did the loss build over days, weeks, months, an increasing awareness that poured in a steady leak like floodwater over sandbags? Just as with the heart attack, she always believed in the moment, though she couldn't say for sure which one. Whether she stopped functioning altogether or just stumbled along, a turning point existed, this I know, and it must have happened that summer because nothing else could have pulled such a stubbornly despondent woman out of such a deep pit. I think the heart attack scared her, and Lee, but the breakdown changed her. Her bottoming out differs little from the prophet Elijah, a man used to winning, who had to wait through wind, quake, and fire before God found him ready to listen. And then the Lord whispered.

I see Josie in her room, weeping hysterical tears over the fact that another day has passed, and nothing has changed with Lee. Nothing specific has triggered this outburst, simply the monotony of the pain that wore down through bone to nerve. She closes the door to be alone, away from the children and the life outside. She paces, arms folded, elbows in palms, and her dress swishes around her knees. Cyclonic thoughts swirl in her head: *What am I going to do? I can't do this anymore. What am I going to do?*

Death would be better than this, than watching someone she loves destroy himself and his family. Maybe she doesn't really want to die, but she wants the pain to stop. Yes, I'm sure that's it. She sits on the edge of the bed and drops her wet face into her hands, rocking and sobbing, until she slides slowly onto the floor and buries her face in the quilt. Then she pulls the quilt and lies down on the floor with it, curled up like a child. *What am I going to do? I can't do this anymore. What am I going to do?*

Images flash through her mind, and she closes her eyes to escape them, but they don't stop. Lee walking in from Wallace's field, sweaty and brown and smiling. Lee sliding gold onto her finger. Shoveling out of those snowbanks on the drive from North Dakota. Following him through the empty farmhouse. Stooping before that black stove and kindling a fire. Telling Lee he was going to be a father, and watching him hold their son for the first time. These images elicit pain now, reminders of the man she's losing.

The space underneath the bed blurs into a cavern that she wants only to crawl into. She thinks about her mother, who dealt with this for forty years and never once complained, never had a heart attack, never packed her suitcase, never fell apart in front of the children. Why is it that her mother could handle it, but she can't? Josie closes her eyes in guilt, the shame pushing her further into that dark space under the bed. Faith did it, Josie recognizes, faith that she knows she doesn't have. All she can do right now is beg, barter, or surrender. She chooses all three. *God help me God help me God help me.*

God, I don't know what to do anymore. I can't do this. I can't. I can't. I want to die. I want to go away forever. I know it's wrong, but I don't care. I can't do this anymore. I just can't. I'm not my mother. I love him, God. At this she sobs uncontrollably and can't even think her prayer. *I love him, and I can't see him do this to himself, to me, to the children, to the farm. How can he do this? How? Please don't take my family away. Please don't take my husband. I just want my family. I just want my husband back. If you save me from this, from all of it, I'll do whatever you want.*

I can be there with her, imagining this moment, because of what she told me and what she wrote, but more so because I, too, have lost my man.

I don't know what happened next. I only know that somehow she got up, and she made supper, and she woke up the next day and did it all again. Was it faith? Hope? Love? I suspect it was mostly release, surrender, trust. Nothing changed with Lee, at least not right away, but her fear dropped, unlocking the shackles, and no longer controlled her. Something she couldn't explain grounded her, something that compelled her to keep going, to love her husband, to wait.

LEE DIDN'T STOP DRINKING just because Josie prayed, but he did stop. The mystery does not preclude the miracle. I like to think he broke with liquor because he wised up and saw it as the right thing to do, but fatigue or fear probably won out more than anything else, fear that Josie and the kids would leave him for good or that he'd kill her with worry. Scared sober, as they say. His son said yes, a threat of the d-word hovered, but she never got around to drafting divorce papers because he promised to change, and then really did, and so she stayed. Ruth left but returned when things didn't work out at home: "I came down here with my brown suitcase," she says. "And your Ma came to the porch door, and then I said I need a place to stay. I said, 'Can I stay?' And she says, 'Well, yeah, but we can't pay you,' and I says yeah, that was fine."

Josie would say that God spoke to her, that He saved her, and I suppose He did. But I choose also to believe that a woman can make a promise and keep it, that she can give everything she has and then some more so that a child of any age can have a few moments or a few years of love and normalcy, that after she told God that day in '45 or '46 or whenever that she'd do whatever He wanted, they came.

The Youth

BEFORE MOST OF THE CHILDREN came Sonny: Sonny who brought some food to the farm's bare kitchen, Sonny who on occasion drank a few too many, Sonny who witnessed a fight and lamented the loss of some good tires. His wife rightly calls him by his Christian name, Herb, but the three aunts have always known him as Sonny, and Sonny he will always be. In his old age he looks remarkably like Ronald Reagan, his fine light hair parted on the side and slicked over, the comb marks visible in neat rows. He stands strong and tall, sturdy and clad in flannel, with wire rims and a soft voice that requires listeners to lean in, as if he's an old radio.

He and his wife, Phyllis, have come to the farmhouse at the aunts' request. Sonny has taken the chair at the head of the table, square in the picture window framing the black walnut tree and the stone fireplace that crumbles away a bit more each time the snow melts. As we fill in the chairs around him, I tell him I want to hear his stories. He remembers no life before the Broadheads. I ask him to think back seven decades and then some, a taxing task for anyone. But he has, I soon learn, the energy for the challenge, enough to dredge up a remarkable repertoire of tales and dates. This explains why the aunts have been saying, "Sonny Kramer'll know," every time they can't answer one of my questions. It bodes well that Sonny has such a strong memory because he was a witness. He saw it all: Lee and Josie's arrival, George, Josie's heart attack and nervous breakdown, the hired men, all that drinking, births, deaths, and just about everything in between. He can verify the truth of most hearsay as well as or better than a lot of fact checkers, and he can fill in quite a few holes.

Sonny may be useful when it comes to assembling Josie's chronology, but his story has its own merit. All told, he lived and worked on the farm over a period of eleven years, 1941 to 1952, the hardest ones on the farm, and at least four of those years were full-time. He came to be Lee's right-hand man. He differed from the others who came only in that he chose to be there; his circumstances hadn't tossed him into the ragtag collection of folks living with the Broadheads. Even if he came for different reasons, he left like everyone else: changed.

Like Lawrence, Bev, and Mary, he was one of three children and home-grown in Breidel Coulee. His dad owned the farm just across from the white house for many years, and then he lived there with his bride and started a family. (Now, Ruth Seebauer Heslip calls it home, having moved in with her husband, Jack, when the Kramers moved out in 1960 to take on another farm.)

He went to Washington School, running home past the Broadhead farm, where the Duchess apple trees still sagged like old women. "Oh, they were beautiful," Sonny says. "Us kids, you know Mom and Dad didn't care, but we'd run home from school, and then we'd pick some apples. Some of the kids picked them for their dinner pail for the next day." It takes me a minute to realize he's not talking about his folks when he says "Mom and Dad." He's referring to Lee and Josie.

Like the Broadheads, he walked to Trinity Church with his folks "ev'ry Sundy." They'd leave out around 10:00 for a 10:30 service, and they wouldn't get home until near 1:00 because they'd connect the dots on the way, visiting with each neighbor. Mrs. Kramer involved herself in Ladies' Aid and often baked five dozen kugels for their events, which even the Catholics attended on occasion: church picnics that lasted until evening milking and chicken dinners in the church basement, where three chickens and three pies gained you entrance. The coulee at that time drew a line between Catholics and Protestants, which convinced some people, such as Catholic Bucky LeJeune, to avoid stepping foot inside the Protestant Broadheads' house. And as the coulee kids passed Trinity Church walking home from school, the Catholics sniffed and jeered, "Hey, what stinks? Must be that barn over there."

Sonny suffered such insults only through the eighth grade. "I feel bad now that I didn't have a chance to go to school," Sonny says, looking down, "but my dad said you need somebody to work on the farm. 'You gotta help me.' Well, some people got a chance to get it right in school." So Sonny's childhood shrunk like many other farm kids,' and he started working for Lee just into puberty. "Lee hired me when I was thirteen years old," he says. "I drove team for him. Shredding corn and filling silo and threshing. In 1946 I left home and come workin' for him. First of April." I notice that Sonny takes extra care in recalling exact dates and even days of the week. He pushes himself to get it exactly right—was it a Wednesday?— before he goes on with his story. I consider some of those details useful, but later he tells me that his mother died with Alzheimer's, and I understand.

His arrival on April 1 puts him in the farmhouse with Ruth Seebauer—who had come almost a year earlier—and just a few short months before Josie's nervous breakdown. The current of the hired men towed along the eighteen-year-old, though Sonny leaned more toward Lee than the rest. He saw the drunkenness, the fights, the problems in the house. One time, he recalls, Lee's brother Leonard, who ran a neighboring farm, landed in jail for drinking. "Leonard needed tobacco help out here," Sonny says, "so we had to get him out of jail." Maybe he went along with such things because it all seemed exciting—because his youth pushed him to live like a man. Maybe because he about worshiped Lee, and where Lee went, he went. He respected and loved Josie, but his relationship with Lee had the benefit of time.

Over his eleven years, Sonny did pretty much everything that could be done on this farm, a thousand things: planting, threshing, baling, filling, draining, building, fixing, cleaning. He also milked. In those days, fifty-two cows required emptying twice a day. Mary helped, and even as a young girl of eight she'd tell Sonny, "I'll get the cows 'round, milk 'em, and you feed 'em.'" Mary stuck with the simpler of those tasks; feeding meant Sonny shoveled full three carts in the morning and three at night from silos with nine- and eleven-foot pits. Before breakfast, they fed and milked the cows, and sometimes Sonny fed the horses. After breakfast, he cleaned out the barn, let the cows out, and put bedding down for them before moving on to other day chores. At night, they repeated the milking, ate some supper, tinkered, and fell into bed, heavy.

I find as the conversation warms that I am strangely drawn to this man. I want to hear everything he has to say. I will sit still for hours, more than once, to do that. He qualifies as an apt storyteller, sure, but something else compels.

I see them together, Lee and Sonny, young and strong and brown from the sun. I see them rocking rotten fence posts back and forth to make way for new ones. I see their arms, pasted with sweat and dirt, stringing barbed wire, looping it, cutting it, nailing it. I see them wheeling sweaty ten-gallon milk cans through the rutted barnyard and lifting them onto the truck, wanting to hug the cool metal but holding back. I see them stacking wood across the entire yard, wood they chopped up on the hill by hand after Lee's chainsaw gave out in a puff of blue smoke. I see them laughing over a frypan, pushing supper with the spatula, nine eggs for Sonny and fifteen for Lee. I see them in their long johns trying to get the furnace going in the middle of the night, doing their best not to shiver on the stone floor of the basement. I see them passing each other on tractors, stopping in the middle of the road to chat a spell about the calf

Sonny Kramer (left) and Lee Broadhead with Lee's new tractor, circa 1949

that's coming or the pig that got out or the pen that needs fixing. Short sentences. Longer pauses. Things that aren't said.

I see them.

MY AUNT KAREN HAS DISAPPEARED into the kitchen, beneath the sound of clanging silverware and sliding drawers. Above this very kitchen, Sonny says, Josie kept her chicks. He never dealt with the infamous chickens, though he remembers that they arrived each spring in several holed crates. Josie placed them upstairs in the spare bedroom above the kitchen, an accidental incubator warmed from the rising heat of the stove. There they stayed—all three hundred and fifty of them—until they grew enough for the coop out back, where they produced eggs and eventually returned to the house, as dinner.

"I *hated* that chicken house," Bev says. "Those *dumb* chickens. I tell you, if you went in underneath, they'd peck you. So I got behind them, and I'd pull their leg out, throw them out and get the eggs."

Mary nods at this. "I hated those chickens," she says, slapping the table for emphasis.

"There was a wall between where the chickens were that went straight down to the basement," Sonny explains, referring again to the farmhouse. "You know Grandma Josie opened that wall up herself. Said 'I'm gonna bust that open.' Was down there with a bar, she had a chisel and a hammer. She'd work a little each day on it getting the rocks out. Once she got one rock out, or two rocks out. It was damp in there, see, and you know what happened when it was damp in there. The *rats* got in there."

"Oh, sure," the women crow scandalously.

"Oh man oh man," Sonny mutters.

"Oh, you couldn't help it," Bev says, batting away the stigma of how it sounds.

"Lee went and put the bathroom in there—"

"That's why she knocked out that wall," Bev interjects. "And then Louis Galster came and did that."

"And we had a water pump, you know, that Red Jacket. BOONK BOONK BOONK BOONK. 'Bout every three months, Lee, on a Sunday night, would work on it 'til 'bout 1:00 in the morning. Repack that pump. But we couldn't buy nothin' either at that time, you know, but he'd repack that pump, and then it'd quiet down a little. Then after 'bout three, four weeks, you'd hear it. BOONK BOONK BOONK. You'd hear it over the cow barn. But anyhow, that's when those rats got started. 'Course it was damp in there. Bathroom was out around the corner—"

"Off the kitchen," Mary finishes. We all lean forward with our elbows on the table.

"And Lee got up one night and put a light on and went out in the kitchen and one of these big rats—stepped on one of those big rats." Everyone groans. "Josie had baked three loaves of bread, homemade bread, and those buggers dragged one off the sink and down the hole where they come up through there." The groans explode into laughter. "Nineteen forty-six I think it was, 4-H Club, D-Con. D-Con. Says, 'I don't care.' They smelled when it dried 'em up, but it got rid of the rats."

I don't know Sonny, but it seems to me that a softened radiance shoots out through his pores as he talks, especially as he talks of Lee. He tries to tell me something Lee taught him while sitting at the kitchen table one morning, but it gets lost in translation. Something about everyone having skeletons in the closet. He can't quite recall, can't quite explain. I don't press him. It's just as well. The memory and the lesson that goes with it are tucked away where they should be.

Karen brings out several casserole dishes, some sliced nut bread, tiny pickles, a creamy salad. *Come Lord Jesus, be our guest. Let this food to us be blest. Amen.* A web of hands stretches across bowls and passes dishes.

I see that the farm served as far more than a job for this boy of thirteen, fourteen, fifteen on up to twenty-four; it gave him the chance to play, something he'd had little of. "I remember when Lee bought that, when he had that Chevrolet," he says. "A thirty-five, thirty-six Chevrolet car he had. And they used to have free shows down in Coon Valley on Wednesday nights. We went down to a free show one night. *Thirteen* of us in the car. There was thirteen, and I don't know who they all were, but we all got in the car, and Ernie Jensen rode on the fender in front by the headlights. And we got down there and we thought, jeez, what's that going on, and here they were going with their chairs, they were going home." He laughs. "We got there at quarter to ten!"

Though Sonny hadn't been able to finish school, he pulled one better and married the schoolteacher. Phyllis Rieple had begun teaching at Washington in 1948, when one room still served eight grades about a mile from the farm, and both Bev and Mary numbered among her students. In 1951, Sonny wed Phyllis down at Stoddard; Josie hosted a bridal shower, and the neighbor ladies collected and bought her a toaster. When Phyllis moved into the white house for that first year, I imagine it was strange for Bev and Mary to nearly live with their teacher, though they don't much recall.

To understand Sonny, I think now, is to understand Lee. Sonny wasn't one of Josie's projects; he was one of her husband's. She had many; he had one. Except I'm willing to bet Lee didn't see Sonny as a project or even as an employee but as something closer, dearer, something he could never articulate. Sonny's presence allowed Lee to be strong, to be an expert, a mentor, an authority. With Sonny, Lee wasn't weak; he was a man—sought out, looked up to, admired. Maybe Josie knew this and that's why Sonny stayed around longer than any of the other hired men.

Sonny left the farm when his brother injured himself on a to-bacco pull in 1947, but he came back. Then he left again when his dad took sick in 1948. "Cancer, right here," he says, pointing to his middle. "Tumor, 'bout as big as a hickory nut." Seems his dad, one of those people who had never been ill a day in his life, woke up one morning with a headache. The doctor went in to investigate but right away closed him back up again, telling him, "Kramer, you're two years too late." He worked through the summer of 1948 and into the fall, until he couldn't work anymore.

"By God, your dad come over prob'ly twice a week every night, stayed with him," Sonny tells Bev and Mary, "and that went to the twenty-ninth of May, forty-nine."

"He was such a nice man," Bev sighs. "He was a *good man*."

Though Sonny had twenty-one years with his father, loved and respected him the way it's meant to be, he spent a lot more time with Lee as a young man than he did with his father. He explains that before he says, "Lee was more of a dad to me than my dad." That way everyone will know what he means, that he loved them both.

The Babies

La Crosse, Wisconsin
1955

LEE AND JOSIE HEAR a persistent knock at their door. According to most storytellers it's the middle of this spring night in 1955, in which case the couple has already retired to bed, leaving the light over the kitchen stove to illuminate the table with a muted glow. They never lock their door, even at night, but the visitor doesn't let himself in. Lee and Josie pad pad pad down the hallway, flicking on lights. When they open the door, the crisp air elicits shivers. Lee's nephew, Daren, stands before them. He holds a paper bag in one hand, and over either shoulder, like a couple of twenty-pound sacks of flour, slumps a little boy, asleep.

After a quiet surprise and a step back they wave him in. Josie walks ahead of him to the couch, though he knows where it is. There he lays his sons. Most likely she instinctively puts on some coffee, as the men pull out and fall into chairs at the kitchen table, exchanging raspy whispers. Then comes the mention of a favor, which stumbles

out in the unfinished sentences of a proud man low. He needs someone to watch his boys. For a while. Their older sisters are at their
mother's parents' in town. It's hard to expect anyone to take four
kids, he knows, and boys'll do better on a farm.

The way it will stick in Josie's mind, and the way the story will
trickle down, Daren has come because his wife, Jackie, left him and
went to Texas, and he wants to go after her, a journey best traveled
alone. To this, Lee and Josie can give only one response: of course.
So Daren leaves with a handshake and a grateful face, his babies
dreaming as the couch presses lines into their cheeks. To the tune
of a disappearing car, Lee lifts one, Josie the other, and they lay the
boys on an empty bed upstairs, leaving the little heads on dented
pillows, their few belongings in brown paper.

Breakfast: a screen door slamming, girls gathering lunches and
schoolbooks, the smell of coffee and bacon or pancakes or eggs.
Lawrence is away, well into his first year at the University of Wisconsin at Madison, majoring in veterinary medicine. Beverly is in
high school, Mary wishing she was. With Lee and Josie, the four
of them create a static electricity in the kitchen, the bustle and the
noise and the hurry.

Into this chaos stumble the two sleepy-eyed boys. The oldest is barely five. The first son. Named after his father but called
Stubby to keep everybody straight, a name that has stuck to him.
His brown hair, cut crew, takes to the light like a wheat field, his
face round and imprinted with a more innocent version of his father's. The embryo of a handsome man. His brother, Dean, is three
and a half but taller. A towhead. He has his mother's big eyes and
Madonna skin.

To be sure, everyone stops and gives a good morning, an offer
for something hot or salty or sweet. The boys stare, saying nothing,
their eyes coming to rest on Lee, who sits at the table with one leg
crossing the next, a work boot at the height of their eyes. One of
them blurts out, "Who is the man with the big feet?" Good-natured

chuckling and laughing follow, Mary and Bev taking special delight in the silliness and their father, intertwined.

The boys have already met Lee and Josie, back before their memories started. There is, perhaps, a small assumption that the boys will remember, fit in, forgetfully happy to be at the farm, instead of a recognition that they have awakened in a strange house with strange people. At the sight of quivering lips and wrinkled foreheads, Lee and Josie say who they are, but the explanation can't prevent the tears that lead to the wailing and a one-line refrain, "I want my daddy!" Reassurance from grown-up strangers comforts little when you're three, or even five, and truth isn't a salve.

One leads, the other follows. Under a chair they go, their best protection. The folks let them be, figuring the boys will warm up—kids always do—that they just need a little time. A walk to school still awaits the two girls, and chores have only paused for Lee. So the bustle resumes, and the boys watch the saddle shoes and work boots and lace-ups cross the floor in a dance they don't understand.

The next time someone looks under the kitchen table, the boys are gone. Interest, concern, panic—Dean and Stub are not in the house. They are not in the yard. They are not in the bushes or the barn or the basement. The family calls and scurries, increasing their speed as seconds turn to minutes. Josie jogs to the road and turns toward the highway, and then she sees a blur, low, partially hidden by ditch weeds, rounding the corner. Her hollering is rhetorical, and she runs as fast as her legs and her back and her heart let her. Older and smarter, watching them and the cars and pickups that seem to fly by just feet from the children, she runs across the field, diagonal, and catches them. She grabs them and holds them tight, the boys still thrashing and dripping with tears and screaming for their daddy.

IT TOOK SOME TIME for the little runaways to feel anything but fear, to warm up to their "Uncle Eee" and "Aunt Dosie." Too young for school and too little to help, play was their work. Inside they built tents from bed sheets, with a little scolding from Aunt Dosie, who had to remake the bed. Almost certainly Mary showed them how she dipped dimes and nickels into a jar of mercury, shining them up, dancing the beads on the table. When Grandma Martina came to visit, they sat and watched Lawrence Welk together, mostly watching her, hoping she'd let them change the channel to *Disneyland*. They planted a black walnut tree in the yard. The animals in the barn proved magical: puppies and calves and litters of kittens. On Easter morning, after an egg hunt in the yard, one of the boys saw a calf lying in the straw. "He rushed up to me, wide-eyed with wonder," Josie wrote, "and said, 'Look what the Easter Bunny brought!'"

Mary Broadhead with Stub (Daren Jr., left) and Dean (right), 1956

Outside, as the air lost its chill, Josie let the boys run all day—the farm supplied endless places to imagine and make believe—or she let them help in her garden. Josie couldn't cook very well, but she could grow. (This came into question once when a visiting pastor found a fence nail in his potato; someone eventually determined that the spike had found its way into the spud underground.) Josie always had a garden, and it seemed to bow to her the way it grew. My dad says she would start hoeing standing erect, and by the end of the row, she'd be hunched over from her back pain. My brother recalls her heading out to the garden, and Lee putting up a fight, saying she didn't need to be out there so much. "God wants me in that garden!" she hollered.

She and Mrs. Winter ran a produce stand out by the highway. Mrs. Winter provided the mums; Josie provided everything else. Josie didn't shy away from the unusual—okra, peanuts, chives—and she didn't do it small. Her spread looked nothing like the doormat gardens you see in the city or suburbs; it sprawled the good portion of an acre with whole rows of each vegetable. Visitors often commented, "You have such a big garden," and Josie guffawed, waving away a portion of the plot, "Well, that's just corn and potatoes."

The boys sat in the strawberry patch and ate until their bellies bloated and their faces glazed. The strawberries, small and soft, dissolved in your mouth. The raspberries, too. Summer squash and sweet corn the color of dandelions. Tomatoes that dripped down your neck before you could stop them. Peppers, green beans, peas, potatoes red and brown. Blackberries grew wild far up on the hill, and once a year they were gathered in boxes and gallon pails, the pickers returning with scratched arms and purple fingers and tongues. And no doubt the boys accompanied Josie on such trips, though if their experience was anything like mine, they twirled and tumbled down the hill with very few berries but wearing a thick coating of mud from head to toe, the fairy-tale image of life-size chocolate treats.

Daren came to Lee and Josie because, as the boys' mother says, "There wasn't anybody else." But the real reason may be because he had known their place well—a place he himself was brought as a boy.

AFTER WALLACE BROADHEAD came Leonard, the second son of George and Maud, born at the turn of the century, ten years and two brothers older than Lee. There's not much to tell about Leonard's young life, but he married Hazel Silbough on New Year's Day in 1922. They churned out their first two sons, Richard and Daren, in the first two years, and Bernard, known as Bud, arrived in 1928. Leonard took on one of his dad's farms in West Prairie over in Vernon County. He ran it, but he didn't own it, which makes me wonder whether George Broadhead didn't test some of his sons first before bestowing his gift. Could be George knew even then that Leonard, like his older brother Wallace, liked to drink. A lot. So much that his wife decided she had had plenty and hauled her boys across the plains and Rockies to California, maybe thinking that would be far enough. But it wouldn't have mattered if they had gone to China, because when Leonard's dad George found out, he sent his son Earl after them. "Those are Broadhead boys," he grumbled at Earl. "They belong here." George worked his influence with a crooked judge in Vernon County, who then awarded custody to Leonard, and Earl legally took those three little boys away from their mama and dragged them back to Wisconsin. From that point on, the family referred to Leonard as a widower.

At first the boys stayed with George and Maud, as George probably had sense enough to realize that the children's father wasn't fit. But when Josie, newly married, learned what had happened, she gathered up Richard, Daren, and Bud, who hadn't even unpacked their suitcases, and took them into her house; if anyone protested, it didn't do any good. She kept them for a year. Then Leonard decided he missed them, or rather that he needed their help on the farm (though none of them was yet ten). Josie reluctantly took them home to West Prairie, where Leonard's methods restricted as much as a belt on the wrong hole. Maybe the bitterness of alcohol or a lost wife prompted his beliefs, but the way he saw it, kids existed to work. After Richard had attended seventh grade for about two weeks, Leonard said, "Can you read and write?"

"Yeah," Richard replied.

"Well, then that's your last day of school."

George must have seen what transpired and made some decisions for Leonard, one being that he needed to go get his act together and stop messing up the family business. He sent Leonard to his halfway house of choice: Lee and Josie's. Leonard took Bud to his parents' house in town and accepted a job at his little brother's farm. Leonard, Richard, and Daren moved into Lee and Josie's in 1934, probably thinking it was just for a few months. They stayed four years.

"Josie was very strict," Daren recalls. "When she said sit down, you sat down. But she was very good to me and I loved her a lot."

Three summers after the Broadhead boys moved in and just before Rural Electric lit up the coulee, some Twites joined the mix. Josie's younger sister, Tina, and niece, Evelyn, both having just graduated from high school, came to live at the farm for a year. Evelyn and Tina were just slightly older than Richard, and the three of them made for a pack of slaphappy teens that summer. They helped out in the barn and the fields, most notably cutting corn, when Evelyn sat on the binder for sixteen days straight, her bottom numb as a brick. Lee slipped them a little money now and then, so they went to movies, and Rich even saved up enough to give the girls airplane rides. "That," Richard says of his time on the farm, "was about the best part of my life." Richard came back to the farm over the next couple of years and worked for his dollar a day, though he told his daughter, Margaret, years later that he would have done it for free.

Leonard, perhaps with his father's help, bought a place in town on Losey Boulevard. But even if he lived there, it wasn't for long. When his father died in 1938, the agreement was that Leonard would get another farm—his own—in exchange for the lot on Losey. This new farm formed a rectangle of a hundred and twenty acres, only a half mile from Lee as the crow flies. Sonny Kramer says, "The farm was good, but you couldn't get to it. There was an old road going all along there, all mud, and then once in a while they had a bridge, and 'course the water'd get high and it'd take the bridge out. Then they'd lay a plank." Eventually Lee and Leonard's brother, Earl, got the county to put a road back there, still named Broadhead Road to this day.

So off the family went, Leonard and his sons, to isolation, to lonely drinking, to hard, hard work that chafed the hands and the soul. "Dad drank a lot, pret' near ev'ry day," Richard says now. "Never got enough to eat or nothin.' I'd sneak down [to Lee and Josie's] and eat." It's no surprise that when the war came, all three boys enlisted. The service provided their escape from farming, from their father, and they probably didn't care that it meant he would lose the farm and have to move in with his mother as a man in his forties. He sold the farm to his brother Earl, who turned around and sold the land the very next day for a profit.

Richard went first, then Daren, both paratroopers in the U.S. Airborne. Bud stayed home at first, too young to join, and he started dating Jackie Fidlin, a policeman's daughter from the north side of town. It's easy to see why Bud fell for the city girl. She wore the looks of a silent film star: skin like marble, full lips, round eyes, and striking dark hair that fell across her shoulders, chopped in a straight line of bangs across her forehead.

But then the brothers traded places; while the marines shipped Bud overseas as a sharpshooter in September of 1945, the army sent Daren home. Daren, whom the government later awarded for bravery with just about every medal in the book, including the Purple

Brothers Daren (left) and Richard Broadhead serving during World War II, circa 1943

Heart, six Bronze Service Stars, and a World War II Victory Medal, had been shot, and shrapnel laced his back. His tour, finished. After returning home, Daren went to the Avalon Ballroom in La Crosse, and there he met Jackie. They started dating, though no one remembers if the love affair commenced before or after she and Bud broke up. Part of Daren and Jackie's courtship entailed a visit to Lee and Josie's farm, perhaps to get the parent-like approval that was hard for Daren to elicit at home. Jackie, though, saw it as simply a trip to the country. "Daren took me out to see the cows and the chickens," she says. Whether it functioned as a test or a blessing, it didn't deter her, and they married in October 1946.

Richard had brewed up some marital escapades of his own. He had married a girl before he went to war, but when he came home after two and a half years, he found her pregnant. "It took me five days to divorce her," he confides, and the judge told her she was lucky to be getting out of the courtroom with her shoes. The same thing happened to him during the Korean War. When all was said and done, he had married five times and fathered an unknown number of children, though he only recognizes two.

Right after they married, Daren and Jackie moved to California. Daren didn't want to farm. None of the boys did. So instead he went looking for work, and they had their first child, a girl, in November 1947. Perhaps because the dust of parenthood had yet to settle, or because she donned the idealism of youth, Jackie persuaded Daren to look up his mother, the same woman who had crossed the continent with her sons twenty years before. "It was a mistake," Jackie says. "She wasn't very happy when we found her."

California didn't work out, so Daren and Jackie returned to La Crosse in 1948. There they produced another daughter and three sons, Daren Jr. and Dean, and another boy. With each baby, Daren had a new job: service station attendant, employee of Gateway Glass Company, mechanic for Casey Car Sales, punch press operator for Auto Lite.

Jackie insists that she and Daren had no marital problems at all. And though Daren won't talk about that part of his life, his brief comments seem to corroborate her story. "I did what I had to do back then to keep the kids together," he insists. "I had to work and make a living and that's the only way I could do it." Maybe Josie's fanciful prairie imagination heard certain discreet phrases that night in 1955, inflated by the hour and the two sleeping babes on her couch, and she drew her own conclusions. Maybe she inferred that the strain of unemployment had drawn the marriage tight. Maybe she just remembered wrong.

Jackie says that she and Daren and the kids went to Texas together. After unsuccessfully trying to find work up north, they sold their furniture and drove their old car to New Orleans and then decided to go to Beaumont, Texas, instead. While Daren hauled himself from shop to shop, selling himself as a mechanic, Jackie worked three night jobs. "It was hard," she says, "because we never really had a lot of money. We had a lot of kids and no money. I worked all the time. Couldn't spend as much time with the kids as I wanted." After six months with no change, Daren piled his four oldest into the car and drove home, thirteen hundred miles north to Wisconsin, because he knew that if things went on much longer, he wouldn't be able to feed them. He just probably didn't know when he drove away from Lee and Josie's that it would be nearly a year and a half before he would come back.

DAREN AND JACKIE SENT TWO PAIRS of red cowboy boots for Christmas. A photograph from December 25, 1955, captures two laughing children, standing in those boots. Dean wears a cowboy shirt and holds a peppermint stick as big as his forearm. Stub digs down into his stocking, a pocket nearly half his height. The family went to church that day, and the boys kept bending down to shine their cowboy boots with their hankies. The parishioners in the surrounding pews couldn't stifle their smiles, knowing the boys' story (though it's uncertain which one), and patiently listened to Dean and Stub tell about their boots again and again. "I'm sure it affected the congregation the same way it did us," Josie wrote. And for a time, the boys forgot that it had been months since they hugged their daddy.

I KNOW THAT IN THE SUMMER OF 1956, Daren and Jackie reunited with their children, but Daren doesn't want to tell me the end of the story. He doesn't want to tell me the middle or the beginning either, not even now, when he's dying. Maybe because he's dying. When Daren told me to stop asking questions, that it's private and no one needs to know all of that, I told him I would leave him in peace, but I wept private selfish tears because he wouldn't help me, because he was impeding my project. As the self-pity waned, I started thinking, good and hard, about what I was doing. These aren't fictional characters, and the story doesn't originate in some Faulknerian county. Many of the players, by choice or default, still live with the memory or consequence of the happenings of decades past, and just because I'm a relative doesn't give me any rights to their lives. How would I feel if some distant cousin I didn't know came out of nowhere and started asking me about the unpleasant details of my past, about the times when I was needy or desperate or ashamed?

Daren, to some extent, was right. This is his life I'm talking about, stirring up, announcing to the family and God and the world. But Daren's story is also Josie's, and in that way it has become part of mine, and joint custody always complicates. A sliver of Daren's life forms part of the journey I'm on, of discovering my heritage and my purpose and unearthing what good came about because Josie took in those two little boys, their father and uncles, even their grandfather.

Maybe Josie felt the same way. She had begun writing about Dean and Stub in the 1960s:

> When I tear off the brown paper, I see beyond and beneath
> The gift and the wrappings, to the man with big feet.
> Two loosely wrapped bundles were tossed on our porch,
> And I questioned the contents as Lee lit the gas torch.

My guess is that she wanted to tell Daren's story, and Dean and Stub's, and the others,' because she wasn't one for keeping secrets. I think she believed that the stuff behind secrets constitutes what makes all of us human. It shows us how far we've come, how much we've learned, how great the heart's capacity for forgiveness, re-generation, and love.

So we tell what we know, and what we don't, and we hope that the air won't tarnish it beyond recognition.

STUB AND DEAN CAME OF AGE in Texas in the mid-1960s, a rough passage, as comings-of-age are. In 1967, as Dean turned sixteen and Stub outgrew seventeen, Jackie left Daren. She puts it very matter-of-factly: "I met another man. He took my kids. He was good to my kids." The family consisted of six children by then, two girls and four boys, though the oldest had already moved out of the house.

Dean graduated from high school early and had already begun working and living in his own apartment by then. "I wasn't going to live with either of them," he says. Stub, barely seventeen, enlisted as a paratrooper in the 82nd Airborne, the same division in which his father had served. He trained at Fort Polk in Louisiana before dispatching to Fort Benning, Georgia, for airborne and wireman training. Just two weeks after his eighteenth birthday, on April 22, 1968, the army shipped Stub to Vietnam, where he served as a wireman for his unit. He missed his mother's wedding to Henry Montalbano that May. By December, the army promoted Stub to senior wireman. He must have done something right, for he earned the Bronze Star, an Army Commendation Medal, a Vietnam Service Medal, a Vietnam Campaign Medal, three Campaign Stars, a Parachute Badge, a National Defense Medal, and two Overseas Bars. The records then show another promotion to message clerk seven months later, but shortly thereafter comes a permanent return to the States. He officially served his country for nearly another year, but before he turned nineteen his tour of duty was over.

What happened in the next six years forms one long sentence, punctuated by a series of commas. The family soon learned that Stub had picked up a bad habit in the rice paddies: shooting up. "I talked to him, I talked with him," his mother says. "I told my mother, and she said, 'Well, tell him to stop,' but it's not that easy." Then Stub called his mother in the middle of the night and said he wanted to get married. He filed an informal marriage with Harris County on February 24, 1970. His bride was Cynthia Cay Evans. She was sixteen. The honeymoon consisted of one long drug binge, according to his mother, and when it ended in three years, so did the union. His mother refers to her oldest son as a hippie and has only one thing to say about that marriage: "Full of hell." Stub and his wife had a baby, and then they separated. No one remembers the baby's name.

Stub was a sensitive kid, and sometimes for people like that all it takes is one incident to mess with their heads. In Vietnam, there would have been several opportunities, the smoldering huts and the independent limbs and the smoke-smeared faces of terror, unfortunately all so cliché now. Take the drugs to forget. Then forget why you're taking the drugs. Then just forget.

The guilt of using, a failed marriage, fatherhood, being home. Wanting to feel just a little number, a little happier. It could have been any of those things or simply a miscalculation that made him shoot extra heroin on Sunday, January 13, 1974. The drugs caused an aneurysm, a blood clot in the brain, and he stopped thinking and moving and breathing, and then he died.

Six months later, Leonard died an alcoholic in Milwaukee.

Four years later, cancer took Bud.

Then cancer took Bud's son, and now it's taking Daren.

Though his heart has given him a tough run, Richard has eluded addiction and parasitic tumors, but his grandson toyed with the same fate as his cousin, Stub, and lost, which hurts just as bad.

Maybe Daren isn't talking because he doesn't see any redemption, and if that's true, I can't say I blame him. Looking at the way things turned out for his father, his son, and his marriage, the question remains: what good did Josie do? What good were her promise, her willingness, her sacrifice, her faith? She didn't prevent much of anything she might have hoped to: husbands lost wives and wives lost husbands, parents lost children and children lost parents, substances stole loved ones, and the heaviest anchors simply couldn't keep anyone put for three generations.

Lee and Josie traveled to California to see Bud as he was dying, and they had certainly been to Texas, though the only surviving photographs were taken long before everything went sour. The pictures show all six children, the boys having grown up to Lee's chest. But something went wrong with the film or the camera, because the pictures are just enough out of focus to look surreal. A blinding white envelops everyone except Dean and Stub, but still the two boys smile from ear to ear.

If Josie reacted to Stub's death—and even Leonard's—the way I think she did, she didn't understand it. She didn't understand why someone would willfully decide to go that direction. The thing that broke her heart, that broke everyone's, is that the boy didn't need to die. Not yet. Not that way. I want to believe, as she did, that sheltering a child or a man, giving him enough love and opportunity, even for a short time, can make all the difference, turn him around. But maybe I recognize—even in cynicism—what Josie didn't: love isn't a free ticket. People still make their own choices. Life happens. But if she had understood that, maybe she wouldn't have kept trying. She would have become bitter and self-absorbed, having given up long ago. How might things have turned out if she had rejected all six?

A LETTER DATED MARCH 27, 1963, found among Josie's papers after her death: *Dear Uncle Lee & Aunt Josie, and the rest,* it starts, carefully written in pencil. The cursive belongs to a teenaged boy, and it slants in all directions.

What going on up there on the farm. Hope you all are having good weather. I've been sick for the last week but who wants to talk about being sick but hope everbody feeling well on the farm.

We plan to move again but it will be in the same old neighborhood. This time we might buy the house instead of renting it. I hope!

Tell Mary heres the picture I promist her. Tell her I said hi! Tell her she better write me O.K. Hope all of you are having fun. Tell Terry I want him to write me and tell Mary I want a picture of her OK. Send me one of all of you OK.

Well I can't think of any thing else to write so I guess i'll be signing off

love Daren Broadhead Jr.

P.S. Write Me! OK.

*   *   *

DEAN REMEMBERS LEAVING the day they buried Stubby, but records show that he actually reported for active duty in the air force a week later. Like his brother and father and uncles, he also earned high decorations in his four years of service—a National Defense Service Medal, an Air Force Good Conduct Medal, an Air Force Outstanding Unit Award. He became a sergeant trained in accounting, based at Bergstrom in Texas.

Dean now works as an executive for a music corporation in New York, a workaholic with two failed marriages behind him. Almost fifty years have passed since his parents picked him up at the farm. He doesn't remember much about that time—he was only five—but he will tell you that his childhood was happy before and after his time with Lee and Josie. He will also say this: "Two of the most important years of my life were on that farm. Always have believed that."

> Now the days have slipped quietly into months, into years,
> And we've all but forgotten the strain and the tears.
> We count it a privilege and a reminiscent repast,
> For our stature was multiplied by this God-given task.
> When I tear off the brown paper, I see beyond and beneath
> The gift and the wrappings, to the man with big feet.

The Boy

La Crosse, Wisconsin
1955

BACK UP TO A SUNDAY AFTERNOON in the summer of 1955, just a couple of months after Dean and Stubby arrived. Lee, Josie, Lawrence, and Mary have just finished eating dinner in the yard. Beverly has left early for college, and Lawrence has come home—at his father's request—for good. The two little boys are gone for the day, most likely in town at their Grandpa and Grandma Fidlins.'

The air simmers on medium-high. Flies light on plates scraped almost clean, taking in bits of bean and meat. Strawberry tops lie scattered on the edges, and sweaty glasses form rings on the table. The sound of the occasional car whirring by on Highway 14 joins the cacophony of birds, insects, rustling grain. Amid the song, an unfamiliar motor catches Lawrence's ears. He turns. There, in the driveway, idles a taxi.

A cab on Breidel Coulee Road has always been the kind of thing that makes a person look twice. It still is. The driver shifts into park, gets out, and opens the rear door. Lawrence motions to the others without looking away. The Broadheads at this point are surely expecting a businessman or a shirttail relative who will soon ask to borrow the fare, seeing as they can't imagine who else would take a cab into the coulee. Instead out steps a child, who at first appears to stumble until it is obvious that he has a limp. Despite the heat he wears a full suit, navy serge, bookended by slicked hair and patent leather oxfords. When the driver hands him two small suitcases from the trunk, the child's arm flashes a gold wristwatch.

The family stares. Before the questions can start, the driver gets into the cab and backs out of the driveway. Lawrence chases him, yelling, "Hey! Hey there! Stop!" Left behind in a cloud of dusty gravel, the child remains planted, scarcely taller than mid-July corn. Except for Lawrence, no one moves. No one speaks.

To think, they could have missed it. If Josie hadn't decided to serve dinner outside, it being so hot in the house, Lawrence might not have seen, and the boy might have wandered who knows where. Who would send a child somewhere by himself anyway—and in a taxi? Maybe if he was thirteen or fourteen, but this boy looks more like eight.

"Lawrence," Josie says, pointing with her head, "go find out what he wants."

The boy stands, catatonic, still clutching his suitcases. Wearing the demeanor of middle age, he stares straight ahead, his eyes dark and empty. "Hey, what gives?" Lawrence says, now next to him. "Who are you and what do you want?" Nothing happens. "Can't. You. HEAR?" he continues, thinking maybe the child is deaf. Mary edges up behind and insists that the boy level with them, sure she will show up her older brother for once. When the stranger remains silent, she and Lawrence hold conference. (Lawrence thinks him a nut, while Mary doesn't know what to think—just that the kid's staring gives her the creeps.)

Josie gets involved. Her back condition causes her to lean toward the boy naturally, but she bows a little more to get closer to his level. "Hello, son. What's your name?" she asks. He does not look at her or respond. "I'm Mrs. Broadhead. What is your name? Where are your parents? Are you lost?" They ply him with questions about his family and his destination, about his leather suitcases stitched with the initials T.N.T., and anything else they can think of. The boy stands with that detached look on his face, almost as if he isn't really there. Lee rests against the fireplace, watching. When Lawrence asks him what to do, he says to call the sheriff.

Now in Josie's opinion, this is some kind of foolishness. God helps those who help themselves, and it's up to each of us to make an effort. This boy is being difficult; anyone can see that. It irks her. Evidently it irks Mary, too, who after another couple of minutes bends toward the boy's face and tries her hand at intimidation. "Now listen," Josie interrupts. Mary closes her mouth and the boy drops his suitcases. When he reaches for them, Josie grabs his arm, maybe a little more forcefully than she intended. "You leave those suitcases right there. They're not going anywhere. A few simple answers and you'll get your luggage back. We can't help you if you don't tell us who you are."

Finally, he speaks. It shouldn't seem strange to hear his voice, but it is. It makes him real. His tone, eerily deliberate, seems far too big for his size. This is what he says: "Mildred sent me here."

Mildred. Mildred. *Mildred?* Never mind the *shoulds* and the *oughts,* Josie can't even recognize her response, the *is,* doesn't know whether to call it surprise, confusion, or wrath. The only Mildred she knows has what people might call a reputation. Even the mention of the woman's name makes her cringe, a woman—if you could call her that—who treats decency carelessly, replacing it with self-indulgent fancies. It's Uncle Albert and Mabel's girl we're talking about, the one taken in after Uncle Edwin widowed. (No one knows yet that Mildred was actually born to a neighbor and not a relative at all.) Millie Broadhead is electric, a live wire, seemingly more comfortable with men than women, which may be why she joined the army, though after two years she still held the title of private first class. The rumor states that she has already been through seven husbands, helping relatives to remember her as "a shady character" they can blame for draining her family's money. All things considered, a boy, a taxi, and Millie, all entangled, is surprisingly possible.

"Mildred? *Cousin Millie?*" Josie asks. "How'd you get mixed up with her?"

"She's father's housekeeper," the boy answers. Josie snorts under her breath but is careful, careful enough that her gesture could be mistaken for frustration. For all she knows Millie could be the boy's mother, and you don't talk down about people's mothers. Instead she works hard for nearly an hour to get a phone number out of the child, after which she bangs through the screen door to use the phone. Lawrence and Mary stay and trade observations. Lee looks at his watch and leaves to do chores. When Josie reappears ten minutes later she knows two things: the boy's name is Terry Tharp, and she is going to town to straighten the whole thing out.

LEE HAS ALREADY STARTED MILKING, so Josie has to wait even though she doesn't want to, even though Lawrence could drive them. She has to wait for Lee to get through the herd, has to wait for him to hose down the milking parlor. She then has to wait for him to pull on some clean clothes, splash his face and arms and smooth his hair, and she has to wait for him to back the Buick out. Even the short trip in to Tenth Street seems like waiting, but eventually they pull up outside a tall red brick Victorian a few blocks from the river, where you can hear the horns and bells of barges and buoys. After they park, they find their way to the right door, the number the man on the phone provided, Lee carrying the suitcases. Josie rings the buzzer and waits some more.

Long seconds later the door opens, and there stands a tall, imposing man with dark hair and shadowy eyes who is only slightly older than they, though no one would guess it. Ironically, he looks remarkably like Josie's father, the way he was in those last years. It's uncanny, really: the same build and coloring, the same proud but beaten shoulders. The same stench of liquor that stings her eyes almost to tearing, blurring time so that for an instant she thinks she is facing him again, wondering what she should say, feeling repulsed and angry and small all at the same time. But her mind brings her to, remembering the taxi and the wristwatch and the waiting.

"We're here about your son," she says.

Her eyes find the backdrop, a living room crowded with heaps of grimy clothes, dishes of rancid food, and bottles of liquor. It quickly becomes clear to Josie that Mildred met this man on the small-town imitation of Chicago's Rush Street seven blocks over. The man, his hand still on the doorknob, steps aside slightly. As the story goes, he doesn't pay his son any attention, address him, or even look at him. One account claims that Terry stayed in the car, but that's unlikely since Lee and Josie assume they are bringing him home. When they cross into the apartment, the man speaks.

"What is the middle of the Bible?" he says.

He can't possibly be serious, Josie thinks, expecting that any second now the joke will be on her. The man motions for them to sit. They do, expecting more relevant dialogue in return, but he only repeats himself.

"Sir," she replies, "I don't know the answer to your question. We have come to discuss your son."

Mr. Tharp begins a five-minute monologue about himself, unapologetically boasting about his achievements and abilities, people he knows, patents he has pending. He tosses around claims of being an executive, a lay pastor, an inventor. He stops only when Millie rushes in from the kitchen and embraces the stiff visitors, gushing through big eyes and cherry red lipstick, her gray-blonde curls stiff as pumpkin vine.

"I'm sorry about the confusion," she says, "I'm afraid Terry's having a hard time with his mother's death." Like watching a drug take hold, Millie sees Josie stutter, suddenly embarrassed, incapacitated by shame. But for once, Millie is not far off. Amanda Olson—Terry's mother, the second woman to bear David Tharp's name—has died, leaving a story strung together by ordinary sadness. Before she had one son, whom she loved, and one husband, whom she feared, she had lived nearly forty years with her aunt—first as a child, and then as a spinster who kept books for the family hotel. When David Tharp, a traveling salesman with a Pennsylvania steel mill, came through La Crosse and stayed at the hotel, he rubbed the tarnish off the promise of the life she had always wanted. Though a few months her junior, this David exuded everything she lacked—worldliness, magnetism, brilliance—and she married him. Would he have told her that he had already been married and divorced with two children back in Pennsylvania? Would it have mattered?

Sometime during the war the graying newlyweds stole back to Pennsylvania, where they had their son in 1945. Before long, they returned to Wisconsin—first to Wautoma and then back to La Crosse, where they found a little place on Cass Street, right on the Mississippi. David picked up mostly machinist and electrician work, while Amanda spent a lot of time at her older sister's farm. Then the drinking started, or he stopped hiding it, and Amanda learned that David grew malicious under the influence, abusive and cruel. Hypertension weakened Amanda's heart, dousing in oil her already flammable home. In the days surrounding New Year's Eve 1954, Lutheran Hospital admitted her, and she died there three weeks later of cerebral hemorrhage, a complication from her condition. She was forty-nine. Terry was eight. Within eleven months, David married a third time (he would marry still twice more before his death), but the two stayed together for less than a year. By the following summer, the summer of the taxi, he had encountered Millie.

But Josie knows none of that yet. She knows only what Millie tells her, which is that it would be good for Terry to spend some time on the farm, get his mind off sad things. That the boy has never been on a farm shouldn't make any difference, and it would just be for the summer. Josie finds herself snared between pride and conscience. She certainly holds no obligation to this woman, or this man. Until she remembers her promise.

Here this child has come to her, this boy with a flask for a father—something she knows all about. She and Lee may just be simple farmers who have only their home and food to give, but they have those things because of the goodness of God, and who is she to hoard them from someone in need? Why sure, there is no question in her mind now that God sent him (*why didn't she see it earlier?*), and she will not, cannot allow herself to turn this boy away.

"Well," Josie says, "if it's just for the summer—"

Millie sings at Josie's response, racing from the room to pack up another suitcase for Terry, just a few extra things. Within minutes she returns, handing a bag to Lee. Then comes the uneasy conversation about Terry: Millie's dismissing his limp with her hand, saying it stems from an old school injury, that he is fine, has no other medical concerns. "He's just missing his mother," Mildred says. They believe her, sort of.

No one remembers Mr. Tharp saying anything else, nor Lee for that matter. The women do all the talking. Once Lee, Josie, and Terry step into the hall, the door closes behind them, and they start toward the car. The grumbling quickly gives way to practicality, and Josie rises to the responsibility that is now hers. Even if she mutters "*housekeeper*," under her breath, to Terry she says, "Come on, now. Let's go home."

* * *

JOSIE ASSIGNED TERRY one of the upstairs bedrooms formerly used for hired help, which weren't around much anymore, kitty-corner from Mary. At first he stayed there a lot, behind a closed door. It wasn't all that unusual that a stranger had come to stay. It wasn't even remarkable that he was a child or had troubles. What remained curious was the way this boy *was*. Lawrence thought they should call a doctor, something wasn't right, but Josie didn't even know what kind of doctor Terry needed. She did know that any old MD wouldn't do, so she took Lee up on his suggestion to give the county nurse a call. The nurse, whose duties normally didn't exceed vaccinations and an occasional influenza outbreak, set up an appointment with the hospital. (With her notable lack of emergencies the nurse most likely tried to be professional but no doubt found the whole incident very exciting.)

Because Terry wouldn't leave his room, it's unclear whether the doctors came to the house or Lee and Josie somehow carted him into town again. The doctors said Terry appeared to show signs of various disorders, including schizophrenia and autism, though no one has been able to uncover evidence saying for sure. His medical records indicate some psychological disturbance from his limp and emotional trouble later in his life, but his doctor saw him as "a nice little boy." He also clearly exhibited brilliance, they said (someone remembers him having an IQ of 150), though one plagued with feelings of guilt, perhaps something to do with his mother's death. They recommended that he continue seeing a social worker and that the county welfare department look into the Tharp home. It seemed enough to Josie. She still trusted doctors then.

Once she had the official word—Terry's condition entailed more than grief—she knew she had been duped into taking him. "I had let the grieving issue convince me," she confessed in her writing, having dismissed her uneasiness of Mildred, which—seen in the rearview—turned out to be a glaring red flag. It seems that cousin Millie and Mr. Tharp sent Terry to the farm because they didn't want to bother with him and couldn't control him. Bev says that she can almost hear Mildred saying, "Oh, let Lee and Josie take care of him. They're good people." Mary says the same.

Josie could have become bitter, but it wasn't her way. There was a child to be helped. Maybe the farmer in her pushed all the self-pity and anger aside. Maybe the Christian. Or maybe it was just Josie, and it never occurred to her to do anything else.

In the first weeks, when Terry came out of his room, he sat on the davenport or in the living room and simply stared. Having the neighbor boys over didn't stir him, nor did invitations to go swimming in the creek. He didn't want to watch the milking, didn't want to feed the chickens. There wasn't any drawing or pretending or running. He spoke very little, smiled not at all, and kept his face in neutral. Except for his little body, he didn't seem like a child at all, at least not any they'd ever seen around the farm or anywhere else.

He had toys, but they remained in their boxes, in the bottom of the dining room hutch, which he had picked out as his toy chest. Every so often, he opened the cabinet. There he sat cross-legged on the floor, pulling out the boxes one at a time, opening them and inspecting the toys, mostly models of planes and ships he had presumably assembled himself. Then after a few minutes he returned the boxes to their places, closed the hutch, and left. It didn't occur to anyone that he might not know how to play, Josie said, since that's something all kids just do.

Terry did touch Dean and Stub's toys, but if the two little ones came near his own cabinet he hurled himself into a rage, an uncharacteristic display of emotion, screaming that those were his toys. Josie tried to explain the double standard to Dean and Stub, telling them to continue sharing even if Terry didn't. "But that's not fair, Auntie," Dean and Stub cried, "That's not fair."

When Josie asked Terry why he wouldn't let anyone else near his things, he replied, "It's all I have." Maybe his mother had given him the toys, she thought. Perhaps those boxes contained all that remained of her. He had no photographs, never spoke of her. Maybe he was really saying, "It's all I have *of her.*" Josie didn't know then that she was right, but she let it lie.

The only known photo of Terry's mother, kept by a cousin all these years and not discovered until I started looking for her, shows Terry sitting between his parents on one end of a patterned couch. Amanda and David lean back, while Terry rests on the edge, nestled between them, feet on the floor. He wears a cowboy-style shirt and dark pants. Anyone can see that he has his mother's nose and ears. Beneath his short bangs pushed to the side, his face frames a temporarily contained energy, as if he had been running around playing and happened to flop on the couch for a moment. David wears a dark shirt and tie with pinstripe pants and oxfords. His hair is just starting to gray. One arm hides behind Amanda, and the other rests on his thigh. His lips are poised to speak. With her graying curls and sagging cheeks, Amanda looks sixty-five, though she is actually about fifteen years younger. One white flower dots her black dress—a funeral, perhaps?—her legs greatly swollen, revealing the secret that will soon take her life. She wears no smile, but she holds on to Terry with both arms—one wrapped around his shoulder, hand dangling down over his heart, and one gripping his other arm.

That picture provides the only evidence that someone in his family ever touched him affectionately. It is also one of a few photos that show Terry smiling and looking at the camera, most of which were taken before he came to the farm, before his father sent him away. In other pictures, he crosses his arms or digs his hands into his pockets, his eyes somewhere else.

Others would hardly describe the boy in that photograph with his mother and father as showing no emotion, or, as Josie later called him, a "boy of many moods." But that picture captured his face before everything changed, before his mouth, shaped like an almond when open, grew to look like a third eye. The fact that

Terry Tharp with his parents, Amanda and David, circa 1953

his lips and two front teeth tilted slightly to the left gave the illusion of a sly smile, but others knew it as more than that. Before
long they had to watch him for reasons other than to ensure his
adjustment.

And the adjustment wasn't going well. As they peeled away
what enshrouded this child, every layer seemed more disturbing
than the last. Indifference gave way to rage, which Josie soon saw
was tangled with fear. It turned out Terry possessed an unnatu-
ral fear of spiders. While it would have been understandable for
Josie to chalk it up to his being a city kid like lots of others she'd
seen, she had to learn the truth from the social worker. The limp
didn't come from an old school injury as Millie had said. He fell out
of some playground equipment as a young boy and broke his hip.
By one account, his parents—read: father—failed to get him proper
treatment, and he walked around on that broken hip for a year until
a teacher finally reported it. By the time doctors treated the leg,
they had to put him in a body cast, in which he lay, alone, for long

periods. Sometime during his convalescence, a spider, or several, dropped from the ceiling onto his body, and he couldn't move to do anything about it. He developed severe arachnophobia from that incident, but the real problem stemmed from the fact that a scared little boy cried, and no one came.

Whether this version is really the case, I can't be sure. Terry's medical records indicate he did fall from a jungle gym on October 9, 1952, and that someone took him to a local physician. But he "continued to get more and more crippled." He then saw a chiropractor for some time. Dr. J. C. Harman's notes state that the family then moved from Wautoma to La Crosse, and Terry's new principal at Washburn School "noticed that [Terry's] difficulty in walking was having a psychological effect on the child." Harman diagnosed him with a rare childhood affliction known as Legg-Perthes disease, which explained the worsening limp, and got him into an orthopedic hospital in Madison in late April 1955. After that, explains Dr. Harman, it was "the plan of the father to take this boy back East, where he will remain under the care of his half brother, who himself was a cripple."

That never happened. Terry went home, and then he went to the farm, and he never returned to Pennsylvania, or, as far as anyone knows, ever met his crippled half-brother.

In time the county welfare department found the Tharp home unfit, and the court granted Lee and Josie temporary custody with the stipulation that the county pay all medical bills and give the Broadheads ten dollars per week for Terry's care. Someone must have considered the arrangement fairly permanent because they ended up with Terry's original handwritten birth certificate from Pennsylvania's Westmoreland Hospital, cased in purple velvet and stamped with a gold seal. This was turning out to be a trial they didn't anticipate. Josie took it out on her knees, Lee took it out on the cows, and Terry took it out on them.

* * *

WHEN SCHOOL STARTED, Terry went off with the other kids from the coulee, though Lawrence more than once had to throw a glass of water on him to get him out of bed. This made it all the more irritating, since Lawrence would have given just about anything to have stayed in that vet program at the university instead of coming home to help with the farm. Lawrence's son, Paul, explains that his father didn't see Terry as anything more than "another of his mother's projects."

At this point they knew Terry was smart, but they didn't know how smart. Besides, schools had not yet developed a focus on genius and special tracks for gifted children or concluded that regular curriculum bores. So no one understood why Terry didn't like school. And now his anger, previously contained, warped into disturbing violence—tripping classmates and pushing their teeth into the water fountain, scattering tacks or oil on the playground, pulling hair, kicking, punching, and pushing others to the ground, no matter how uneven the match.

Terry, at least once, indicated his rationale: he felt others were picking on *him*. To the reasonable person, Terry's logic made no sense, but his situation earned him some leniency and explained away some of his behavior—a young child, disabled, motherless, pushed out of his home by an alcoholic father, suddenly living on a farm with people he didn't know. Teachers held conferences; parents complained. There was talk of putting Terry in a special school, but June Matzick, a niece by marriage, says Josie "fought like mad" to keep him out of there. June remembers Josie saying, "If you lived that life you would probably be that way, too." Terry stayed where he was.

His tendency toward violence and paranoia at school at times contradicted the behavior he showed on the farm. Terry had started to warm up to the dog. He had taken to Lawrence's cocker spaniel, and Josie often found him seeking Tammy out after school, encouraged by his ability to teach the dog to speak or beg on command.

But then Terry's true behavior revealed itself. One afternoon as the family grilled on the outdoor fireplace for some neighbors who had stopped by, Josie looked into the yard and saw Terry sitting with the dog. He carefully forked a slice of meat off the plate and fed it to Tammy while cooing and speaking gently to her, except that he was petting her head with one hand and viciously grabbing at her neck—strangling her—with the other.

Such sociopathic cruelty would be the last stop for a lot of people, the place where they cut their losses and untangle themselves from the sticky mess before it gets any worse. But to Josie, this resembled any other problem. It had a solution; she just had to find it. It was still a little early to hope for an answered prayer, let alone a miracle. To keep herself motivated, she cut out sayings and tacked them inside her kitchen cabinets, near her typewriter, by the phone, all to remind her to keep believing that something good could happen. Sayings like, *All that is necessary for evil to triumph is for good people to do nothing!* written on an index card. Or this one, cut from a Christian publication: *Hope is wishing for a thing to come true; faith is believing that it will come true. Believe that for every problem God will provide you with a solution.* And perhaps the most telling, a page titled "Risk It," which ends like this:

> But risks must be taken; because the greatest hazard in life is to risk nothing
>
> The person who risks nothing does nothing, has nothing, and is nothing
>
> He may avoid suffering and sorrow, but he simply cannot learn, feel, change, grow, love, live
>
> Only a person who risks is free

She saw it as her responsibility—obligation, even—to intervene when she saw need. "If we humans take violence into our hands and do nothing to stop the violence," she wrote, "it will worsen.

The only solution is to take the problem to the Lord, ask for forgiveness, and make restitution." She wanted each child to know this message, believing that its truth would set them, and her, free.

But Terry was not yet free. After the dog came the kittens, which belonged to Dean and Stub. Terry relished devising creative tortures for the two little boys or manipulating them into deviance that resulted in sure trouble. Dean recalls Terry trying to drive a pencil into the top of his head and forcing Stub's head into the wall or the blunt end of a nail. On an afternoon when Terry had harassed them for hours, Josie took the little ones into the cow barn and showed them the newborn kittens. Just as she expected, the warm mewing balls with eyes still partially closed acted as the perfect salve. The boys gently held the squirming babies and squealed, safe and content, and Josie returned to her work. But with the children out of her sight, the incidents continued until she had to bring the two boys into the kitchen, where she was making bread, to keep them away from Terry. Together they sculpted sweet rolls, dipping the hot dough in melted butter and brown sugar, their fingers and mouths sticky with unlicked grainy goo. When Terry's absence from the house stretched into suspicion, Josie went looking. In the barn she encountered not Terry, but the kittens lying still and cold—all strangled to death. Dean and Stub found out soon enough, and the three of them wept at the meanness, the loss.

"When the tears stopped," Josie wrote, "I was tired, so very, very tired."

She wasn't the crying type, and beating wasn't her style. Mostly she got good and mad, and everybody knew when that happened. For some, adult or child, a good yelling could scare them straight into holiness. But not Terry. When he showed no sorrow, no regret over the mass murder, she didn't know what to do. So she probably did the only thing she believed would work—yell for her own sake and then just pray some more and hope God would answer a little sooner.

That night, once she had put the boys to bed and Terry in his room, Josie sat down in the kitchen to plan meals. While poring over her list, pencil in hand, she heard screaming from upstairs. She raced down the hall and looked up, and there stood Dean and Stub in their pajamas, wailing and covered in wireworms and other insects. A revenge. Josie pulled all the creatures off them and plopped the boys into the bathtub. She dried them with mismatched towels, rubbed witch hazel on the red areas, and tucked them back into bed.

As their tears dried and eyes closed, she marched over to Terry's room, where she found him working on a model. She grabbed him by the arm, dragged him into the bathroom, and plunked him down into the still-full bathtub, clothes and all. She then turned on the cold water and left the room yelling, "I've had enough of your viciousness! Stop it! Stop it! You hear, stop it!" She ran downstairs, hating herself for losing control.

"That incident really got to me," she wrote. "I felt so incompetent, so unfit to handle a child that was a potential threat to our safety. I prayed and prayed. I just had to live up to my bargain with God."

The behavior had to stop, this Josie knew, but punishment had proved completely ineffective. Penny Bruckner, one of Lee's nieces, says, "She'd send him to his room, but that never bothered him. He'd rant and rave and carry on, but then he'd enjoy staying up there." Josie had already sought help in a dozen places—books and experts, universities and preachers, to name a few. She'd had it with the doctors, who told her to do this and that, all unrealistic, since in the end they didn't have to live with the boy. She had no idea how hard to push him—was this adjustment or manipulation, illness or outright rebellion? He posed a riddle she couldn't figure out, and she was not used to feeling inept. "I did not have the heart to label a child devious or dangerous," she recalled. "To me a child was a child, on the whole sweet, innocent, and lovable. Or so I thought until Terry came into our lives." Watching Terry became a shared family task by default, a gang of "rubberneck spies," trying to catch him in his acts. He must have known, as they later found a hole he had sawed through the planks in his closet floor so he could listen to conversations below. You can still pry up those boards.

Josie knew how to fight hard. Maybe the time had arrived. She had been reading psychology, trying to figure out this Terry situation, and she had not yet considered some more aggressive tactics, like shock therapy. Perhaps he needed a healthy dose of humility. She wasn't sure about that, but she knew she had nothing left to lose. She told Terry that the next time he behaved badly she would retaliate. The morning after a series of bullying incidents, including pricking the two little boys with needles just because they got too close to him, she placed a dead spider in his cereal bowl. He came down to the table, poured milk on his Corn Flakes, and was lifting the spoon to his mouth when he saw it. He instantly gagged, and vomit spilled over the table into his lap. Josie, seeing what had happened, ran to her bedroom and wept over what she had done.

After wiping her face, she returned to the kitchen, where Terry still sat, pale, trying to clean himself up. She grabbed a towel and tried to help. She said she was sorry, explained that she did that because, as she told him, if he did something nasty, she would do something back. She thought this would show him that it just isn't nice to pick on boys littler than him. She never thought this would happen. Terry just stared at her, except this time he looked like a child—helpless, vulnerable, small. He got up from the table, went to his room, and stayed there the rest of the day. The incident did nothing to curb his behavior, and Josie abandoned her plans to try anything like that again.

Terry offered no explanations for his violence, experimentation, revenge, or whatever it was, and it defied all of Lee and Josie's logic why a boy they were trying to help would continually seek to hurt them. The social worker said that these acts formed a funnel for Terry's displaced anger toward his father, something Josie still vastly underestimated. She wondered only how a child this young could dig a well so deep.

Terry Tharp at the La Crosse farmhouse in the late 1950s

IT PROBABLY SEEMED ALMOST insignificant that Lee and Josie's twenty-fifth wedding anniversary fell in the middle of all this Terry trouble, but the neighbors had been counting for years, waiting for the chance to honor the Broadheads with the greatest tribute in La Crosse County: a mock wedding.

A mock wedding involved a giant anniversary party during which friends humorously re-created a couple's wedding. Just like a real wedding, everyone brought gifts and food, and after the ceremony, someone produced a fiddle or an accordion, and guests danced well into the next morning. They had the first one down by Shorty Kish in September of 1949, an idea dreamed up by Chet Dahlby. So he'd have a permanent venue for such events, Sonny Kramer's second cousin up on the ridge cleaned out his barn, added two bathrooms on the side, built a stage, and called it The Party Barn.

The instigators usually developed an elaborate secret plan of research and preparation almost more fun than the wedding itself.

They recruited casts, wrote songs, sewed costumes, and penned vows to the tune of, "Do you promise to be faithful unless it's to-bacco harvesting season?" A man always played the bride, a woman the groom. The cast also included preachers, attendants, guests, and mothers of the bride with wet washrags to simulate tears. On the big day, the entire party snaked along coulee roads and simply showed up at the couple's house without warning to present their full-blown production.

The day of Lee and Josie's mock wedding, Josie stood near her flapping laundry when she saw the cars coming. She hollered at Bev and started throwing sheets and clothespins into the basket. "Get rid of the laundry! Here they come! Here they come!" The cars filled the drive and spilled onto the road. Folks propped two chairs in the middle of the living room for the honored couple, and they watched as Louis Galster, a large fellow draped in white with painted lips and hairy legs, swooned over a woman drowning in pinstripes and a red wig. Everyone laughed, and then they rolled up the rugs and carried them out, and the dancing began, with Norman Schroeder on the accordion. For a few minutes, Josie forgot all about how hard her life had become.

A photograph taken later that same year, in July of 1957, shows a grinning Lee ready to leave for a mock wedding as somebody else's bride in a floppy hat, long dress, and chiffon—lots of chiffon. Terry sits on the step in the background, watching as if confused.

THOSE WHO LIVED IN THE HOUSE slogged over to Trinity—now part of the United Church of Christ—with the family, even Terry, and surprisingly he went without resistance and rarely caused a disturbance. On the one morning he refused to cooperate, he sat in the living room after breakfast, rocking and staring out the window at the cow barn. "Terry," Josie said, "hurry up now, or we'll be late for Sunday school." He continued pushing the chair with his foot, slowly lifting his toes off the ground, ignoring a second request while Josie rushed around. Then Terry said something that made her forget all about church.

"My father killed my mother."

Josie stood there, not knowing what to do, not knowing what to believe. There had been stories of David Tharp chasing his wife and son out into the cold of winter in nothing but nightclothes, stories of Terry going to the neighbors' because he feared going back in the house with his father—all easy to believe now that she had seen what the man was like. Even if this child was so mixed up that he really didn't know reality from nightmare, he understood this to be true. No wonder he felt angry. She stopped; she had no words. Terry never spoke to her of his mother's death again.

Creases marble the one photo of Terry's father that survived Josie's house, as if someone had balled it up and thrown it away. It shows David in a long, dark, double-breasted winter coat, white collar and knotted tie peeking through. He stands behind Terry, who can't be more than four or five, also in dress coat and hat, chinstrap undone. Terry appears to be struggling with his father, feet pointed sideways, arms in motion, head looking down, but David holds him by the shoulders. They stand in front of a stout evergreen, the only noticeable life among a background dotted with telephone poles, houses, and dead trees on the hill in the distance.

In all the time Terry lived at the farm, David Tharp never came out to visit, though Lee and Josie made sure they got the boy to his father's place. Even Sonny Kramer, who still worked closely with Lee during these years, often drove Terry into town on his hog feed runs. Josie seemed to understand to some extent why, even if Terry blamed his father, he still gravitated toward him. The way she saw it, cliché as it sounds, blood is always thicker than water. Maybe her seemingly endless patience and hope stemmed from the fact that she grew up with a father she loved and hated at the same time—a man like a tornado with a bottle, who would do and say terrible things when the liquor took charge. But one key difference separated Josie and Terry: Josie had an ally in her mother for a lot longer.

For a while Josie and her family swayed between hope and defeat, watching the incidents progress in severity, from abusing animals and toying with preschoolers to deeds of unadulterated wickedness, as when Terry chased Lee's nephew, one of the many nieces and nephews who stayed summers, with a kitchen knife. An incident was bound to go too far. After everything Terry had done, it would make sense for the incident to involve the Broadheads. Instead, the Kramers got it. Like most of the neighbors, they had tried to support Josie, as she had always been so good to them, and they were not without compassion. Even when Sonny and Phyllis tell of it now, they drop their voices. It's easy to understand why. While the accounts differ, two things remain certain: the Kramers invited Terry over to play with their younger son, Jerry, and sometime that afternoon Terry planned or tried to hang Jerry from a tree.

Something interrupted the plan either before or during the attempted lynching. Though Jerry was unhurt, the neighbors immediately petitioned to have Terry removed from the coulee, which might have happened even if Terry had shown remorse and given a plausible explanation. Josie contacted the social workers, who recommended that Lee and Josie put Terry in a children's home. Josie recognized it as the right thing for everyone, but she couldn't help feeling that she was quitting. She hated this about herself even if she couldn't argue that he had proved to be a danger many times over, and she wept when he went away.

They sent Terry to La Crosse Children's Home, and everyone relaxed, said it was best. Things returned to the way they had been, but the family failed to realize that to Josie giving up on Terry amounted to the same thing as giving up on everything that mattered. To walk away from something—anything—condemned her character and the life ahead of her. She had always known that if she worked long and hard enough at something she'd find a way around, over, under, if not through. It's what she was known for, how people remember her. And if in Christ Jesus all things are possible and no one is beyond saving, then who was she to say, "I can't"? Ironically, though she refused to say those two words, she cemented her philosophy to them, claiming that she alone could do nothing apart from the God who made her. So putting Terry in a home surpassed quitting and hemorrhaged into a lapse of faith. Lawrence noticed the effect of Terry's absence, even if he didn't completely understand. Lee saw it, too, and hoped it would pass. Mary felt good about him being gone, so relieved that she didn't care.

Josie remembers that just a few months after admitting Terry, a young, impatient messenger from the children's home stopped by the farm. The notes of a Dr. A. G. Brailey indicate that Terry lived at the home for a year and a half, but he was wrong about another date, so his accuracy may be in question. Regardless, the home wanted to know if she would consider taking Terry back. He was now *their* Terry, and their Terry had gone into a rage at the home, cutting bed sheets into pieces and shredding feather pillows until the staff restrained him. Her promise to God had not been about Terry, but the promise had become that to her. Because she must consider other factors, because he wasn't *her* Terry, she didn't agree right then. The man turned around and left, clearly inconvenienced; the home, expecting and hoping for an agreement, had sent Terry along in the backseat of the car, in case they could make the transfer that day. If Josie peeked out the window, she might have caught a glimpse of Terry, who undoubtedly stared out at the yard, expressionless.

Josie called a family meeting to discuss the things they knew and the things they didn't, including that vow she had to consider. By now the very mention of it must have sounded like manipulation—how could you say no to something like that without feeling guilty?—even if she didn't mean it that way. They didn't ask the neighbors. Maybe they hoped that a few months had healed the damage enough on all sides. They talked some more before reaching a decision. By now I suspect Josie only had to look at Lee. Without a word, he would get the car, and they would bring Terry home.

WHEN TERRY CAME BACK, they all tried to act enthusiastic to see him, probably for Josie's sake. The inwardness, the docility had returned. As a welcome gift, they bought him six models, knowing that only building intricate planes, cars, and ships interested him. It's easy to see why models drew Terry in. They allowed him to construct a world of tiny plastic and metal parts with glue and paint and tweezers, a world like ours except smaller—one he could control. Each piece had its place, fit together the way it was supposed to according to plan. Models entailed no surprises, no challenges that couldn't be overcome with a patient hand. And most importantly, he didn't need anyone else's help. Terry was good at them, and fast. But when Josie asked him a few days later how he liked those models, his response shocked her.

"I finished them," he replied.

"Finished? All six? They were the most complex ship and space models the store had. You're a genius, Terry! You should consider displaying them at the library." He walked off. Josie shook her head and returned to the kitchen, thinking out loud how different things would be if she could just harness that ability.

Soon after, Josie set out to do some gardening but could not find her hoe. She checked the machine shed and the barn, finally finding it near the outdoor fireplace, of all spots, dull and powdered with soot. "Who on earth used my hoe to clean out the fireplace?" she wondered aloud, walking back to the barn to sharpen it.

Once she got to hoeing, she straightened up and noticed a large cloud of black smoke coming from the yard. "Mercy!" she said. "Something's on fire!" She dropped her hoe and ran toward it, her first thought the hay barn. From that angle it would have been tough to tell the origin of the smoke. As she neared, she saw

Terry stuffing something into the fireplace. "Terry!" she yelled, but he continued feeding the fire. As she neared, she saw that he was breaking up his models and burning them. "Terry, Terry, what are you doing?" she screamed.

The air reeked of noxious plastic smoke, and Terry continued packing the ships and planes into the firebox. Orange ashes floated up through the chimney toward the hayloft, and she ran to stomp them out. "If that hay catches fire, the whole place will burn," she hollered. "Put the damper down!" He ignored her, so she ran over and poked the iron handle. Immediately smoke shot out the front, and Terry started to cough, still trying to stoke the fire. She moved him back and held him, smothered by fear and disgust, until the fire died down. She later said that this pain, this complete inability to reach him, watching this annihilation of a life, was a despair unlike any she had ever known.

When the embers had cooled, she went back and pulled out a miniature flag from his steamship and the tip of his spacecraft, all that had survived the blaze. She sat on the edge of the fireplace, turning the flag over in her hands, wondering why he did it. He hadn't burned just the six new models. He'd burned them all.

WHEN SHE CAUGHT HIM in the basement, she knew to suspect something. No one ventured down to that cold, dark place, a cavernous unknown, unless it was absolutely necessary. Only mice and spiders liked it. Terry turned around, startled at her presence, and thrust his hand behind his back.

"What've you got there?" she asked, hands on her hips. He slowly held out his palm, and in it lay a bottle of poison. "What were you going to do with that? Were you going to hurt somebody with it? Hurt yourself?" He looked at her blankly. "Well, why don't you just go ahead and take it? Go on, I dare you to take it." She had placed no forethought in her comment and for the moment, no regret. She didn't think about how it would be to watch him die. She didn't pray. She didn't think about the fact that his standing there came about because God had prevented her from dying. She only wanted it all to stop, everything, the cruelty and the fires and the confusion and the death. She wanted to win for once, to be right, to see everything she believed about God and people and life proved true—that no one is beyond help, that everyone has a turning point. She wanted to rest.

It seemed like hours that they stood there. She couldn't see anything in his dark eyes, but she knew he did not fear her. Did he fear anything? Was he even human? Could a real live person keep on acting like this? Terry dropped the bottle on the table and ran up the stairs.

Josie wept.

She noted later that Terry seemed almost rational after that incident. Maybe because she had called his bluff. Maybe because she had shown no fear and earned some of his respect. Maybe because inside he was still a child who wanted to know love and live.

Terry might not have been bluffing. He told his doctor years later that he tried to electrocute himself by "wrapping a lamp cord wire around one wrist" at age fifteen. Did Josie ever know?

She begged God for some insight into this boy who resisted every effort, defied every attempt, and yet seemed to need it all. Where did she go to pray? Did she go to her room? Did she walk the fields? Did she just turn inside herself, continuing on with all that life required of her, her mind off having a conversation with God? Wherever she sought Him, she told the Lord that she didn't know what to do. That she thought He wanted her to take Terry in, but she just didn't know how she was helping him. That she wanted to keep her promise, but she just didn't know how. Most of all, she said, "Help." I see her sinking to the floor of her bedroom, her head buried in the quilt, only one of the many times when she, for just a few moments, released her tension and collapsed against the bed. If her body shook with sobs, only God knew, and that's the way she would have wanted it.

* * *

NOBODY CAN ESTIMATE ACCURATELY how long this all went on, how much Josie and the rest tolerated—can it really have been three or four years? However long, he was still fighting, and so was she. Whether he was at it again, the usual, and she simply wanted him to go away, or she just couldn't get into town (too tired, too busy, or too empty), she shoved her good typewriter, broken, into Terry's hands.

"Go up to your room and fix it," Josie spat. He looked at her, looked at the typewriter, picked it up, and went to his room.

"Mom, you must really be desperate," Mary said. Josie said nothing.

A few days passed. The family went about their chores. The house stayed quiet, save the screen door banging, the chopping and stirring, peaceful, almost happy-like, with—

Thud.

Josie turned around to see Terry standing near the typewriter. She probably frowned, still a little sore to see him, but she wiped her hands and walked over to the table. When she tried it out, after putting the caps lock on, letters appeared across the paper. ASDFJKLASDFJKL. MRS. LEE BROADHEAD. Maybe even TERRY NEIL THARP. Then she laughed and kissed him on the cheek, a rare display of affection for them both. "What else can you fix?" she asked. No one knows for sure, but I like to believe that at that moment Terry smiled.

A SET OF TOOLS BECAME HIS SAVIOR, mostly, even if Josie would argue it was the Good Lord. Terry fixed things, radios and mixers and adding machines and farm equipment, and that kept him busy and mostly out of trouble. But not entirely. He still had difficulty keeping his grades up, and in his junior year of high school, he transferred from Logan to Central. Around this time, he went to live at St. Michael's, another home for troubled kids in town. Relatives say that when St. Michael's admitted him on June 18, 1963, purportedly for Terry to finish out his senior year with some help from social workers, he moved out of the farmhouse for good. Why he went to St. Michael's only then, after he had been at the farm for so long, is uncertain since it seems he had started to change. Perhaps a new program had opened, or he needed mental health care, or maybe Terry simply wanted to go.

He graduated from Central the following May. He couldn't go back to the farm, because all the bedrooms had filled, and the only alternative would have been to live with Lawrence and his new bride, Karen, in the white house. He tried the air force in the fall, but he made it through only twenty-three days, not even long enough to survive basic training at Lackland Air Force Base in Texas. After that, he dabbled in courses at La Crosse State and went back and forth to the farm, depressed. In the spring of 1966, his social worker, Curtis Nedova, through the Department of Welfare, recommended that he see a doctor about possibly gaining admission to Mendota State Hospital for proper diagnosis and treatment after Terry inhaled carbon tetrachloride in an apparent "suicidal gesture."

The doctor's notes say Terry's "classwork and performance has apparently largely disintegrated. He has skipped many classes and examinations because he finds it impossible to concentrate and so on." Then the notes stop, so whether he received the care remains a mystery.

He had grown to be tall with dark, wavy hair and statesman glasses. He wore plain clothes—white-collared shirts and T-shirts, dark slacks. He remained quiet and still didn't look people in the eye, but most found him to be polite, even pleasant. Even if he was mean as a child, he generally hadn't been rude, just minimalist. Terry's social skills might not have matured at the rate of his peers, but he did have one friend, Michael Broadhead, Wallace's grandson. Close in age, both he and Michael had trouble with their families and were painfully shy. When Michael got a job as a telephone lineman in Racine, Terry tagged along. Terry bought an old Volkswagen and rented a room in town, but with Michael gone on the job so much, a local electronics store diverted a lot of Terry's attention. An innovative venture between seventeen-year-old Jim Fumo, his sister, and their father, J. J. Audio Capital sold records and stereo equipment catering to the under-twenty-eight group. Radio stations were playing The Who, The Stones, and Jefferson Airplane, but the equipment captured Terry's interest more than the music. He spent so much time at the store that the Fumos offered him a job. Within a year they made him manager of that store, another branch, and a start-up in Burlington called The Back Room.

The Fumos informally adopted Terry, a young man still rough around the edges, who still kicked at the floor when something made him mad, but a man becoming known as a dependable, trustworthy, ethical employee, one that customers liked. Jim remembers that Terry even started to take an interest in one particular customer, a girl.

One morning during the fall of 1971, Terry set off for The Back Room, calling Jim at J. J.'s to say he was running late. Sometime that morning, the door at J. J.'s opened. Jim looked up, slightly surprised to see a policeman standing at the counter.

"Can I help you, officer?" Jim asked.

"Do you have a Terry Tharp working for you?"

"Yeah, he works up at the Burlington store—"

"So, you do have a Terry Tharp employed here."

"Yeah," Jim said, suddenly concerned.

"I'm afraid I have some bad news," the officer said. "Terry was in an accident."

"Oh my God. Is he okay?"

At this, the officer held out a set of keys so mangled and melted that they were almost unidentifiable. "I'm sorry, son," he said, "but he died."

* * *

Terry Tharp at The Back Room in Burlington, Wisconsin, circa 1971

AT AN INTERSECTION on the outskirts of Racine, just outside a church, firefighters had the blaze out and had begun cleaning up. They had taken away in a body bag a seventeen-year-old who had sped through the stop sign. They had gathered the debris that had scattered when the cars collided, exploded, and ricocheted into a telephone pole. They had watched the tow trucks haul away the remains of the vehicles. And they had found Terry, who had been thrown from the car, dead on the scene from massive injuries.

A squad car turned left onto Breidel Coulee Road and pulled into the farm. The sheriff got out, walked over to the folks sitting in the yard, and held out to Josie a scorched leather billfold, the one she had given Terry for his twenty-fourth birthday. The wallet still reeked of smoke, and she held it to her chest and wept.

TERRY'S CHARRED BODY traveled back to La Crosse, where it waited while Lee and Josie arranged the funeral. Terry's father could not stay sober long enough to do it. They held the service at Trinity on a Thursday afternoon in late October, on a day when leaves in jewel hues floated gently to the ground as if through water. Lee and Josie purchased a plot so Terry could be buried in the church cemetery, right there on Highway 14, less than a mile from the farm. All the neighbors came, even those who had petitioned for his removal, even the boy Jerry, now a man. Some of the social workers and nuns showed, as did two of Terry's cousins from his mother's side. Michael and Lawrence served as pallbearers. Beverly sang. Terry's father stumbled in, drunk, but he was there, too.

After the funeral Reverend Warner sent the seventy-six dollars and fifty cents in memorial money to Winnebago Children's Home at Josie's request, but the matter of the will remained an issue. David Tharp insisted that Terry's will be turned over to him, but Lee and Josie had learned enough to give it to their attorney instead, even if David seemed to be genuinely wrestling with what had become of his life.

The three of them attended the reading of the will, during which they all learned something very important—something they had not anticipated: Terry had left everything to his father. Josie's was a forgivable reaction: *How could he do this? How could he do this to us? We cared for the boy for all those years, and he left everything to the father who* abandoned *him, whom he believed killed his mother?* Someone who doesn't understand would think her upset about the money (though Lord knows there couldn't have been much anyway), or maybe about not getting due credit for what she had done. But when Josie heard those words, I believe she saw only a boy who had found one last chance to get back at her and took it. In that moment she didn't think about why, if he was angry with his father all that time, he chose to hurt them instead of his father in the end. Neither did she consider other meanings for Terry's action. After so many years, someone could reason that she had formed calluses to protect herself from this sort of thing. But she hadn't. The way it stood, this was the only explanation, and it hurt her.

She almost didn't hear the lawyer explain that the money Terry left his father could be used for only one reason: treating David's alcoholism. Time muddied what actually happened next. One account says David roared in anger. Another says that when he heard the conditions, "he broke down and wept bitterly," but then accepted them, handing Josie a medallion with the Ten Commandments on it and saying, "My boy would want you to have this. It belonged to his mother." She knew that one of the ten is, "Honor your father and mother." Regardless, somehow in his last act Terry managed to honor all of the people who filled those roles, living or dead.

No one knows if David Tharp ever got his hands on that money, if he got himself straightened out. But everyone knows that he died alone eighteen years later, and he was not buried next to his son.

In the will Terry hoped Lee and Josie would understand, and there he said the two words that Josie had not heard from him since he arrived that day in 1955, sixteen years earlier—the two words he had been unable to express any sooner: thank you. Josie sat, silenced by humility, her face shiny with tears. She knew then that her prayers had been answered. While some would see only the sadness in Terry's death, Josie saw where he had come from— that he had, when it mattered most, learned to love and forgive. And that is why, for the rest of her life, she referred to it not as a tragic end, but as her finest hour.

Footprints

Burke, Virginia
2005

THE OTHER DAY I watched a beekeeper at work. He hunched over the hive, pulling out each frame, its combs like pieces of coral. He removed them in a sort of plié, with thousands of bees flying around him, landing on his clothes, on his bare arms and legs, and in his hair. I wondered how many times he'd been stung. If it hurt. If it would hurt me as much as it did when I was a child, the last time I remember it happening. I stepped on a bee in our backyard once. Another time a friend and I climbed up into her tree house, which the wasps had taken over and in no uncertain terms told us to get out. (We cried, and then her mother served us ice cream.) And then a bee stung me up at the farm. It got me on top of my foot, probably as I ran barefoot through the clover. Someone wanted to pull the stinger, my dad being the likely candidate, but the mention of tweezers or needles prompted the best show of force I could muster—crying, proposed bargains, and outright refusal—which the enemy camp countered with ultimatums. When it came to pain, I inflicted an ordeal on my parents that rivaled any test of endurance. This time Josie saved me with a home remedy. If I remember correctly, it involved mustard, oatmeal, maybe some vinegar, an old bread bag, paper towels, and a rubber band. She assured me the poultice would do the trick overnight, and I slept in my bed on the upstairs landing, foot rustling on top of the covers. My parents took aspirin.

The next morning my mom washed my foot, which revealed a swollen red welt. "Stinger's still in there," she said. I howled, pleaded, and begged, but in the end they heated a needle and pried the thing out.

UNTIL I STARTED MESSING AROUND with her past, I had never questioned the notion that I wanted to live the kind of life Josie did: caring, sacrificial, inspirational. Extraordinary. So I sought her secret and looked to her leadership, hoping to find the element I've been missing. But in looking for Josie, I've stumbled onto myself, and I don't like what I see.

As I uncovered her life, piece by piece, I couldn't help but hold what I found up against mine. At first the process resembled a matching game—*I do that! That happened to me!*—and all appeared hopeful, trouble to triumph and all that. But I couldn't sustain the comparison; the more closely I looked at her life, the blurrier mine became. I see now that her life can stand up to scrutiny under a microscope, but mine can't. Her flaws are more forgivable because her strengths stand so straight. She and I may be related and share qualities, traits, and even some misfortunes, but the similarities end there. Her actions jettisoned her ahead, leaving me on a cold trail, hiding behind my words, drowning in my dreams.

Confession: I fully intended to investigate Josie so that I could tell the stories she wanted told. But the truth shed its veneer almost immediately, and I saw that this whole Josie search is all about me.

Typical.

I suppose Josie knew that, and her last gift to her middle grand-daughter was to let me learn from her life. It took me only eleven years to figure out how to open and assemble it. In gluing her story back together, I hoped it would remove the stinger of aimlessness and confusion I've had inside me for years, and bring down the swelling for good.

Without the needle.

And maybe I could have the kind of life she had, that kind of impact, that kind of legacy.

After all, I'm stubborn, just like she was.

I'm task-oriented, just like she was.

I express myself in writing, just like she did.

I can't rely on my beauty, just like she couldn't.

I've faced the pain of losing a husband, just like she did.

I've had to deal with the loss of my would-be children, just like she did.

I look at life seriously, just like she did.

I don't like to accept failure, just like she didn't.

But after looking at Josie, more questions than answers clutter and crowd: What hardships have I survived and for what ends? Do I really know what hardship is? How many have I helped? What would go in my obituary if I died today? Would the paper even print one? How many people would come to my funeral, and what would they say?

The truth is that I want noticeable results too quickly, and I give up too easily.

I've allowed my failures to dilute my passion, my boldness, my courage.

And just like an insolent child, I want what I want, and I haven't been willing to give that up.

What will it take for me to release my grip? Will I release, or will I be like the rich young ruler, who walked away from Jesus because he couldn't let go of what he loved, sad?

I've been thinking about how my mom has felt all these years living behind such a tall shadow. My mom respected her parents, did her chores, stayed active in the 4-H and church, and graduated from high school. Then she went to college, got married and worked a little bit, had two babies. She secured miscellaneous jobs for money. She raised her children. Now, in her later years, she is nearing retirement with her husband of four decades and anticipating her days of rest. I think she would say that her life has been good—for which she is grateful—but average.

She started out like many young idealists, trying to make a difference in the world. But she stopped working at twenty-eight to be a mother, giving up her job in Gary, Indiana, and moving to a white Cape Cod, but she never returned to that first job: a social worker who, ironically, removed neglected and abused children from their homes. She never again watched the car drive away with screaming children pressed to the rear window, their cries silent through the glass for the mommies and daddies who couldn't love them.

I don't think my mom has felt pressured to live up to her mother, although many of the things she does smack of Josie's influence. I've seen her light up the eyes of the elderly and make children squeal with glee. Her extra bedrooms rarely echo, and the parties she and my dad throw are famously large and raucously fun. She brings meals to shut-ins, sends care packages to soldiers, and volunteers to watch other people's children. I recognized this sort of thing during my childhood, but it quickly disappeared beneath the sacrifices she made for my brother and me. She has settled into this way of life as she has aged, looking more like her mother in deed. I wonder how this all started: Is it like the child who grows up learning to write thank-you notes and then simply does it as an adult because it's inbred? Does she do it because it's who she is or because she grew up knowing no other way?

I see Josie in my mom the way I see my mom in me.

In the past couple of years, I've started to sound like her, like most girls start to sound like their mothers. I unconsciously wanted to be my mom early on. Maybe that's because I was afraid to be myself, or I didn't know who I was. Maybe because I had grown up in a home that, while not necessarily stifling, didn't encourage experiment, risk, or individuality. That's how it was on the farm, and that's how it was in my house. I hadn't even recognized the box that contained me until well into my twenties, and by then, I found the patterns that much harder to separate and break. Eventually I realized that even if I wasn't myself, I wasn't her either, and all of the above had to go.

Here I sit, ten years later, still trying to figure out who I am, still trying to convert my life from average to extraordinary. So I revert back a generation and look at Josie. Despite the fact that Josie and I share the spirit of frustrated visionaries who focus only on what they have yet to accomplish, who share so much more than blood, I'm starting to grasp that I can never be Josie, so where does that leave me?

Sometimes I wish I'd left Josie alone.

Mary Broadhead Bilen at the La Crosse farm on her wedding day, July 25, 1964

The Mother

La Crosse, Wisconsin
1958

JOSIE MUST HAVE BEEN THE ONE to prepare the room.

Did she snap new sheets, fluff the pillows, and pile a couple of extra quilts at the foot of the bed? Did her rag run along the bureau, night table, sills, picking up bits of gray? Was it she who pulled the ceiling chain, noticing the dust on the bulb and massaging it with her rag before it heated? Who else would have done it the way it needed to be done? Yes, I am sure she opened the window to let spring in, and cool air gushed through as if she had just opened the icebox. Her broom reached into the corner and gathered up the dust bunnies, and she swept them into the dustpan. She must have been the one to prepare the room for her mother, to transform the space into a hospital room, a hospice, a tomb.

AFTER HER HUSBAND DIED IN 1932, Martina Twite remained in the granary house for thirteen more years, until her son, Carl, won at auction a two-bedroom house in Carson. He paid four hundred dollars for it. She moved with her brother, Carl Hanson, affectionately known as Uncle Carl or Old Carl, who had shown up from Minnesota sometime after their mother died in 1926. Carl had left the family farm in the charge of their older brother, Martin Hanson, but the farm had grown more debt than crops. Martin, who had experienced a mental breakdown thirty years earlier, did not last. Lonely and displaced, fearing complete loss of the land, he hung himself in 1928. The church initially resisted burying him alongside his parents, but Martina, Carl, and their sister Jorgina pleaded until the church relented. No one knows why Carl went to live with Martina, or the reason he said to hell with the family farm and deserted it for six years until the sheriff repossessed the land.

For a man like Uncle Carl who liked the finer things of life, it must have been a rough transition to come and live with his sister on the prairie. Photographs almost exclusively portray him in well-tailored suits, showing off cigars or a hand of cards, though judging from the debt he had incurred on his father's farm before coming west, he and his brother-in-law must have had a lot in common. One of Benhard's daughters, Lily Twite Bachmeier, describes Carl as "a kind and gentle soul who seemed to chew, snooze, and play solitaire most of the time." She might add "stubborn," since getting him away from his checkers to help out with chores was like trying to pull a mule out of the barn and into the rain.

Old Carl died on December 5, 1944, a handful of seasons after their move into town. The obituary claims his end followed months of heart and stomach trouble caused by sunstroke, although the family insists that sitting on a barrel of acid did him in. Despite the fact that he liked his drink just about as much as her husband had, Martina considered it a great loss.

The house simply echoed after that, too lonely to keep, so Martina spent most of her time alternating between daughter Manda just outside Carson, son Henry in Milwaukee, and Josie in La Crosse. Her children and grandchildren knew that when Grandma Twite came, all dancing and card playing ceased, which left plenty of room for Bible reading and talk about Jesus. Often she knitted, drinking cambric tea, and sometimes she told about seeing her daughter Clara fly up to heaven. She employed her grandchildren to write for her, letters to her sons and daughters. "I slept with Grandma," Mary says proudly. "Every night I'd say, 'Grandma, tell me a story.' She'd always sing that song, and I remember she'd tell me about heaven, about pearly gates and streets of gold." The song Mary means is, of course, "I'll Away."

Martina Twite, likely taken in North Dakota in the early 1940s

Carl Hanson and his sister Martina Hanson Twite, likely taken in North Dakota, 1931

But not everyone thought of sleeping beside Martina as special. Another granddaughter, Bernice Johnson Steinley, says that when as a teenager she stayed with Martina in the Carson house, "It was the most ghastly thing I ever had to do." For as long as anyone can remember, Martina slept in long underwear, under a stack of quilts, with a scarf around her hair and a pungent smear of Vicks across her forehead. Once Bernice painted an unsuspecting Martina's fingernails red during the night, and Martina thought the devil had come after her.

Just about everything Martina did made Beverly roll her eyes. The woman dressed in layers of wool, even in the summertime. She drank tomato juice every day as if receiving an oral blood transfusion. And as the girls did dishes with lye soap, Beverly washing and Mary drying, Martina asked again and again whether they had run enough water over the dishes. Bev repeatedly answered, "*Grand*-ma, I *rinsed* it."

Beverly and Mary Broadhead at the La Crosse farm with their grandmother Martina Twite and their dog Pepper, 1949

But then the unexpected happened. Confusion overtook Martina one day at Josie's, and she stopped speaking, went numb. They rushed her to the hospital, and the doctor said she had suffered a stroke—an odd turn, seeing as Josie remembered her ill only once, years before, while watering the cows. As Josie wrote:

It happened the year we had a long dry spell. The creeks had dried up, the wind had died down so the usual windpower stilled the wind mills so we had no alternative but to pump water by hand for those cows. Mercy, have you ever pumped water for thirty-six water-crazed cows on a hot summer day with flies buzzing overhead, making the cows nervous and ornery. One trough full of water was only a teaser and with a herd of over thirty pushing their weight around it was near catastrophe. There was a mighty tussle of wet noses, sharp horns stabbing one another in the stomach and flanks and if you happened to be in the middle of that mad herd as Ma and I were, well to say the least, it was unnerving. To make matters worse the cows would sling their heads about, spattering watery slime in our faces, while at the same time their tails were swishing more filth at us and with the whirlwinds kicking up dry dust around our faces, we reeked yuck from the tips of our hair to the soles of our shoes. There we were pumping water by hand at full tilt until our arms ached, trying desperately to make room for the calves, but the cows bunted and tore the flesh of them fiendishly. Ordinarily those cows were gentle, cud-chewing milkers but now they were dangerous, actually splashing out more water in their greed than we could pump in. Ma decided to fill an adjoining trough and in so doing the water-crazed cows bunted Ma into the sloshing mud beneath their feet and they very nearly stampeded her to death. If it hadn't been for Uncle Carl I'm afraid Ma would have never survived. We finally got her out on dry ground, a safe distance from the bawling crazed cows, removed her outer clothing. She was a mess! She looked more like a black grotesque oddity than a human being. We washed her clean, brushed her long hair and checked her limbs and body for injuries, all the while she kept up a steady babble about going to school and buying silverware. We were far more terrified than we wanted to admit, but we carried her into the house and set her on the couch, praying silently that Reverend Norlie would drive in. He was due as Ma had cooked up special foods just for the occasion. I can't remember all the things we did to keep from breaking down for we knew without a doubt Ma had lost her mind so we tried to break that death-like pall that settled over us. We somehow managed a tortuous night of watching and praying. As the night wore on we noticed Ma had drifted into a sound sleep. By morning time we were wretched and lifeless but when the flaming orange sun peeped up over the horizon Ma awoke with her usual energy.

Not this time. Conversations zipped back and forth along phone lines, among those who understood, Manda and Henry and Josie, dancing around the hesitation that comes with uncertainty and shame, the niceties, and the words that no one dared speak. In the end, Josie took her. Josie agreed because of principle and promise, though maybe she found it easier to say yes because she thought it wouldn't be long now. Martina had repeatedly insisted upon not being a burden to anyone, but it is difficult not to default to that state when you cannot feed, clothe, or bathe yourself. Because Lee needed Lawrence and Beverly was finishing up college in Illinois, Josie's only possibilities for assistance included Mary and Terry. Between school and regular chores, Josie had no help, and the task would require all of her faith and a loan on some of her mother's.

Now I envision Josie looking out the window on this day in 1958 and catching the ambulance as it pulls into the driveway. She rushes out the front door and waves at them to stop so they can bring her mother in right there. The driver parks and gets out to help the second paramedic in back. Josie peers in as they open the doors. There she sees her mother, covered except for her head, enshrouded in white as if entombed. Josie knows that her mother chills easily anyway, but now her skin has thinned almost to transparency, her legs no bigger than Josie's arms.

"Ma, I'm here, Ma. Everything's going to be all right now."

The paramedics carefully roll the stretcher out from the back of the ambulance and don't bother to put the wheels down. She is as light as a stack of spring dresses. They carry the stretcher up through the front door, which Josie has propped open, and she directs them immediately to the left, into the master bedroom, where a hospital bed waits.

Josie watches as they unstrap the canvas and lift her mother gently onto the bed. They remove the blankets, and before they cover her with the bedding, Josie once again stares at the shocking frailty of her mother. Looking back at the paramedics—such a contrast with their fleshy arms and rosy cheeks—she thanks them, and they go, leaving her alone with her mother.

It has been a long time since they lived together—more than thirty years, in fact. In a way Josie has missed it, not being able to borrow strength as readily, but then her feisty temper can live without a gentle and quiet spirit admonishing her. Though they have the same faith, their dispositions differ as much as knife and spoon, Josie's manner all the tougher in contrast. But saying she *would* left no room for *won't* or *can't*. Martina is here to stay. She has come to die.

Lying there, her mother still radiates beauty. Gone is all the color from her face, from her eyes, replaced with white and gray like the sky right before a storm. Josie knows that her mother, tired as she must be, gave away the reins of her life long ago, placing herself in the hands of God. Together they must simply wait, a course they both know something about.

LONG BEFORE THE IDEA of Josie but only six years after Lincoln saved the Union, she was born Martina Christina Hanson—or Smestad, depending on whom you ask—a purebred Norwegian in Wilmington, Minnesota. The land she knew as a girl still hugs the Mississippi River in the southeast tip of the state, Houston County, where I have driven and walked, where crops carpet deep valleys and high ridges, lush and rolling and very like those her father had plowed before coming to this country. Why Martina's father chose the land of ten thousand lakes we can only conjecture now, but history reveals that he might have been caught in a riptide along with thousands of his countrymen coursing west to find land. For Scandinavian immigrants coming down through Canada who were weary of travel, new poverty (a ticket to America could cost a year's wages), illness, and death, the short journey from the river provided welcome relief and made Houston County not only a place to begin but a place to rest. Martina's father might have settled here rather than somewhere else for one more reason, one more convincing than plat maps and homestead claims: quite simply, it reminded him of home.

Left to right: Frederick, Jorgina, Carl, Martin, Marie, and Martina Smestad Hanson, likely taken in Houston County, Minnesota, circa 1890

Martina fits all the modern stereotypes: she not only lived in Minnesota, but she farmed and attended a Lutheran church. As the oldest daughter, the second child of four still alive, she held her title well. A soft-spoken leader by example, young Martina worked inside the house, later assigned to gardening, milking, and tending hogs and chickens when her sister could assume the household duties. At ten or eleven she differed from other Norwegian girls in that she did not take a job. She didn't need to. Instead she worked the fields alongside her father and older brother. Though it would have taken her from home, a job might have been easier.

Martina's father proved to be a good farmer, thrifty and wise. One of the well-known Five Brothers who settled the county in 1853, he spent his first nights in America sleeping under the night sky, owning nearly nothing but the land beneath him. Over the next thirty years he chose well for himself and his new family, and some would say luck followed him, though he'd have attributed it to the goodness of God. Besides his wife and four children, he had aging parents to support, but their table never lacked food, nor their feet shoes, and he had the means for his daughters to drape their bosoms with long strands of pearls. Music filled their house, with Martina's brothers Martin and Carl on the fiddle and the piano, and their mother singing. Martina's mother worked just as hard as her husband, and together they gave their children the gifts of faith, education, and something even rarer: childhood. Martina finished eighth grade and still apprenticed with her father, quickly becoming skilled in things physical and mental. Later she must have believed that her father and mother could have given her no better inheritance.

As she grew, she developed the body of a dancer—grace in her arms and neck, a dramatic comparison to her mother, a round woman generally photographed with layers of an ample skirt ballooning from a chair. Martina's shoulders drooped sharply, as did her sister Jorgina's, unintentionally implying timidity or weakness.

Twirling to fiddles on a wooden floor, probably at a house party, a twenty-two-year-old farmer named Martin Tvedt first saw Martina. Three years her senior, he had been born to the second wife of a Norwegian immigrant in Houston County. Lips and books remain quiet on the subject of Martin's childhood, but we know that on Sundays he sat in the pews of Wilmington Lutheran Church, and he learned two languages from necessity—English at school and Norwegian at home and church. After fourth grade, the farm needed Martin more than Martin needed school, so from then on sowing and threshing instead of mathematics and composition filled his days. The burden must have weighed heavily on young Martin, as it would be several more years before any of his four younger brothers could join him in the fields. If the Tvedt home regarded happiness or peace as common during this time, the photographs don't tell, but Martin worked for his father into adulthood nonetheless, when his sandy hair and blue eyes looked down instead of up at the man who had raised him. Six feet tall and not quite thin, Martin assumed an imposing stance, and his face had taken on a proud and hard cast.

Martin courted Martina for a year before the Reverend Reque, a Lutheran, married them on September 16, 1891. Martin's brother and sister acted as witnesses, as did Martina's sister, Jorgina. The wedding picture shows the groom in a suit and boutonniere and the bride in a ruffled dress and delicate cape, flowers near her heart and in her hair, a slight grin between. He faces the camera, his left arm bent stiffly for his bride, his right behind his back. She faces him, allowing her left hand to reach across her body and gently grip the arm waiting for her. The groom makes no effort to smile. "The knot having been tied," the front page of the local paper noted, "a large number of invited friends accompanied the happy couple to the home of the bride's parents, where a wedding party was celebrated in grand old style. The presents were many and valuable and guests were unanimous in their expression that they had been treated to a happy social time lasting not less than twenty-four hours."

Martin and Martina Twite on their wedding day in
Houston County, Minnesota, September 16, 1891

Until now, Martin had earned his keep from farms and roads,
and though he showed skill at blacksmithing, stone masonry, car-
pentry, and dynamite blasting, he wed before he could become an
experienced tradesman. He didn't seem to much like farming, nor be
very good at it, but he was bound to it when he received the generous wedding present from his well-meaning in-laws: a fully stocked
farm adjacent to the Hanson land, one hundred sixty acres with livestock, equipment, and a house ready for living in. The land records
tell a different story—that Martin purchased his farm the following
spring for one thousand and forty dollars from Hosea Pease and his
wife. Either Fredrick Hanson gave Martin the money to purchase
the farm, or the family embellished the tale down through the years.

Assuming that the farm was a gift, Martin's son Henry later said that his father didn't deserve that farm, didn't know what he had. That may be so, but the Hansons also probably didn't realize that sandwiching their new son-in-law between their well-farmed land to the east and the west could produce an expectation that Martin, even at his best, would never reach, even if he wanted to.

If Martin had broken all the rules then and just said he didn't want to be a farmer, things would have gone much better all around. But he didn't, and this likely started him drinking the wrong way, this feeling of being trapped in incompetence, caged up with it as if serving time together. Drink would have been part of his heritage, and hers, undoubtedly accepted and even encouraged, but the nights of violent drunkenness and staggering walk couldn't have started before they wed, at least not as severely, since chaste and principled Martina would surely have taken God's name in vain before she married an alcoholic.

Perhaps not without a tinge of the bittersweet, they conceived their first child before news of the union could reach relatives in Norway. Martina bore daughter Minnie the following July, and her belly stayed swollen with life for the next several years: Clarence came in 1893, Manda in 1895, Benhard in 1897, Clara in 1899, Peter in 1901, and Henry in 1904. All the babies were born at home, probably with a neighbor's help, as Martin had a bone to pick with doctors.

The family became rootbound, even after three-year-old Clara died from choking on a kernel of corn, so Martin found a new farm at Beaver Ridge, halfway between Caledonia and Spring Grove and overlooking Beaver Creek, including a more modern house with several upstairs bedrooms, a large summer kitchen, and a forty-foot windmill. It borders that state park now, where the blue-ribbon trout stream I drove through twists its way through the valley. In January of 1905, Martin and Martina, pregnant with the son who would one day buy her a house, loaded up their wagon with all their belongings and their six children, aged two to thirteen, and moved fifteen miles to their new farm.

Martina, if she had any joy in those first years of marriage, had it here, disguised as relief. She now lived farther from her family, but life in the new house eased simply because she had more room and, increasingly, more help. (She bore Carl here, and the second Clara.) The belief that Martin would do better here, that maybe he wouldn't need to drink as much, likely refreshed her as if she had plunged into that cold-water spring in the valley below. Martin had proven himself as a poor farmer, but it's hard to tell if it resulted from him drinking so much or being just plain bad at it. The family survived anyway, even with the deep dent the bottle made in their savings and the resulting legal problems. The three oldest children, Minnie, Clarence, and Manda, only thirteen, twelve, and eleven, already worked outside the home, and Manda had started with pint-sized jobs at age six. In addition to the cleaning and feeding and the endless laundry, Martina gardened and raised chickens for egg money. She also picked berries, canned, and baked. She plucked feathers for pillows and mattresses, stoked fires, kneaded dough, churned butter. She made toys. She helped with butchering, and she carried out the chamber pots. She watched the children the best she could, tying a rope around little troublemakers who were prone to wander up windmills and yell, "Hi, Mama!" from the height. And each night she prayed with the children and put them to bed before sitting by the fire to knit and sew clothes, quilts, and socks in the quiet dark. She crawled beneath the covers late and left them before sunup the next morning to start again.

A bigger house meant a mortgage—the place had cost five thousand, twice as much as the first farm's sale price—and Martin's inability to pay led him back on the road to blue-ruin. When he drank he didn't work, which made the mortgage even more elusive and the load for Martina and the children much heavier. Regular trips to the table at breakfast, dinner, and supper became ice in hot hands; chores came first for the children, before meals, even if Martin failed to live by the same standard. They took turns working Sundays, not that they went to church regularly anyway. The children had to stay out of school to work, especially for planting and threshing, and by the time they returned to their studies during the cold months, at best they were far behind. Perhaps the family hid the bleeding ulcer Martin's drinking was creating; perhaps they didn't. Perhaps Martina's parents helped with clothing and pencils and the occasional sweet, as photographs show well-clothed daughters at confirmation in white blouses and large hair bows, sons in jackets and ties, though the finery can't disguise their faces, sad and too tired to smile.

The Martin and Martina Twite family, likely taken in Minnesota, circa 1910, just before the move to the prairie. From left: Martin, Clarence, Peter, Manda, Benhard, Henry, Carl, Clara, Minnie, Martina

Despite Martina's prayers, her faith, her clinging to the God of miracles who would not leave or forsake her, the tension in the home thickened, as if someone had left the fireplace damper shut. The family choked on it, stumbled around in it, feared it. Even so, and maybe because of it, Martin funneled his sternness into disciplining the family. He enforced simple procedures, such as mealtime, when the food always began with him, and the children had to eat everything placed before them, even bitter rutabaga tops. Or when he sat down to read his Norwegian weekly, the *Skandinaven*, and forbade all talk. Failure to comply resulted in severe tongue-lashings, whippings, or worse. Only Clarence, the oldest son, defied his father and exhibited enough boldness to fight with him about the main problem—the drinking. It had reached a point at which Martina couldn't have vanilla in the house, because he'd drink even that. Liquor transformed Martin into a mean drunk, and though no one has said that he beat his wife or children, Martina, upon hearing him trip his way up the walk—late, drunk—hid her babies.

Where he did his regular drinking remains a secret, as he rode into Caledonia, five miles from their farm in Beaver Ridge, only once each week. Caledonia in 1909 thrived with train tracks and smokestacks, steeples and houses of stone and brick. It also, as Martin soon learned, contained a courtroom, a judge, and a jail. The night that liquor unchained his demons and he bloodied another man into the hospital was the first time Martin faced an unyielding foe—the law. Then came a hearing, but more importantly a choice: Martin could go to jail for thirty days or vow to stop drinking. He didn't want to stare at the inside of a cold stone cell for a month, but it's hard to say whether he felt the same way about the bottle that made the mortgage, the failure, and his family shrink to a manageable size. Martin made his decision, and then the judge made his: he let Martin go.

From the way things went after that, it seems as though Martin meant what he said, and the law had scared him into sobriety. He must have known that he lacked the strength to stop drinking and provide for his expanding family, to farm and pay the mortgage, so the news that the government would give free land to homesteaders in the Dakotas resembled the prospect of bare feet after miles of shoes and blisters. The talk that had blown on the westerly winds across Minnesota told of other Norwegians settling in and around Bismarck, men and their families who had traveled from other corners of the Midwest, having won a fair price for their land, or immigrants who had sailed straight across the sea. State reports and magazines had dangled seductive numbers from just about any area that could be measured. Successful creameries dotted nearly every county in North Dakota, they said. Railroads, spreading vine-like throughout the state, winked, smiled, and printed booklets extolling homesteading up north. The land, they said, would never go hungry. The soil would "grow crop after crop of grain without impoverishment, and without the aid of fertilizers." Pages of letters and testimonials, all good, spit-shined these claims, like this one from a man in Mandan:

> DEAR SIR:—For the benefit of the renters in the East and those who say they are too poor to come a little farther west and get a home of their own, I say—"Shame!" There is no man but what can come out here and get a good home if he only has a little get in him, and if he hasn't that he is no good anywhere.

Since its birth in 1899, North Dakota had grown like a thundercloud over a lake. Double-digit wheat yields drew the desperate and enterprising, enough of them to increase the population by more than 80 percent by 1910 and the number of farms almost as much. Though the value of land had more than tripled, in the end, Martin's younger brother, Peter P. Twite, a young Minnesotan bachelor, likely tempted and teased Martin into the westward endeavor. Peter had staked his claim in 1905 and was proving up just at the time Martin got interested. Peter's letters home probably offered just the lure Martin needed. If his little brother could make a go of it, so could he. It worked: in the spring of 1910, Martin Twite left Houston County, Minnesota, in pursuit of the land that matched what he had to believe measured up to nothing short of a real-life fairy tale. But he sold the farm first—for two hundred less than he had paid for it five years earlier—ensuring that there would be no turning back.

When Martin left, the family had good reason to believe he wouldn't return at all or that he'd end up lying in a muddy gutter behind a saloon, bloody, sick, or dead. Their minds played tug-of-war with relief at one end and worry at the other, and talking with God likely helped the family know which to stick with. Martina's prayer, if she muttered any for herself, might have included the wish that he would stop drinking for good this time so that they wouldn't have to move after all.

Martin did come back, and when he did, he told the family to pack. Though he was sober, still they fought—they probably screamed and cried—but in early May 1910 they got on a train with a man they didn't trust for a land they didn't know. Saying good-bye to their families proved to be a grief in itself, and six hundred miles might as well have been six thousand for the distance it would put between them. They left the dead and the living, and when they would see each other again, no one knew. In just months Martina's father would die, but there would be no money to travel back for the funeral.

The two oldest daughters, Minnie and Manda, stayed behind to work for one year before joining the family, then the only income for the whole lot of them. The teenaged girls lived with their maternal grandparents and uncles, the younger of which had taken over their father's farm and, judging from a photograph taken during this time, did so successfully—at least at first. Uncle Carl stands behind his nieces, arms resting on a chair, his face warm with fatherly pride and a hint of one-upmanship. Fashionable hats sprout from the girls' coiffed heads, lace blouses and jewelry beneath. Their eyes, big and unencumbered, stand out, but Minnie's phosphorescent smile steals the photograph, all aglow.

For two days and two nights in May of 1910 the Northern Pacific rattled, the grass blurred outside, and the smell of coal wafted in through the windows. Far away, lights of farms and towns twinkled like stars hung too low. With two daughters left behind to work and one in the ground, there were eight of them, including three children under age five. When the sign outside said Almont, North Dakota, the family got off in the dark and climbed into a hayloft to sleep. The next morning they filled a covered freight wagon and rode twenty-five miles with a rocking and bumping that made sleeping or reading or talking next to impossible, their destination the brand-new town of Carson.

If they had arrived just a couple of years later, the bleary-eyed travelers would have seen hints of modernity: the Hotel Carson, the newspaper office of *The Carson Press,* the First State Bank. The children might have glanced into the postmistress' window or peered into the billiard hall when Martina turned her head. Close by would have sounded the clink of the blacksmith's shop, and the chatter of men in the hardware and furniture store. The creations in the windows at Velora Griffith's dress shop would have offered a temptation for the little girls and perhaps Martina, and the men with razors to their faces would have intrigued the boys. Martin, in his boyish excitement, would have bought the children a sweet from the general store, tens of sticky fingers becoming brown with the dust that coated everything like sifted flour. But not much of anything stood there when the Twites arrived.

They picked up their belongings—nothing they couldn't carry, shoulder, or drag—and followed Martin out of town to their new home. The family walked one mile south over the first hill, trudging along until he stopped, I expect about where I did. Then their hearts fell, hard and fast. A wide depression lay before them, surrounded by low-lying hills, as if God had swept and left the lumps under the rug; turning in a circle revealed only more flats and slight rises and far-off buttes, concealing any trees, lakes, and people they might have hosted. Only a tiny structure straight ahead and another off to the side interrupted the sea of grass. As the family neared, they noticed Louse Creek winding to their left and saw the dwelling for what it was: a small hut made of layered grass with walls two feet thick, coated inside with dried clay the color of dirty feet, whitewashed with lime, atop a cold dirt floor pockmarked with the tiny claws of field mice, muddy ceiling drip, and the ring of frozen water pails.

The government, under the Homestead Act, had given Josie's father one hundred sixty acres and whatever was on it, including the ten-by-twelve sod house and a granary a tad longer just beyond. Martin paid eighteen dollars in filing fees and a promise to plow fifteen acres over five years, though the folks in Washington changed their minds in 1912 and shortened it to three years. That someone had already broken twenty acres and raised two sod structures suggested a homesteader or squatter had come and gone. The family claims that Martin paid a man named Thompson forty dollars for the plot, but if he did, it was only to get the man to leave because no Thompson ever owned the land as far as I can tell. Martin had to have that land, the northwest corner of section twenty-eight in Thain Township, because his younger brother, Peter, had the southwest. Five years into prairie living, twenty-eight-year-old Peter still slept in a sod house, kept his livestock in a sod barn, and stored his harvest in a sod granary, although he had put in a well, staked thirty acres worth of fencing, and single-handedly managed one hundred twenty acres of crops over those five growing seasons. But Peter didn't stay. Not long after his brother arrived, Peter sold out and returned to Minnesota, leaving Martin's family in what some folks called "the desert." But Martin Twite buzzed with determination.

He had long ago seen himself as a pioneer, an American, and to prove it, he had changed his name from Tvedt to Twite.

That first year Martin saw nothing but green—on the prairie and in his future bank account. He built a new house and an addition, which looked like two pieces from different puzzles forced together. One side measured fourteen by twenty-two feet, with plank siding and a slanted roof, while its appendage, a smaller twelve by twenty feet, looked more like log cabin construction with a flat top. The windows interrupted the walls in strange places hardly worth mentioning. It seemed thrown together, the quickest way to get the family out of the granary, the overflow sleeping quarters.

That year he got his wife pregnant.

He built a barn with a henhouse and added onto the granary. He bought a team of horses named Ben and Tony, one cow, a few chickens, and some pigs, and he planted wheat, oats, and potatoes on the already broken land. The family met their neighbors, most memorably Austrian royal Jon Polzer on the east, the man with rags for socks who came over once a week for milk and gave each of the children a nickel. Martin constructed a privy twenty-five yards behind the house and dug the fourteen-foot well I looked into, though his son Henry said, "Waste water out of the cow yard could not have tasted any worse."

Martin and his three sons nailed together new furniture—benches, tables, a homemade counter with a dishpan on top. Martina stitched mattresses of straw and learned to operate a new stove. The older boys discovered places to hunt and trap muskrats and mink. They planted one hundred trees along the ridge and near the house.

The younger children started at a one-room schoolhouse, carrying lunches in half-gallon or Karo syrup pails—sandwiches of bread, butter, syrup, or molasses. When not working or studying, they ran in search of places to play, collecting glacial seashells on the buttes and arrowheads left behind by the Indians already on the Standing Rock reservation twenty-five miles southeast. Martin's sons and daughters ran the ridges of history, of Sacagawea and Sitting Bull, of Custer. In the evenings Martin continued to read the *Skandinaven* by kerosene lamp, except now it came by train to Almont, then by wagon train to Old Carson—the same way he had come—and the news was many days old.

And during this time not one drop of whiskey came into the house, by bottle or by breath.

Martin didn't know, and the agricultural industry didn't discover for many more decades, that each cow needs twenty acres for grazing. That means even if Martin used all of his land for cattle, whether Herefords or Holsteins, he could sustain a herd of only eight cows. The prairie unveiled many more things Martin didn't know, things he hadn't thought through or had chosen to ignore in his intoxicating ambition. Traditional plows didn't work as easily there; the rampant buffalo grass tangled like steel, and the plows needed sharpening every night, something only a blacksmith could do. Even if a farmer broke ground in one season, he couldn't count on planting until the following year. Most could not afford the luxury of building fences, with lumber so expensive and far away and, more significantly, the shortage of trees. And though enough creeks ran through the county, trees had trouble growing because not enough rain fell. One report I consulted said that a successful farm needed twenty inches of annual rainfall, but the central region of the state averaged only sixteen. The rain they did receive was cyclical, and a dry year could turn the topsoil into dust, blown away by the wind. The topsoil that stayed, initially virgin and rich with nutrients, soon became anemic without crop rotation. Frosts hung onto spring and jumped into fall, shortening the growing season and converting farming into a race.

Martin might not have considered that the rails of the Northern Pacific branch still led to nowhere, and no roads or bridges offered an alternative, only cow trails that would vanish under the first snow. To keep the family warm they would have to burn chips of dried cow dung and fill their lungs with the stinking fumes, and to keep their cellar from freezing they would have to pile horse manure up against the cellar walls. Even then, the frost would layer a quarter-inch thick on the windowpanes, creating a muted darkness inside the house, not unlike a foggy twilight, for weeks. The blizzards would ground the snow into talcum that flies into eyes and freezes eyelids shut. With illness and ice damage, the savings for spring planting could dwindle to pocket change.

He might not have thought about the smell, that the difficulty of bathing with a frozen pump and so many eyes in the house would lead him and many of the children to bathe only once or twice per month rather than go through the experience of washing after two or three others. Some of their neighbors, they would learn, washed even less.

Each spring the roulette wheel would spin.

The droughts would bring dust that coated the clothes and the stunted crops and the insides of mouths and lungs. The parched seasons would mean lower yields, if any, and worry over how to feed the cattle and horses, let alone the family, until the next spring. Once the well dried up, they would desperately shovel through the bottom of Louse Creek, like a dog digging for an old meat bone. And then they would just have to pray, and ask for a credit at the mercantile, because they would have nothing else.

Locusts, on a scale to impress even Moses, would be just as bad. The grasshoppers, in their sheer volume, would snap tree limbs and create a slick worse than mud, causing wagons to slide on the roads. The hoppers would come in clouds that darkened the sky, slowly moving across the horizon as if enjoying their form of torture, and descending with a dread equally as dense. They devoured anything green, eating the crops away, leaving a wake of naked stems and branches. Hail the size of grapefruit or fires like spilled acid devoured whatever the hoppers left untouched.

Martina watched all of this, understanding that her deliverance would never come from this land; saviors weren't plentiful here.

Josie and Martina waited two years: from 1958 to 1959 and into 1960. What roiled in Martina's mind for those two years apart from a good deal of prayer and meditation on Scripture, I have to wonder. As her shrunken life allowed only a few new memories, her imagination could work only with what had happened, what had been. Of course she had primarily known monotony, interrupted with punctures and gashes of the severest kind, so maybe more of the same didn't bother her. But questions, so many questions, haunt even the most faithful among us; why would she be any different?

She had raised her children in a violent and poor home. She had lost her husband and both of her brothers, all of whom troubled themselves with drink or worry or both. Two of her sons, with a third in question, had become alcoholics like their father. More than a couple of her grown children wanted nothing to do with the church, and a couple had converted to Catholicism. She had lost three small children to illness and accident—unnecessarily?—and a grown son to tuberculosis. Clarence—oh, dear Clarence—had gone away. And now she had buried her firstborn, too.

Just before Christmas in 1952, Martina rode in Minnie and Wallace's car with four other family members. A savage snowstorm fought for the roads. Between Viroqua and Westby, Wisconsin, near Tri-State Breeders, the weather won out; with the poor visibility and the slippery roads, the car hit another head-on. When the ambulance arrived, the paramedics took one look at Martina and decided she, being so much older and frailer than the others, should go in the ambulance. But Minnie was the frail one, bleeding where no one could see, yet she rode in somebody's car to the hospital. The minute she entered the emergency room, engulfed by a rush of warm air, she collapsed and died.

Minnie had lived out a chain of disappointments, and a freakish death at age sixty, when she still emanated beauty and grace and generosity, left a cruel irony to knot the end of the string. A mother is not supposed to see her children die. Martina knew nothing else to say except, "Why wasn't it me instead of her?"

What if she had been sitting elsewhere in the car? What if she had spoken up? She should have known that Minnie needed care more urgently. And the others? What if she had gone to the doctor behind Martin's back? What if she had prayed harder for him to stop drinking? What if she had loved Clarence just a little more?

Perhaps how she wound up being a burden to her children, Josie especially, the one thing she wanted to avoid, posed the greatest question. And she was a burden, not simply an inconvenience. No paid staff cooked and served her trays of food; no bedpan or catheter substituted for the bathroom. No nurse changed her clothes or bedding, read to her from the Bible. Her daughter did it all.

I imagine Josie talked to her. She had to. Her mother's eyes returned her gaze, even if no voice consistently accompanied them. Talking to her helped Josie remember her mother as a person, not an obligation; a gift, not a burden. So she talked to Martina about Terry, about news from Beverly and church. She might have even gossiped under her breath once in a while, at least what she would consider gossip, since her mother's room acted more as a confessional than a rumor mill. And the times when she sat and had patience forced on her, during feedings especially, perhaps they relived the silly moments. *Ma, do you remember when . . .*

Certainly Manda and Henry, Josie's two most reliable siblings, offered support, albeit limited since they lived many hours away. One of my favorite pictures from this period shows these two with their mother during a visit to the farm. Martina sits in a wheelchair in front of the farmhouse, and the expression on her face suggests she is trying to speak with some urgency or difficulty. Someone has pulled her white hair back in a limp ponytail; one hand grasps her bedclothes and the other the chair arm. Henry leans toward his mother, his hands on his knees, looking into her face. Manda stands at her shoulder looking down, one hand on the chair and one on her hip. Even the black-and-white of the photograph exhibits the signs that neither Manda nor Henry is young anymore; their hair is whitening, their middles thickening, and their eyes hidden behind plastic and wire frames. Though the camera didn't catch either of their faces directly, it's easy to tell that they can't stand to see their mother this way, that it pains them to the quick. Josie noted their names on the front of the photograph, and underneath her mother's name she wrote, "Sick."

Whether because of pragmatics or stubbornness, Josie alone acted as her mother's hands and legs, clinging to what she considered her duty and promise as stubbornly and unflinchingly as guilt clung to her. Her insistence on doing the right thing, on not putting her mother in a home, shadowed her reason, her view of her limitations. She willingly and adamantly took the responsibility of caring for her mother, but over time that commitment came to possess her. "It just about killed her," Mary says.

One of Josie's nieces, Lily Twite Bachmeier, remembers Josie telling the story of when a neighbor came by, a story that formed something like this.

The neighbor lady stops in on a Sunday morning to take Josie to church, seeing as Josie hasn't been in some time.

Josie, we've gotta go to church.

Josie doesn't want to go. Promises, obligations, sickness, chains. Excuses.

Josie, we've gotta go to church.

Does the neighbor lady notice how Josie has withered? How some of the lines on her face look as if you could stick a butter knife in them? Josie's hair has coarsened, her skin become almost jaundiced, pressed in by a fatigue as heavy as the air in the room, a staleness like the inside of a vault, curbing even the joy at seeing her neighbor, her friend.

Josie, we've gotta go to church.

Does the neighbor lady invoke or question Josie's Christian faith?

Something—persistence, guilt, or loneliness—makes the caretaker give in.

The two women drive off to Trinity. When they open the doors, they hear the organ humming and see Reverend Birkner making his way toward his seat in front. Parishioners scuttle to find their pews, facing forward. A couple of latecomers touch her elbow and say hello, good to see you, let's talk after the service.

Josie stops in the doorway, letting herself take in the place and its people. The neighbor woman stops, too, perhaps thinking this was a good idea, just what Josie needed. But then Josie speaks.

She points to someone in the congregation and names that person's pet sin. Drunkenness. She points to someone else. Carousing with someone else's husband. Lying. Cheating. Points and names, points and names.

Then she cries.

And cries.

And cries.

"I want to condemn these other people," she sobs, "and I'm trying to starve my mother to death."

The neighbor lady doesn't understand right away but comes to see that under the strain of caregiving Josie has fed her mother less and less food. A smaller cut of meat. Fewer carrots. Half a roll. She did it not because Martina's appetite had decreased but because Josie hoped her mother would pass on. She simply couldn't bring herself to say until now that she and her mother are starving each other.

She intended, if the word applies, liberation, not malice. Josie's niece, in the retelling, says Josie didn't even know she was doing it until that moment at the church, that it had been unconscious. She had taken no break since 1955. Dean and Stub had arrived, then Terry, and finally her mother—nearly five years of backbreaking caregiving. The story didn't surprise my mom when I told her, but it surprised me. That she would stubbornly cling to a responsibility until it turned on her strikes me as foolish, not inspiring. I have since seen it happen to other caregivers, people who narrow their worlds out of obligation or guilt or a twisted form of love, constricting their own oxygen supply. People who become living martyrs who can't live with their situation but can't live without it. So perhaps Josie was no different. She felt her burden, and it affected her—promise or no promise—because she was human.

Josie made it right. With a renewed focus on her faith, she determined to care for her mother until a natural death came. It came on January 28, 1960. As the winds blew powdery snow into chest-high drifts around the farmhouse, Martina Twite simply stopped breathing. Pneumonia. They called the ambulance. They shoveled a path down to the road. Then they carried her out the same way they had carried her in. She left behind her Bible—still at large to this day—and a note scrawled in blue that says, *If there is any moneys left from what I have saved up, it should be turned over to mission to carry on God's work.* The moneys totaled twenty-two dollars, and with the two hundred that poured in at the funeral, Josie distributed part to the church for building Sunday school rooms and purchasing cherub choir songbooks, part to a radio ministry, and part to the New Wilmington Cemetery, where they buried Martina in the frozen ground.

Josie and her sister, Manda, fought terribly over where to bury their mother. If any of the siblings could match Josie in stubbornness, it was Manda, who had a will of cast iron. Manda felt the burial should be in North Dakota, next to their father and sisters in the cemetery in Carson. Josie felt it should be right there in Minnesota; her mother had started there, and she should end there, next to her folks, her brothers. I would guess that her insistence stemmed less from principle than from pragmatics: sending a body six hundred miles cost money, and she was simply too worn down to make the trip.

Josie won because she had assumed the caretaking, and the funeral was at Trinity. At the funeral, Bev Larson from Cashton sang Martina's favorite communion song in Norwegian, and Bev and Mary sang "Old Rugged Cross" with a little help from Uncle Waldo and his daughter Joan. A sterile obituary listed only the facts, the dates and places, the generations that survived her, the sum of her life: "She was born July 18, 1871 in Caledonia, Mn. In 1891 she married Martin Twite, who preceded her in death. Most of their married life was spent in North Dakota on a farm."

For many years Martina prayed three things. First, that she would see her son, Clarence, again. Second, that she wouldn't be a burden. And third, that her brother, Carl, would stop drinking, though that prayer probably expanded to include her husband and sons at different times. But Martina received no miracles. She never saw her son. She weighed on her daughter until the last breath. And the bottle had the last laugh: on her grave, her name is inscribed for all time as MARTINI TWITE.

The Eight

JUSTICE IN THE LIFE and conduct of the state is possible only as first it resides in the hearts and souls of the citizens.

I am certain Josie didn't miss those words.

I picture her tilting her head back, reading and rereading the words painted in the plaster cove above the white-haired judge. Hypocrisy! The citizens have displayed justice; the court has not. The court, the county, the state—the whole lot of them. It should read: *Though justice may vanish from the life and conduct of the state, it carries on in the hearts and souls of the citizens.*

Her eyes lower to movement at the front of the courtroom. They are hearing another case: unfamiliar words spoken, papers passed, suits standing and sitting. She doesn't know much about this Judge Martin Gulbrandsen, but he has yet to impress her. County judge for twelve years now. An older man, close to retirement, Norwegian, Lutheran. Father to five. He should understand.

The iced branches outside just beyond the bench jerk slightly, like the leg of a napping dog. It's warm in here. She could almost fade off for a few moments—

TOCK TOCK TOCK.

The gavel startles her, and the bailiff speaks, a chesty baritone ring. "In the matter of Edward and Irene Broadhead," he begins. Josie rises and walks toward the front of the courtroom, feeling a swell of anger as she reads the quotation again. Her thighs press, almost bounce lightly, slowly against the walnut banister. On one side of her stands Lee, on the other their nephew, Edward Broadhead.

Judge Gulbrandsen lifts the folder before him and studies it to refresh himself. "Says here that the county has deemed unfit parents Edward and Irene Broadhead, and in the interest of the children, the county would like to remove the eight children from the home and place them in foster homes." He flips between pages. "Apparently the welfare department has identified several homes willing to take in these children, seeing as no one family can be expected to take all eight."

"That's not true, your honor," Josie says. She adjusts her glasses, which are part brow line, part cat's-eye.

"You will speak when spoken to in this courtroom," Gulbrandsen says sternly from his platform. With Josie standing, the two are at eye level, about ten feet apart. "Who are you?" he continues, as if seeing the three for the first time.

"I'm Josephine Broadhead, the children's great-aunt, and this is my husband, Lee, and this is the children's father, Edward." Ah, yes. He has seen this woman before, and it wasn't pleasant then, either.

"The county has decided, Mrs. Broadhead. We have informed the parents," he says, motioning toward Edward, "and this hearing is merely a formality."

"That's why we're here, your honor," says Josie, gripping her purse and the banister with both hands. The two round mirrors on the back wall reflect her dark gray hair and widening middle wedged into a fitted dress.

"I don't think you understand what I'm saying. The children are already placed with foster families who plan to adopt them."

"But you can't break up a family. You just can't. Edward has tried to work with the county, but this county has failed him. If you people had—"

"That's enough, Mrs. Broadhead," Gulbrandsen interrupts. "There will be no disrespect in this courtroom, or I'll hold you in contempt."

"What I'm trying to say, your honor, is that Edward has done everything he could possibly do to keep his family together. As you probably know, he's already lost one son, and he's fought like the dickens to get that son back. But instead of that happening, he ended up losing the rest of his children. And there's just no sense to it. No sense." Her eyes widen; her nostrils flare.

"But it's all here, Mrs. Broadhead, in the report. The parents are unfit. The children must be removed. It is our responsibility to look out for these children, regardless of how tough a time the parents have had."

"Then give them to us."

"Begging your pardon," the judge chuckles, "but you want to take all eight children. At your age?"

"You said you couldn't find anyone to take all eight. Well, Lee and I will. We've got a farm out in Mormon Coulee with lots of room—our kids are grown now—and we've had experience caring for troubled children. You can't break up this family. Not when there's relatives and a good home waiting to take them in."

"But there's the problem of time, Mrs. Broadhead. These children need to be moved immediately, and you aren't certified foster parents. We don't know anything about you. For all we know, we could be shuffling this family from one dilapidated situation to another."

"We've been foster parents for one boy going on ten years now. You can check with La Crosse County. I think you'll find our records to be acceptable."

Gulbrandsen leans back in his chair, his black robe reflecting the sheen of the overhead lights, each of which looks like a scale. He absentmindedly rubs the routed edge of the bench, worn light and shiny. The judge considers what he has heard. Nobody tells him what to do. This is his courtroom. If he gives in to this woman, he not only discards the county recommendations and all the arrangements set in motion, but he also defers to a nobody—a woman, at that. But if he doesn't concede, it will soon be known that he had a chance to keep a family together and didn't, and this matter will not die quietly. The state could get involved. It will get messy.

Josie looks over at Lee and then at Edward, each of whose mouth straightens into a tight-lipped line, expressing at once worry and fear and love.

"All right then. The court remands the eight children of Edward and Irene Broadhead to the care of Lee and Josephine Broadhead, pending verification of their qualifications as acceptable foster parents."

TOCK TOCK TOCK.

Josie is pleased, mostly. She got what she could. But Edward can't help himself. He throws his arms around Josie and weeps.

MAYBE IT DIDN'T HAPPEN exactly this way. Josie did go to court, and she did argue with Judge Gulbrandsen, and she did convince him to give her custody of those eight kids. I have visited that courtroom, seen where they stood, sat, fought. Other than that, I couldn't really say, since the court has destroyed its records, and any known witnesses have died or vowed silence.

Or maybe, like Josie, I have an overactive imagination.

AS THE SECOND OF TWO surviving sons born to Minnie and Wallace Broadhead, Edward was tied by blood to both his uncle Lee and his aunt Josie. A birth date in 1922 made him old enough to remember when Josie came to live with him during her high school years. The Dakota prairie lay claim to his childhood, but after George died in 1938, the will offered Wallace a choice between the Dakota farm and one in Wisconsin. After nearly twenty-five years of struggle, there was no question: he chose Wisconsin.

Edward and the younger kids moved with their parents, while the older son, Lenoth, stayed behind and took over the Dakota farm. Minnie and Wallace tilled the land a handful of years in Vernon County, Wisconsin, before deciding to retire from farming in the early 1940s and buy a house in Viroqua. They offered the farm to Edward on March 1, 1951: one hundred ninety-eight acres, "more or less," for twelve thousand dollars, payable at five hundred a year without interest. So the second son took over the second farm.

With a hat pulled down over his face, Edward looked like any of the other Broadhead boys. He shared their thick, fair hair, and his eyes formed two blue slits, just like theirs. A sturdy build and a naturally stoic face presented an air of strength and confidence, though his brow sloped slightly downward on either side, suggesting sadness.

Edward had already been married to Irene Miller for four years when he assumed control of his father's place. Irene, slightly shorter than Edward, also claimed a farm in Vernon County as home. Born in 1926, four years and a day after her husband, she seemed to enjoy a happy and normal childhood. Photographs with her good friend, Gunnel Lavold, show her posing in a two-piece bathing suit or grinning widely in a photographer's booth in Red Mound, the girls' temples joined in girlish affection. Irene's dark hair cascaded to her shoulders, full and wavy. Her brows arched at the outside corners, framing eyes that became narrow when she grinned. Her mouth curved up sharply at the ends, showing only a few teeth but proving that she knew how to smile for the camera.

Despite her lipstick and open-toed shoes, she appeared plainer than Gunnel, less petite than her other friend, Dorothy. But she attracted Edward's attention, most likely at the dance hall across from the Viroqua Dairy. They married just after her twenty-first birthday in 1947, and they had their first child the following summer. No one remembers where they lived those first four years. Perhaps they lived on the farm so that Edward could prove to his father he could run it.

When they did take over, Edward and Irene raised Holsteins and tobacco—fairly sure ways for a farmer to make money. The children came with just about each new planting season. Susan was born at Vernon Memorial Hospital in 1948. Michael followed in 1949. Curt came in 1951, Eric in 1953, and Jill in 1955. Two years later Nancy arrived, followed by Bobby in 1958. But then number eight, Mark, came home in August 1960, and everything fell apart.

Caring for eight children under the age of thirteen is enough to cause anyone to panic, and Irene did. One relative says, "In those days we blamed so much on Irene, being Catholic, for having so many kids." But Irene wasn't Catholic, she was Lutheran, and it wouldn't have mattered if she had been Mother Mary because she needed some kind of help holding down that household.

Postpartum depression evolved into a nervous breakdown. Edward and Irene, realizing she needed help, gave baby Mark to Irene's brother and sister-in-law, Don and Dorothy, to care for while Irene recovered. With only two other children, the Millers were happy to oblige. By the time the baby started to walk a year or so later, Irene's strength had returned sufficiently for her to take the child again. She and Edward never dreamed of any problems with the exchange, but as the story goes, when Irene went to pick up Mark, her sister-in-law said, "You have so many. Let us have this one." In other words, her brother and his wife refused to give the baby back.

Josie wrote, "I'm not a swearing person, but this is one time I'd like to have sent a car-load of something at Welfare. They did absolutely nothing to bring back her baby Mark. If they'd of did something about it, I feel this whole case would have turned out differently."

Three more years passed without legal intervention into the "kidnapping." Edward sought help from the county judge, Martin Gulbrandsen, and the county sheriff, also a Gulbrandsen. He approached three Lutheran ministers and numerous friends and family on both sides. Josie, having learned of the situation, accompanied Edward to many of these places. One time, the children's attending physician, Dr. Gorenstein, asked the Millers to bring the baby to the hospital so that he could "properly diagnose" the case, working with the Broadheads and likely intending to turn the baby over to Edward. The Millers failed to show.

Edward, desperate for ideas, went on a payment strike, refusing to pay his bills until the law returned his child. "What alternative did Edward have?" Josie wrote. "Irene was becoming erratic. They were fighting constantly over the baby. What affect did this have on the children in that household?" His plan backfired; Edward lost his livestock, and the Land Bank threatened to repossess the farm. Edward's father, Wallace, who had originally owned the farm, began foreclosure to prevent the bank from getting the land, or he would have lost out, too.

Presumably trying to help, a local family took one of the boys, Bobby, for an unknown length of time. Forced charity. According to Irene's friend Gunnel, Mrs. Mina Ellefson drove down to see the family for a visit and came back with the boy. Mrs. Ellefson brought him back to Edward and Irene only "upon threats and then reluctantly." Once she had him back, Irene favored Bobby above the other children, except Jill, who had undergone a serious eye operation, presumably because Irene feared she would lose him, too. Soon someone else diverted the attention from Bobby and Jill: yet another baby, Allison, number nine.

Folks claim that neighbors began to complain of children ill fed and clothed, and that the fighting over the baby Mark never stopped.

Gunnel Lavold remembers taking baked goods down to the family, giving them a wood stove, a bed. She recalls a sparsely furnished house and a grime covering what few items the house contained. When Lee and Josie took bags of groceries down to the house, the kids tore into them without even waiting for their great-aunt and uncle to leave. Rumors still circulate of how bad it really was up on that farm, of Irene burning straw to keep the family warm, of dirty children hiding underneath porch stairs and the like, but no one knows for sure except those kids, and, like Daren, they aren't talking. I can't blame them, since no one wants to remember, let alone broadcast, this kind of ugliness. But this much we know: the county intervened at last, and Edward begged Lee and Josie for help, and they all marched into court in January 1964.

Their appeal worked, and that same month, those eight kids, Susan to Allison, aged fifteen to one and a half, moved to Breidel Coulee. Josie was fifty-two, Lee fifty-four. I have heard Bev say more than once, "Mom always said that the Lord sent her Terry to prepare her for the eight." Tears work their way into her eyes by the end of that sentence. Every time.

SOMETIME AFTER, AN ADOPTION WENT THROUGH, and the state of Wisconsin promptly blacked out Mark David Broadhead in the B birth index and squeezed him between some Ms. They typed out a new certificate showing that at his birth on August 7, 1960, at 2:33 in the morning, his mother and father were Don and Dorothy Miller. No one would ever have to know.

"WHEN THE CHILDREN CAME TO US they were very much disturbed," Josie wrote. "They were quarrelsome and frightened. The damage done to these children can probably never be erased. Each had their distinct impairments." Keeping an eye on all eight varied little from trying to hold an armload of live fish. Susan, used to being a surrogate in her own mother's emotional absence, bucked

Josie at every turn. Just a few short months later, she finished the school year at Central High in La Crosse and then moved to Minneapolis before her sixteenth birthday to live with the family of Delores Broadhead Carlson, her father's cousin. Being in the drugstore business, the Carlsons were considerably well off. Probably Josie made the arrangement, as Susan's presence had led to a civil war within her home. With Josie now nearing a normal retirement age, the generation gap threatened defeat even before she had begun, and she didn't need any other counterforces.

Even before Susan's departure, Josie first dealt with practical matters, starting with the furniture. She had purchased a living room set, referred to as "the green set," but the way these children behaved, she knew it would become "the brown set" in no time. She traded with Lawrence and his wife, Karen, who had bought a couple of Beverly's ratty daybeds. Those kids could climb on those daybeds all they wanted, but the long, curved golden sofa purchased specifically for Mary's upcoming wedding that July stayed off-limits.

She found them all places to sleep upstairs; the kids could choose from five bedrooms now that Terry, Martina, the hired help, and her own three kids had vacated the house. Four boys and four girls made division simple, though the ages still complicated matters. Many of the kids wet the bed, and they had grown used to either sleeping without sheets or sleeping on the same ones night after night. But in Josie's house, sheets, blankets, pillows, and pillowcases topped their new beds, and if anyone wet at anytime, the bedding came off. Josie found herself training the kids to strip any wet beds daily and toss the covers down into the basement for washing.

The boys got crew cuts, the girls pageboys. They went shopping, purchasing clothes and shoes needed for every size, school supplies, and more food. The laundry piled higher than it had with the hired men: dozens of mismatched socks and pairs of underwear, heaps of shirts and skirts and dresses and pants. She strung clotheslines in the basement stairway, and there she hung all the socks and underwear, a mystery for the children to solve themselves.

The kids also didn't know how to sit for a meal. They grabbed food when they saw it, when they were hungry, presumably because they had not known for a long time—some of them ever—when to expect the next meal. The children jumped off the bus from school, rushed into the house, and ravaged the kitchen for something to eat. Josie soon discovered that she needed to have a full supper hot and on the table when that bus pulled up so that she could teach them to sit and not only eat a meal but eat it properly. In the morning, she often fixed pancakes, and the instant she placed a stack on the table, the older children stabbed and horded, leaving empty plates in front of those with shorter arms. Josie said, "I will keep making pancakes. There will always be food here."

Every morning, like a scene from a 1950s happy household television show, she made the children sing. Allison, nineteen months, didn't sing. She didn't talk, either, for quite some time. "The kids were all close together and they were the most quarrelsome-hittingest kids I've ever seen," Josie wrote. "Why they fought to kill, and they fought over everything and nothing. I had to figure out ways to keep the kids from hurting each other. Man we tried everything and I mean everything! Finally we learned music did something to them. I've got the world's worst voice but the kids didn't know that so we sang and we sang. We played games with music before they went to school, after they came home from school, every chance we could . . . even tiny Allison after she learned to walk, joined in. She got so she could sing and say all those little nursery rhymes. She was sharp as a whip, no kidding."

Into this chaos Mary came walking in May 1964.

The lilacs blooming next to the barn greeted her as she emerged from the car, newly graduated. She was glad to be home, even for a little while, even if it meant being separated from Dennis. They were to marry July 25 in town and then move to Indiana, where she had a social work job waiting for her in Gary. They had met at

Elmhurst College, where Bev had attended, and where Mary had started as a freshman the summer after Martina died. Dennis, the only son of a steelworker from East Chicago, Indiana, had studied history and played football. He had been working in the steel mill with his father since his graduation a year ago to save money for the two of them. A thoroughbred city kid, he still didn't quite know how to operate a tractor, and the dent in the garage post proved it.

Lawrence and Karen had already been married for two years by now, having met on a blind date. Lee and Josie's first grandchild had arrived in September 1963, named Judith Lee, after her grandfather. As Lawrence still worked for his dad, they lived in the white house. Like his grandfather Martin Twite, he knew his future had solidified: he wouldn't be a vet, he would be a farmer.

Beverly was scheduled to come home soon, too, flying in from Europe, where she had been working for the USO. She would arrive in time to help whitewash the barns (fronts only). Beverly herself was to marry just a year later; she would wear Mary's dress and wed in the same church, but with a flair that is all hers, drape lace over her head.

Mary knew about the kids, but it took mere seconds for pride and expectation to turn into disgust and resentment. Piles of dishes lined the counter. *Piles*. A series of thuds traveled across the ceiling above her. She could make out screaming and yelling, laughing, a radio playing somewhere far off. She wandered into the dining room, stepping over balls and dolls, schoolbooks and stray shoes. Underwear. Her expression sagged sour as one question quickly formed: how was she going to explain this to her soon-to-be mother-in-law, a very proper Romanian woman from Indiana?

She sulked for a few days and then made it clear to her mother that those kids would *have to go* before the wedding. She had shared her house and her mother with kids for a long time. This was *her* time, and she didn't mind saying it. Josie agreed; the children would stay somewhere else the weekend of July 25.

Mary soon learned the difficulty of this task. She watched her mother juggle music lessons and 4-H clubs and softball leagues. Simply getting the children to church in one bunch created a challenge, and they went often, as the kids participated in confirmation and church programs. Little Trinity Church, for its part, upon learning of the situation, responded with food and clothes and gifts. The first Christmas, Josie recalled, "the gifts came pouring in from every one until the little tree was all but covered. Proof positive of Love's power. The generosity of the people again made such a deep impression on us that I vowed that these little ones that was taken from their house in a turmoil of bitterness, should if at all possible be reunited with the ailing parents."

IN A CRUEL TURN OF EVENTS, Irene found herself pregnant again during the whole legal battle over her children, and she delivered another daughter that May. Almost immediately after giving birth to Kimberly Christine, Irene was transported to a hospital in Mendota. The authorities allowed her to take the baby along so as not to produce any further trauma. "By this time," Josie wrote, "both parents were emotionally and mentally ill people. The Vernon County stipulated the father pay 50.00 per month for the support of his children. Edward refused on the grounds that the whole proceeding was wrong. He openly accused the Millers of kidnapping his child. His wife was now erratic and accusatory. What affect do you think this had on the children?" Regardless, six weeks into the arrangement, a social worker called Frank Patterson at the Northern States Power Company, where he worked as a lineman, and told him to get ready for a baby girl.

"We heard things and it was none of our business, and we didn't let it bother us," Frank says now. "But maybe it encouraged us to try to adopt Kim. We didn't know a lot about the circumstances, just that she was a sweet baby and started out that way, and all's we were going to do was take care of her. . . . We always told her of her circumstances, that she had parents, that we were just takin' care of her. I mean, she always understood that, that she had parents."

After the hospital released Irene, she and Edward moved the thirty or so miles to La Crosse. Josie claimed that they came to see their children often, though her family remembers differently. They say that Edward came to the farm occasionally, as did Irene, though she couldn't make herself get out of the car. Whether at the farm or at church events, such as confirmation, Karen says, "[T]here was always a Plan B because they never knew if [Irene] was going to blow her top."

But they called. "[Irene] called every day, sometimes several times a day," wrote Josie. "Irene resented me (I had replaced her as the mother figure). She repeatedly told the children they didn't have to listen to Josie, they didn't have to work because I was being well paid for this service and etc. We understood her condition and when she used abusive language on me I would explain to the children how badly their mothers nerves were so we could keep the lines of communication open between us and the children."

The Pattersons visited, too, bringing Kim to play with her brothers and sisters. "I was so thankful that she was brought up to know them," says Frank Patterson. Normally a soft-spoken, steady man, here his voice cracks, and his kind blue eyes water. Josie brought the other kids to the Pattersons', and Edward even stopped by once, though Frank says Irene never did. The Pattersons, who had taken in five or six other foster children, adopted Kim when she turned eight, and she lived with them until she reached adulthood. "I always wondered if we did the right thing," Frank says on his decision to adopt Kim. "I just didn't know. I know I wanted to very badly, but you're taking away part of a family."

In July of 1964 Lee and Josie drove to New York to pick up Beverly when she returned from Europe, leaving some of the children with Lawrence and Karen and some with Edward and Irene, for which they had obtained permission from the county. Josie wrote about it in a letter to another family member: "We knew [Irene] loved her children dearly and we hoped this would convince her we were doing everything we could to help her out of her situation. She was lucid but terribly emotional, asking constantly for her baby Mark. So we went to New York, when we returned and went down to pick up the kids and Allison couldn't talk. She grabbed ahold of Lee and hung onto him for dear life and just stared at him and me. It was the most heart-breaking sight you ever saw. We brought her back and took her to first, Helen Hanson. You remember her. She had been our County nurse for years on end. She was a friend of ours. Well then we took her to our doctor. Both diagnosed as some kind of shock she had gone into. She was that way for the next two weeks. She came out of it. Thank God for that. We never did find out what caused it. The other kids were too small and Irene and Edward never did tell. I rather suspect it was the emotional atmosphere of the home."

With Susan off in Minneapolis, life at the farm settled down for the seven. A photograph taken that first summer shows Beverly's then-boyfriend Bruce standing next to Dennis and Mary, who balances Lawrence's baby girl Judy on her daddy's back. On the ground in front, Allison sits straddling Beverly's legs in a striped green dress, and Eric leans against Bev's shoulder. Nancy and Jill nestle together in matching red tank tops and cat glasses, Michael and Curt squint above white T-shirts, Bobby wears a toothless grin, and Terry Tharp, recently graduated from high school, squats on the very edge. Lee and Josie stand almost to the side, Lee looking at the camera, Josie looking at her family.

EDWARD AND IRENE COULD NOT KEEP JOBS in La Crosse, and they continued arguing about Mark. Shortly thereafter, Edward left Irene for good. He moved to St. Paul, where he worked construction as a cement finisher. Irene, staying behind, became a waitress at the Stoddard Hotel and got pregnant with her eleventh child.

A son, Aaron Will, was born, and most folks deduce in whispers that the baby could not call Edward his father. Like Mark and Kim, the state gave the child to a family—this time in Bangor. And, like Mark and Kim, the government crossed out his name in black ink, and he was a Broadhead no more.

Josie: "When Aaron Will was born and turned over to the La Crosse Welfare and the children heard about it. They were crest-fallen and bewildered. Jill became violently ill. She threw up for three days, not talking all during that time."

While Kim had regular contact with her eight siblings, Mark and Aaron remained sequestered. It's hard to say who knew what, when, and how much. Kim and Mark attended public school together all the way up, but no one ever discussed the possibility of their being related. The Pattersons didn't change Kim's name until they adopted her at age eight; the Millers followed a similar path, formally adopting Mark when he entered second grade and giving him the choice whether to keep Broadhead or take Miller. He chose Miller, the only family he had ever known. But for a time, two Broadhead children attended school in Viroqua, not knowing they shared the same parents. "I was an early teen when I grasped that Kim was my sister," says Mark. He didn't know about the other nine until he turned sixteen.

When Kim came home from college one time, she accompanied Frank and his new wife, Marge, to a Viroqua High School basketball game. The opposing team: Bangor, the town where her half-brother Aaron lived. "We were playing them that night, and I remember her just *scanning*," Marge says, "she was just panning, trying to see if she could see one that resembled the family, because it really bothered Kim that she never knew that *one*."

Irene moved to St. Paul, though not to reconcile with Edward—at least that was not the confessed reason—and this dealt yet another blow to the children. Jill, especially, took it hard. "We couldn't reach her," Josie wrote. "Her grades in school fell and her whole attitude changed." Lee and Josie kept in touch with Edward and Irene, but the custody situation never resolved itself. "As for the parents," Josie continued, "at this point they are sick and bitter. Whether or not it is possible to restore the mother to normal functioning only knowledgable men can advise. As for the father . . . he is very bitter and has a deep seated unhealthy resentment which has completely absorbed his being. Whether a restoration of his rights would correct this . . . again only knowledgable men could advise."

As with Terry, maintaining guardianship for the seven involved no end of meetings and formalities, counseling sessions and caseworkers. The children's caseworker was Miss Eslinger, and you can believe Josie had a slew of angry questions for her and the children's counselor. She wanted Miss Eslinger to explain to the children "how all this trouble came about." What happened to their mother when Mark was born. Whether that was unusual. How it's possible to hold onto a child "without a court order and against the parents wishes." What this would do to any parent or any child, but especially to these children. What effect losing the cattle and the farm had on them. What the county did about it, any of it, and whether the county was "justified in terminating the rights of the rest of their children." How the county thought the children were affected when they learned they were going to be "scattered all over" (as Jill put it). Why they didn't receive professional counseling earlier. Why Kim and Mark had no visitation rights. What could be done now. Whether their mother could be helped. Whether their father could replace what he had lost. And finally, "Do we have the legal right to ask these questions or would you automatically remove these children from our home rather than solve the problems around which impaired the self image of all the childrens creative personality and which has impaired some of the childrens image for a life time?"

* * *

THE BOYS, OVERALL, handled the transition well—resilient, as people often say about children. The oldest, Michael, then fourteen, is remembered by a schoolmate as responsible and a "nice, nice guy." Compliant, shy, and helpful, in his own way he shepherded the younger children. Bobby, the youngest, developed a reputation as a "spitfire" and an "instigator," spoiled from his time with the Ellefsons. But Eric, only Eric, possessed the unique capacity to make Lee and Josie laugh, cry, and holler at the same time.

Eric Lee: a blond blue-eyed boy with a round face, a nose to catch sun and freckles, and a smile that pushed his cheeks into little pink globes. At ten he was "a very emotional child," beginning each sentence with "me." *Me want something to drink. Me want that book. Me don't want to go to school.* He began collecting flashlights so that he could stay up after lights-out and read comic books under the covers. Ever curious, he constantly found himself in trouble for doing what seemed good sense to him—things that didn't cause any harm but made any adults around him have to work extra hard.

The La Crosse school district had a crowding problem during this time and had begun busing students to wherever they found space. Because the farm kids came from outside town and had to be bused anyway, the district deemed them the best candidates for movement. Farm kids could be transferred to a different school each year. The children became even more ostracized as the new kids, the "dumb farmers." So the farm kids largely kept to themselves. "Seems like those boys got picked on a lot," says Jean Schmaltz Henderson, another farm kid who had classes with the Broadheads.

Eric became friends with another farm boy, John Oelke, and the two stuck together like gum to a hot sidewalk. They rode their bikes—how they got bikes in town remains a mystery—from Logan Elementary over to Super Ice Cream, later Bev and Bruce's place, after school. On Sundays, they paid for a matinee at the Rivoli and stayed to watch it twice before getting home for chores. Getting home on time posed no problem, because Eric loved the farm. He took every chance to feed animals and help Uncle Lee with field work. As he developed an interest in mechanics, Lee let him play with car and tractor engines. One time, Eric had been working on a Ford tractor and took a carburetor to school. He stashed it in his locker, planning to get a part that afternoon. Sometime during the day, a voice boomed over the school intercom: "ERIC BROADHEAD. COME TO THE OFFICE IMMEDIATELY." As John tells it, laughing, the fire department had already been called, and when Eric reached the office, he found the principal dangling the carburetor out the window, explaining to Eric that he couldn't bring parts to school anymore because they leak gasoline. (A foul-smelling puddle at the base of Eric's locker had apparently caused all the commotion.)

It was, I think, because Josie stood up for him that he loved her so. When he stumbled against some disciplinary problems in high school, Josie supposedly raised hell with one of the school counselors because she felt Eric wasn't getting enough support. If she allowed him to be a boy and gave him the space to become a man, then teachers and administrators, paid to do the same thing, should be no different.

Josie allowed Eric to have sleepovers, at which the impish little host would gather his guests around him, look both ways, and reveal a pillowcase full of flashlights, one for each friend, preparation for lights-out. One time Josie and Eric planned a sleepover for another boy who lived in the next coulee, Tom Moldenhauer. Tom's father, Frank, worked as an electrician, as his father had before him, and often ran wire out at the Broadhead farm. Frank married three times, all wives he shipped in from overseas—Japan, the Philippines. He fathered seven children with the first, and they all lived in a tiny cement block shack, what Josie called a "tool shed." He controlled and beat his wives and children, molested his daughters, kept Tom in a hole in the floor for no good reason—happenings that continue to haunt Tom to this day and drive him to his knees for comfort and deliverance.

So with seven troubled kids in her own home, Josie invited another and threw him a birthday party as he turned twelve. Tom had to beg his father to stay overnight even then, a wish eventually granted. That permission represented one small light among all the darkness, since that party turned out to be the only one Tom ever had.

THE FARM PROVIDED A PLACE for boys to be boys, where all four of them could run and be useful and tinker and drive and learn what they needed to be men. Josie's strictness, seeming to grow with each new batch of kids that arrived, dished them what they craved, needed, lacked. Lawrence's son, Paul, proposes—partly tongue in cheek—that they were simply Broadhead boys, meaning that they understood the idea of a strong woman and took it in stride.

While the boys flourished, the girls rebelled.

Everything that worked with the boys backfired with the girls, and when one girl had finished her clash, another waited, and then another, and another. Sometimes they worked in force against their aunt. Though the girls didn't necessarily have farm chores, Josie expected them to help out around the house, to follow the rules, leaving plenty of opportunities for rebellion, nagging, and hollering. "I think Grandma was too strict," says Lawrence's daughter, Judy Broadhead Stromwall. "I think that's what the kids as a family would say."

The girls arrived with their own problems. Josie had to deal with highly sensitive and spoiled Jill. She had to manage tomboy Nancy, "a good shot with a .22," according to Tom and John. She had to address little Allison's refusal to speak. Though the boys stayed through high school for the most part, the girls stayed with Lee and Josie only until they were old enough to leave, which is not difficult to understand considering that they had been displaced like water in a wake. They joined Susan in the Twin Cities as they reached ninth grade, which didn't come soon for all, including the little one, Allison. Ninth grade for her still waited a full thirteen years away, long enough for Lee and Josie to begin viewing her as their own child. June Matzick, Lee's niece by marriage, says of Allison, "Oh, Uncle Lee loved her. Oh, did he love that child." In 1975, Lee and Josie tried to gain legal custody of Allison, but Susan replied, in her father's name, "I do not approve of transferring the legal custody of Allison." In this same letter, even eleven years after the original foster care arrangement, Susan also writes, "I would appreciate receiving the custody status of Mark and Kimberly."

But until these children left, Lee and Josie cared for them and threw them parties, gatherings of children pulling taffy and playing cards. Lee and Josie fed them, clothed them, took them to church and school and the doctor and 4-H. And though her days continued no less hectic, Josie directed her gratitude toward her husband. "Not many men will accept all these kids that aren't his," she told me years afterward, but she should have said that not many men on the verge of retirement will take in enough kids to keep four homes busy. Everything works out for a reason: the same quality that had steered her husband away from conflict all those years enabled him to parent a whole new generation.

In 1970, Lawrence bought the farm from Lee and Josie, and they swapped houses. (They also swapped furniture because the long gold sofa wouldn't fit into the white house.) Lawrence and Karen and their family moved into the farmhouse, and Lee and Josie moved to the white house with the five remaining kids. Josie had nearly reached sixty, but her days had not slowed. For one of her writing classes, she had to keep a daily journal. Two days of the typed journal survive, most likely recorded that year, giving us the most detailed glimpse of her life with those kids.

Listen:

Saturday so got up at 7AM. Hollered at kids (girls) Boys were over to the farm.

Washed up stray dishes in sink. Weighted myself. Same.

Took folded clothes upstairs.

Got angry because kids have slung their clothes everywhere.

Sorted and arranged everything up there neat and clean.

Made kids clean out drawers and rearrange in neat order.

Put the looking glass on the bureau.

Had a pocket full of pins, thread, pencils, pens, and junk to replace

Had breakfast with the family. Listen to Bobby and Nancy's account of Octoberfest.

Karen called and didn't know if she dared take the baby to parade.

I offered to baby-sit. Sort of broke up parade plans for our kids.

Karen called back and said neighbor wasn't going; that she'd drive and our kids could go

Kids could only go if everything was cleaned up and in order.

Lee and Eric brought over the bookcase; put it in the basement family room.

Bobby had job of taking books down there. He was angry as usual, stopped around.

Allison had to wash up the dishes.

I cleaned up the front room and bedroom.

Finished work and got dressed and was over to Karen by 10:25 (all of us)

Helped Karen dress the baby. Took him in car. Karen drove our car to town.

I stayed at Bev's with the baby while the rest went to the parade.

I ironed as I baby-sat and watched the Saturday morning comics

Ate lunch at Bev's. Helped tidy up luncheon dishes.

Jill came. Nancy, Bobby and Allison stayed down town. Going home without them.

Was about to leave when the three kids came. Went home.

Got the Tribune, went and laid down on the bed to read as I was tired.

Fell asleep and slept for about 1½ hour. Relaxed by doing a stretch exercise.

Went downstairs to mend and saw a mountain of clothes. Such kids!

So washed, and mended clothes. Sorted out summer clothes to put away.

Bev came down. Visited with her. [Bev's son] Steve came, staying overnight.

Lee came down. Visited for awhile.

Phone rang. Jackie wanted number of the hymns as she has to play for SS.

Came upstirs. The kids had left a mess with their eating. Scolded Nancy.

Made Allison do up the dishes. Nancy wash woodwork.

Neighbor came over for berry plants, visited a while. Brought back tomatoes containers.

Steve decided not to stay so Bev took him home.

Called Jackie and gave her the number of the hymns.

Went downstairs and finished up the mending.

Came upstirs with a basket of clean clothes and folded them and sorted into piles.

Lee came in. Eric came in looking for something. Bobby got kicked by a cow, in foot

Scolded every ody because dining room rug was soiled. I've got to get a bigger rug there.

Ate some bread and milk with Lee. Eric had a hamburger. Bobby a roll.

Go up and washed the dishes, made up a ammonia solution to wash rugs.

Cleaned rug good and then washed it with conditioner.

Went downstairs. Took out last load of clothes. Sorted and ironed two pants.

Washed ice box and few spots Nancy missed.

Listened to news: Bobby soked his foot. Jill scolding as shampoo was all gone.

About ready for bed. Lee is in bed so are the kids. Nancy babysitting.

Will do a few muscle excerise, read a little and fall asleep with a prayer on my lips.

Good night journal

Arose at 5:30.

Made the bed. Did my stretch excerise. Tidied up the room.

5:45 hollered at kids and turned on light

Tidied up kitchen.

Hollered at kids again at 6:00 oclock.

Hollered at Bobby at 6:30 to get at his music. Girls working on their chores.

Nancy dropped the vaccum cleaner down the stairs. Fixed up Electrolux for her to use.

Scolded Jill. Picked up scatter rug and sewed it up. Sewed Allison's coat.

7:00 oclock and Bobby hasn't gotten at his music.

I gave Eric and Bobby a ultimatum: No TV for a week.

Eric went over to the farm for milk. Hollered at Bobby to bukle his shoes.

Big kids went off to school in sour mood. Nancy was angry because she had to write a letter

Allison finished her lunch, ate her breakfast and started on her music.

Got all the letters for Michael into the envelope . . . ready to mail.

Saw Allison off to school.

Was tired, wanted to lie down but couldn't.

Lee came in for breakfast. Visited with him as he ate.

Ate a bowl of oatmeal and a few strips of bacon.

Washed up the dishes. Went downstairs and made up a strong lye solution.

Took out the bathroom window and took it downstairs and applied the solution to woodwork

Let it set for about an hour. Then went down and scraped off old paint.

Washed it off and took it upsatirs on the cement roof to dry.

Brought the solution upstairs and applied solution to upper window in bathroom.

When window was dry. Painted it. Came in and scratched off paint on other window.

Washed off solution. Let dry and painted that too. Went and laid down to read, slept.

Made some telephone calls to get a Brownie sitter.

Went down to church and baby sat for about 10 little kids.

Played games and all sort of things for a hour with kids.

Came home and told the kids to make lunch as I was going to sand the cupboards.

Kids were still in a bad mood. Had to holler a couple time to get them going.

Allison helped me sand. After sanding varnished all the cupboards. Cleaned up mess.

Washed the floor. Got dressed had to take Allison to music.

Scolded Nancy for not having her lesson so made her go without supper to practice.

She was angry and was quitting music.

Nancy has to baby-sit at 7:15 for Karen. I had to be at a Homemaker Project meeting.

Drove to meeting but stopped at K-Mart and bought some thinner. Saw Bev and Steve.

Visited as I looked over some drapery material. Steve said where's "Grandma?"

Left K-Mart and was late to the meeting. Project meeting was on Drugs/Took notes, talked.

Came home. Lee was up. Asked about meeting. Eric furious because he had to go to bed.

No TV for him . . . or Bobby. Myabe they'll get up and do their chores. Gave them a scolding

Admired the smoothness of the varnish on woodwork.

Did my muscle excerise. Drank a glass of buttermilk . . . a nightcap.

Got out the typewriter and wrote my journal.

Got undressed. Will read until sleepy. Say my prayers and thank God for a fruitful day.

Good night Journal

PS. Killed a few box-elder bugs . . . on dining room door (also a wasp and a fly)

Visited with Karen when she came over . . . Judy looking for leaves.

Sorted out the bad cucumbers in garage.

Took out the garbage and dumped the paper.

Brought in the blankets from the line.

Sewed up the davenport pillow . . . recleaned the blue rug (corners and etc)

HER TOLERANCE DECREASED as her age increased. *There was an old woman who lived in a shoe. She had so many children, she didn't know what to do.* Her pitch wavered between extremes, like a broken volume button on a radio. Josie by her own admission shouted a lot, and teenagers and yelling don't get on too well. "She'd holler a lot, but you know, everybody needed it," John Oelke says, including himself in the mix. But she dished out punishment inconsistently. She'd holler and toss ultimatums around like Frisbees, but at times she'd talk through consequences and let the kids make decisions for themselves.

"One of the kids I caught smoking cigarettes," she told me. "I sat the kids all down at the table. I said, 'Okay, now there's that cigarette. Now you can smoke it if you want to,' I says, 'but you're going to hear the consequences. You may get cancer. And if you do, are you big enough to accept that? If you can, then you go right ahead and smoke your nose out.'"

Despite her sternness, all of the boys, as they left the farm one by one, came back. Eric visited the most, Michael on his motorcycle, Bobby in his Ford Pinto. If the girls returned, they didn't do so as regularly or perhaps with the same motives. "I think the girls came to flash their hippie boyfriends in front of Grandma and piss her off," says Lawrence's son, Paul.

Eventually the kids all lived in the Minneapolis area. They sought out their stolen brother, Mark, and welcomed him, though his demons ran too deep, and he slithered away. They keep trying, although he insists to me that he was never one to care about family. Aaron found his brothers and sisters, and even Lee and Josie; after a stint in the navy and a divorce in Chicago, he meandered up to the Twin Cities in search of connection and found it. They lost Curt to an alleged suicide in 1990, a drowning in the St. Paul River. They lost Eric, some think, to schizophrenia and then to the wind; he disappeared, and though he surfaces now and then, he always goes away.

All the girls married and have children. When Kim wed, all three of her mothers attended the ceremony: her adoptive stepmother, her adoptive mother, and her biological mother. None of the boys ever wed, except for Aaron, who divorced. They have held jobs with railroads and corporations and the government, and they get together for Memorial Day cookouts. They send Christmas cards to Mary and Beverly and Lawrence. But perhaps what says the most about them is this: they pooled their money to support their father and their mother, Edward and Irene, in old age. They have decided that their mother bears no blame for what happened, choosing to believe that she suffered from a medical condition; choosing to believe that it was not her fault, that she couldn't help it; choosing to let everything else go—a level of forgiveness that few ever attain.

"That is one of the neat things that has happened with the kids," Bev says. "I mean I think they see that they are a family within themselves, and I think for whomever has done it, they have created that unit, that they are a family. And they don't care about anything else outside of that, they really don't care, and they really don't care to get into the history of what their life was because it's probably very painful for them." Sometimes Michael rides down to La Crosse on his motorcycle and stops in to see Beverly, but the other kids stay away. They avoid family reunions and visits. It would have hurt Josie to know this, but she would have focused on the greater good.

"There were times that they ganged up on me, you know," Josie told me. "It's normal. But whether I did good or I didn't do so good, they'll have to always admit that we held them together."

Vista

Burke, Virginia
2005

So what do I make of this woman I called Grandma Josie and the trail she left behind?

She had no secrets. She wielded no magic wand, no anointed apron, no book of spells. Instead, she crafted finest hours from typewriters and prayers, pasted families together with plays and pancakes, and loved folks with vegetables and letters and bedpans until they died. She embraced monotony, accepted obscurity, and worked with what most would consider small change. It was a choice on her part; she'd wanted greatness, too. But in her imperfection and disappointment, she welcomed the ordinary, and the extraordinary came to her.

In other words, unlike me and my bee sting, Josie submitted to the needle.

This is the very thing that made her remarkable, the very thing I have not been willing to do. Any time the tiniest pain ekes its way into my space, I tend to howl and cry victim. Then I hole up and have a long visit with pity. Next I decide I am doomed to a meaningless invisible existence, that God must be punishing and humbling me forever. Faced at last with the choice of change, an existentialist purgatory, or death, I determine to revert to that which brought me measured success decades ago: *I'll show them.* Whom, I have no idea. The others in my generation, I guess, the ones who have written books and led companies and started movements.

Make a difference.

Be happy.

Do anything to avoid the needle.

So I jaunt here and there, looking, seeking, striving, envisioning greatness, accomplishing nothing.

If her life were mine, would I consider it enough? Would I consider it enough to help a pair of preschoolers or a rejected boy? Would I consider it enough to cook and do laundry for a bunch of misfits? Would I consider it enough to shelter a family of eight children, some of whom don't even like me? Would I consider it enough just to love people in very concrete ways, to serve and give as they

Josie Broadhead in Florida
in the late 1950s

come across my path, spending myself on them? I haven't been able to say that I would, and that's one of the most shameful admissions I've ever made.

In looking for a life of greatness, of humanitarian wow, I see now that I deluded myself into thinking it would be possible to help lots of people without much personal cost. Maybe some slide into significance, but I suppose that most have to work at it, one day at a time, one person at a time, as cliché as that may sound. And the truly great never think of these steps as a means to an end but as *the* end. Your life *is* the big thing, pain and all. Stop looking, and start living. And, with a little bit of grace, you get to the place where you can weep because your daughters don't recognize their lunches for the candy bars hiding within.

The paradox of a Josie life is that it traps as it sets free. It's losing to find, dying to save, being willing to step into the trap, the dungeon, or the cage because that's where the people are, where the need is. Your dreams stay on the outside. They may rust a little, and you might even let them rot completely because other things become more important. The paradox is true—I see it in her—but it's as if it taunts from the other side of thick glass blocks that don't end, give, or shatter. To do much of anything significant—healing, nurturing, helping, empowering, curing, teaching, even writing or inventing—involves people at some level. *If I speak in the tongues of men and of angels, but have not love, I am only a resounding gong or a clanging cymbal.* That means I must give away my time, my money, my space, my life. I must be willing to close myself in with people. And all their needles. That is the only true call, the only real way to an extraordinary life.

I'm not Josie, and this is no longer her world. It may not be for me to do exactly as she did, but if I use that as an excuse to avoid accepting the ordinary or loving people, then my problems run much deeper than I know. *If I have the gift of prophecy and can fathom all mysteries and all knowledge, and if I have a faith that can move mountains, but have not love, I am nothing.* Maybe being Josie means to give not simply because the need exists but because love is extravagant. And as much as I may try to believe otherwise, that is never ordinary.

Love is patient. Love, be patient with me; the blind are just starting to see.

Found

La Crosse, Wisconsin
2004

I AM SITTING IN THE La Crosse County Recorder of Deeds office, a place I have visited countless times before. Like their neighbor across the Mississippi, they, too, line their walls with stacks of books—land and birth and death and marriage—and I have been digging up more details to verify or contradict Josie's accounts and those of everyone else.

I open the death certificate book for 1991 and page through scores of carbon copies to the one I'm looking for: Lee Walter Broadhead. The typed words tell me that he died on December 18 at 10:21 a.m. in the emergency room, except I know it happened differently.

AFTER HE SOLD THE FARM to Lawrence in 1970 and traded houses, Lee was supposed to retire. By age sixty-one he had worked enough for two lifetimes. Retire he did—four or five times. Still he worked at the farm every day he could. He'd ride his bike over, drive or walk

263

the quarter mile to help his four grandchildren and their mother with milking in the morning and at night. He did understand that he was no longer the boss, that he now worked for his son; he came because he wanted to, because he couldn't let go.

Lawrence didn't have the same passion as his father; perhaps he farmed by default, because he was the oldest son in a generation that took their fathers' places. "I think Dad would teach you, and then Grandpa would come and reteach you," says his oldest son, Paul. Surprisingly little conflict occurred between father and son over how to run the farm. Mostly they talked. Everyone would pull up a five-gallon feed pail and sit around to hash things out. "You knew that you'd arrived when you could sit down and have a feed pail conversation with Grandpa and Dad," says Paul.

Lawrence quickly went into debt, buying expensive tractors and raising new buildings and pursuing his innovations. Lawrence bought the first silo press in Wisconsin. Had a round hay baler before a lot of other folks. Put in a milking parlor, used liquid manure, bought chisel plows before any other farms in the state. But Lawrence acted first, thought about consequences later. He liked to be on the cutting edge, or, as Paul says, "almost on the bleeding edge." His other son, Dean, agrees. "Dad had a lot of great ideas. I think the bad part about being a visionary or a dreamer is that you're a little bit too far ahead of the curve. In terms of business, it's not always good to be doing that." But Lawrence kept with it until near the end, because that's what he knew. Despite any resentment he might have had, when he was dying of pancreatic cancer in 1999, he had his sons help him into the truck and drive him around the farm one last time.

Lawrence's kids learned to farm the same way he had. Father faced oldest son after his first day of kindergarten and said, "Well, you're in school now, so it's time to go to work." I once asked Lawrence's kids about what they had learned *not* to do from their years on the farm.

A "retired" Lee Broadhead on the La Crosse farm in the early 1970s

"Be a farmer," Judy replied, laughing.

"Judy's not so far from the truth," added Dean. "We knew that farming was a tough business."

"I realized early on," Judy continued, "that it was a hard life for everybody because it's always there, you always have to take care of something. And it's a hard job, it's dangerous, and you don't make any money. But on the other hand, what's a better profession, to live out in the country. You own a piece of land, and you've really done something that's made a difference."

"All I know," said Dean, "is that my grandpa and my dad both were missing fingers, so I thought I should find a new profession."

The same silo that took Lawrence's finger caught fire in the early 1970s, provoking in him adult-onset asthma, a death sentence for anyone working in a cornfield or hayloft and what eventually made it near impossible for him to continue farming. That same silo lashed out at Lee in May 1980 as he worked the silo unloader, a conveyer belt that carried silage (fermented corn and stalks) from the silo to the cows in the barn. By that time of year, the silage would have dwindled to the bottom third of the sixty-foot silo. Like any machinery past its prime and left in the rain, the unloader threw temperamental fits. When the huge cast-iron wheels jammed, Lee climbed up the conveyer to fix them, but his rubber work boot caught, pulling his whole foot into the still-moving gears. He somehow worked himself loose and crawled to the middle, where he pulled the cord attached to the emergency switch, but the damage was done: no blood seeped from his foot, but the foot had hinged parallel to his shin. He crawled down the conveyer belt, dragged himself out from behind the silo, and hollered until Karen heard him. He kept his leg.

Just ten months later, when Lee was sixty-nine, the doctors performed quintuple bypass surgery on him, but he carried on like the ox he was for another twenty years until his heart finally gave out. His medical records show that the doctors recognized heart problems as early as the late 1960s, but his body of solid muscle and his iron will probably did much to stay the inevitable. The doctors continually told him to stop working so hard, though that hard work most likely kept him alive a lot longer than any relaxed schedule. But on December 17, 1991, he and Josie went to bed. He got up once during the night to use the bathroom, said he wasn't feeling well. Came back to bed and lay there. When Josie leaned over to check on him, instead of the usual warmth from his arms, chest, breath, she felt a coldness through his shirt, through the sheets. Myocardial infarction, the death certificate says: a massive heart attack.

I suspect she waited until the morning to call Lawrence or Beverly simply because she wanted to stay with him a little longer, to lie with the man she had shared her bed with for nearly sixty years. To feel his companionship, his presence, his hands one last time. She said later, "He went over to the farm, he cleaned out pigpens, ate lunch, took a nap, and died in his sleep. He did everything he wanted to do." Josie called her children, and then she called Ruth Seebauer Heslip, who rushed right over. This is the same Ruth who had lived and worked in Lee and Josie's house back in 1945. Who had—like Josie—become a foster parent; who now sews quilts so sick children in the hospital have something warm and homemade around them. Who, just five years later, lost her husband, adopted daughter, and granddaughter in one year but continued to crawl on faith and the same strength that got her through her time at the farm.

Just days before Christmas, with white on the ground, Trinity Church hosted the funeral, and then we all drove the hour south along the Mississippi into Vernon County. Up we went into the hills of Retreat, winding along to Walnut Mound, the Broadheads' cemetery, which sits on a hilltop overlooking farms in every direction, some of which once belonged to Lee's father and uncle, George and Albert Broadhead. The hole dug for Lee fell into line with George and Maud, Albert and Mabel, Mildred, Edwin, and so many of the others he had known and loved. The mahogany casket, draped in roses, waited, ready for us, ready for its last step. I don't recall what the minister said, what I wore, who stood where. I don't know who cried, who didn't. I kept looking at the trees; an ice storm had passed through the night before, coating everything in crystals, and the rising sun transformed the cemetery into a city of diamonds. The light dazzled off gravestones and branches and plastic flowers almost supernaturally, tempering the sadness with an exquisite beauty that seemed a unique but fitting gift. At last we said amen and crunched through the snow back to our cars, leaving Lee to rest under the shade of a walnut tree not all that different from the one that Dean and Stub had planted, the one that had sheltered him on the farm all those years.

I REPLACE THE BOOK ON THE SHELF and move through the volumes to 1994, a book the color of ripe cherries, with gold lettering. I pull it out and take it back to the counter. Again I flip through the pages until I find the name: Josie Broadhead. Received November 28, 1994. Died November 20, 1994, 12:00 p.m. Someone checked the box for nursing home as place. I begin to cry. Chronic congestive heart failure, dilated cardiomyopathy. Other significant conditions contributing to death but not resulting in underlying cause: depression, chronic atrial fibrillation. I recognize nothing new here, but tears crowd my eyes because a woman who lived such a life died alone, died sad, died in a place other than her home. And I wasn't there for her.

After the last of the eight left home, Josie began dipping candy at the store Bev and her husband owned in town. She and Tina worked for free, and the occasional chocolates that Lee and Waldo would sample when they came to pick up their wives. She continued volunteering with 4-H and church (Women's Guild, Centennial Committee, Sunday School). She gave speeches to women's groups about her "house of confusion," and about loving children. She traveled to the Holy Land. She entered the Ms. Senior Wisconsin pageant (lost). She planned family reunions. She spent much more time writing.

When Lee died, she tried to keep going, though losing him about scooped out her heart. "They really were a partnership," says Paul Broadhead, "in that she said 'let's do this,' and he would do it. He was the hands. She didn't move much, she sat down, and he did less thinking, she did more talking, and I think once Grandpa died, she got lost." Josie wanted to stay on the farm, but she could no longer live independently. Her heart problems had caught up with her, lessening her strength and mobility. So her children decided in 1993 that she should move into Shelby Terrace, an assisted-living facility in town. She reluctantly agreed because Bev and Lawrence still lived close by, and they would come every day to see her. "I really think that when she went to that Shelby Terrace, she thought that was where old people go," Dean says.

Immediately she tried to make the best of it. "From this day forward it's a new beginning," she said, "and God's gonna carry me through." She took her typewriter with her, and at the top of each new page she wrote, "A new beginning." She started organizing writing groups, to the dismay of the social coordinator, who sulked and suspected a slight coup. "They're just waiting to die," Josie said of her new neighbors, "but God's not through with me yet. When I see a starving little kid, I think it doesn't have to be. We can help one another."

Josie Broadhead at Shelby Terrace in La Crosse, Wisconsin, circa 1993

Although Josie, after caring for her mother, maintained that she didn't want to be a burden to her children, she became exactly that. In her loneliness and worry she called Lawrence six, seven, ten times a day, and Beverly just as many, almost begging to come live with them.

"She started this, 'Beverly, I'll, I'll stay at your house. I'll buy you a sofa.' Went through this whole thing," Bev chuckles. "And I said, 'No, Mom. It won't work, 'cause I work.' And the next morning the nurse came, and she said, 'No, Josie,' she said, 'you need to have more care,' and that was hard for her." Tears prevent Beverly from saying any more.

Josie's ability to write and speak declined rapidly after the move. She could not maneuver the pen or her typewriter, and it became too difficult to write anymore. She had spent her entire life doing, and she didn't know how to simply *be*. A depression settled in, and the doctors prescribed Ritalin and Prozac. She told her visiting nurse of suicidal thoughts, thoughts of despair, hopelessness, and valuelessness. They moved her into the adjoining center, Bethany St. Joseph's, and it only got worse.

When her friend Hilda First came to see her in the fall of 1994, she found Josie sitting in the cafeteria with her head buried in her arms on the table. Such a slight woman now, so thin, pale, small. Her clothes hung on her, sizes too big, without sense. Lawrence and Beverly stopped Hilda and said, "Tell Josie to let go." Hilda said all right and walked over to her friend.

"Josie," Hilda said, "you've got to let go."

"I just can't," she replied. "There's just so many people, so many young people I need to help."

Hilda sat as long as she could, listening, exhorting, chuckling a bit. She hugged Josie, and then she left, knowing she would not see her friend alive again.

Soon after, on November 21, 1994, Josie did let go, reluctantly, because she could no longer hang on. It's no surprise, really, how she died: her enlarged heart did her in.

BACK IN VIRGINIA, I sit down to write this chapter. Stretched out on my couch one afternoon, I begin to type. As I write first of Lee's death and then Josie's, polite but unfeeling tears give way to uncontrollable weeping. I sob for well over an hour, my face and shirt wet, tears dripping down on the computer, puddling on the pillow next to me. I type through the blur, writing the story, pushing the words onto the screen. A pile of damp tissues rises, and when I stop to blow my nose yet again, I ask myself about this sadness, about these tears. We buried them more than ten years ago. I have uncovered nothing new about their deaths. Days have elapsed since I looked at the death certificates. And then the answer softly reveals itself: I weep from grief because I have at last come to understand what I have lost.

Each time I revisit this chapter I weep anew.

I CLOSE THE RED BOOK and put it back on the shelf. The next day I have Bev and Karen take me to the cemetery. The October sun warms our hair and cheeks, calling the ladybugs out in great numbers. We walk down Broadhead row and find the grave for Lee and Josie, a serpentine slab of black granite resting on a roughly chiseled pedestal. BROADHEAD it says, framed by an etched cross and a spray of flowers on each side. LEE W. is on the left, JOSEPHINE on the right. PARENTS OF: LAWRENCE, BEVERLY, MARY. Bev pulls a few weeds from around the grave, and I wonder how Lee got his wife to agree to lie next to her father-in-law for eternity. I consider how her children, grandchildren, countless friends and relatives, and many of "the slew," as she called it—those who had lived at the farm for days, weeks, months, and years—flew and drove great distances to pack the country church and stand at her side for the last time.

I remember the flowers against the blue carpet of the sanctuary, the stillness of her face. I played "In the Garden" on the piano just before the service started because I could think of no other gift to give her, an irony I missed until now.

> I come to the garden alone
> While the dew is still on the roses
> And He walks with me
> And He talks with me
> And He tells me I am His own
> And the joy we share as we tarry there
> None other has ever known

I wish that she were here with me. That we could pull up a chair and talk around the kitchen table one more time. I have a feeling, though, that words would not do. Being near her might be the only way to express what I have found, what she has taught me, what I have developed for her. But these points matter little since I have her no longer, only what she has left behind, only what I have managed to dig up, recognize, preserve. Perhaps death took her away, but the great sleep has also granted her peace, freedom, and rest, and I cannot begrudge her that. As I walk beneath the walnuts, I look back to where she lies and smile, knowing that her writing may be finished, and her mortal voice may be stilled, but from atop this crest in Vernon County, she still speaks.

Epilogue

Burke, Virginia
2005

SOMETIMES AT HOME I sit at my desk with the windows open, and the smell of cut grass wanders up and through, teasing me, calling me, pulling me back to Wisconsin. I gave in this summer, after more than two years of chasing Josie, and once more drove the thousand miles back to La Crosse. As the farmers' fields in Ohio and then Indiana appeared, I rolled down the windows and stuck my left hand out, palm open, as if I could grab the stalks as I sped by. Queen Anne's lace lined the highway, pretty little doilies, and the fragrance of freshly mowed hay filled the car, intoxicating me with its familiarity, its beauty. Corn looked good.

I went alone. I went, not because of family obligations or outstanding research questions, but because I wanted to. Even though the farm sits quiet and mostly lonely now, and one by one the old white buildings disappear, replaced by rock gardens and wild grasses, I wanted to laugh over buttered lefse with my aunts again, suck on rich chocolate from the candy store, run my palms along the farmhouse banister, and breathe in the dust of the coulee. I wanted to look into the faces of some family members who had lost their wife and mother. And I wanted to bring my great-aunt Tina a balloon.

I also wanted to see Josie.

Josie Broadhead, circa 1930

On a cloudy Friday afternoon I drove along the Mississippi and turned off at the sign for Victory, heading up into the heart of Vernon County, looking for the little cemetery that crowns one of the ridges. Up and down, up and down I rode on the waves of the old roads, past Albert and Mabel's rotting house, past the Methodist church, with its oversized bell out front inscribed with the names of my great-grandfather and his brothers, through miles of striped fields that Broadheads once plowed and walked, boys and then men who allowed the rich soil to filter through their fingers and fly into the wind. The cemetery appeared as I crested the final hill, and I turned in to the gravel just before the bend in the road, stopping right in the middle of the path. I shut off the car and got out.

I was alone.

Nearby cows bellowed a muted song while the flags stuck in the dirt near veterans' graves flapped in a wind cooler than usual for August. Even in the soft grass my feet seemed an intrusion, so I slowed and lightened my step. I walked to the Broadhead row, recognizing Lee and Josie's stone from behind. I glanced at it for a moment and then meandered through the markers of my family, as if they were a garden lane, remembering the stories I had heard, the pictures I had seen. I now knew the people behind these names.

I returned to Lee and Josie's grave and squatted in front of it. A blurry me stared back, shining across their names, across the dates of their lives as an old movie projector shines on a person standing in its flickering path. I wanted something. I crouched there, gazing at the likeness of myself, hungering for something I could not identify. No, I could identify it. I simply couldn't have it. I wanted her. I wanted Josie. I wanted to tell her about everything. I wanted to tell her about the two years of getting to know her. I wanted to tell her how she had made me question everything my life is about. I wanted to tell her that a weariness had come upon me, the weariness of fighting with my mind against something that refuses to move, a weariness that rolled over me like a dizzying, disorienting fog, absorbing all my excuses and stubbornness and pride. And I wanted to tell her that when the fog dispersed, because of what she had taught me, I did what I should have done all along.

I submitted to the needle.

It hurt.

All I did was say all right, let's give it a try, maybe there's another plan here, but as I unfurled my fingers and released my expectations, my sense of obligation, my need to commandeer the world to my whims, my numbness dripped and thawed, making room for a rough form of compassion and a contented sense of possibility. I looked at what is right in front of me—teaching, writing, infertility—and for the first time recognized them each for what they could be: grand and holy adventures.

I had finally seen for myself. Seen and understood and began to accept. Simply began.

I wanted to tell her about this, to thank her. I hesitated for a few minutes in the disappointment, overcome with longing, and knew then what I had to do. I leaned forward on my knees and onto my hands and lowered myself until I lay flat on the damp grass just over her coffin. With my cheek to the cool earth, I closed my eyes and breathed in the loamy smell of new and old growth sprinkled with recent rain: the smell of farm, of garden, of her. For a moment, I forgot the fluttering flags and bawling cows, the murmuring walnut trees and humming locusts. I forgot my own breathing. I forgot the resident insects crawling over my hands, an unexpected interruption in their work, the blades of grass cutting a design into the side of my face and crunching in my ear. And for that moment, it was just she and I.

I didn't tell her everything. Instead I whispered simple words: *Thank you, I love you.* I said them again and again.

And it was enough.

Reading Group Discussion Questions

1. Author Wendy Bilen starts the book with a description of Carson, North Dakota. Of all the ways she could begin the story, why do you think she chose to start with that landscape? What role does place play in the book?

2. Bilen says in chapter one that "I'm looking for my grandmother not because she is lost, but because I am." What is she really after? In what way does seeking the past bring hope or direction for the future?

3. Instead of writing a straight biography, the writer puts herself in the story, describing the journey she takes to uncover her grandmother's life. What effect does that addition have on the telling of Josie's story?

4. It is often tempting to venerate the dead, remembering or calling attention only to positive aspects or happy memories. Does Bilen fall into this trap and sentimentalize her grandmother? If so, where? If not, how does she avoid it?

5. Part of the enjoyment of reading is being able to imagine what the author is describing. However, Bilen does some of this work for the reader by recreating scenes, such as the morning after Lee and Josie's wedding in chapter two. What do you think of this approach? Why would Bilen choose to use this device instead of simply sticking to what she knows or allowing the reader to imagine?

6. How does the early part of the book dealing with Josie's childhood figure into the later story? What ties do you notice between her upbringing and her later choices? (For example, did watching how her mother and father dealt with her sisters' deaths have anything to do with Josie's later compulsion to help others?)

7. At times Josie makes what some would consider startling choices, such as when she dares Terry to take the poison. Give another example of one such choice and describe your reaction to this behavior. How does it change your perception of Josie, if at all?

8. We learn in chapter eleven about the author's own family difficulties. Why would she choose to integrate this information into the story, and what effect does it have on the narrative?

9. In chapter twelve, Josie has a classic turning point and calls out to God for help. How is this moment similar to or different from other such incidents in memoirs or biographies you have read? What role does faith play in Josie's choices?

10. Of those who came to the farm—the youth, the babies, the boy, the mother, the eight, or any of the others mentioned—which story most resonates with you?

11. In chapter sixteen, the author confronts some of the questions that have arisen since she started her search for Josie. She ends by saying, "Sometimes I wish I'd left Josie alone." Do you think she really means that?

12. Bilen realizes in chapter nineteen what Josie's "secret" really is. Why is it so difficult for the author to accept? Discuss whether the chapter ends on a despairing or hopeful note.

13. In the final chapter, Bilen says she weeps whenever she revisits the story of her grandparents' death, explaining that "I weep from grief because I have at last come to understand what I have lost." What has she lost, and how does that idea converge with a chapter named "Found"?

14. Bilen ends the final chapter with this sentence: "As I walk beneath the walnuts, I look back to where she lies and smile, knowing that her writing may be finished, and her mortal voice may be stilled, but from atop this crest in Vernon County, she still speaks." What do you think she means by this? What does she believe Josie is saying?

15. In the epilogue, Bilen revisits Josie's grave and describes an unusual way to connect with Josie. What kind of closure does it bring to the author's search? What is your reaction to this scene?